Praise for *Invent, Reinvent, Thrive*

If you are looking to be inspired as an entrepreneur, read this book. The stories and insights are wonderful.

—Philip Kotler, author of *Market Your Way to Growth: 8 Ways to Win*; Professor of Marketing, Kellogg School

Lloyd's book is a well thought-out presentation of entrepreneurial pitfalls and opportunities supported by unique interviews of relevant role models.

—Samuel Zell, Chairman, Equity Group Investments

Invent, Reinvent, Thrive by Lloyd Shefsky is full of wise and practical guidance for both would-be and continuing entrepreneurs. Its central theme is well documented through a succession of highly readable and informative anecdotes. His discussions provide wonderful advice that will aid anyone embarking on or continuing in an entrepreneurial enterprise.

—David Ruder, former Chairman, Securities & Exchange Commission

Lloyd Shefsky's book *Invent, Reinvent, Thrive* provides important personal and professional perspectives on change and how successful entrepreneurs purposefully change themselves in order to succeed. This book is a valuable resource for anyone looking to make a long-term commitment to personal growth and success.

—Frederick Waddell, Chief Executive Officer, The Northern Trust Company

If you think business books are boring, this is your chance to prove yourself wrong. Storytelling is an art, and Shefsky brings that art to business. It's part of why he's a popular teacher, speaker, and valued consultant. More importantly, *Invent, Reinvent, Thrive* is a treasure trove of valuable lessons. I highly recommend that it be read by everyone in the business world.

—Stan Kasten, President and CEO, Los Angeles Dodgers; former President of the Atlanta Braves, Hawks, and Thrashers and the Washington Nationals

Our company's direct experience with Lloyd Shefsky motivated and guided us to declare our highest ambition to "Build Forever." He inspired us to methodically pursue Brown-Forman's never-ending greatness, and this book can do the same for others. I highly recommend *Invent, Reinvent, Thrive* to all businesspeople.

—Paul Varga, CEO and Chairman, Brown-Forman Corporation (Jack Daniels, Finlandia, Southern Comfort, Herradura, Early Times)

In *Invent, Reinvent, Thrive* Shefsky has once again distilled the secrets utilized by successful entrepreneurs in growing their businesses. The richness of his stories and the wisdom they convey read like a playbook for how successful companies can grow and thrive despite adverse circumstances. This book captures the essence of what's required to flourish. I'm looking forward to implementing a number of the insights I've gleaned from this book at Edmunds.com and guarantee that once you've read it, you will do the same.

—Avi Steinlauf, Chief Executive Officer, Edmunds.com

For me, *Invent, Reinvent, Thrive* was a page-turner. Writing that moves one from story to story, shedding light on the challenges to entrepreneurial reinvention and family business efforts to succeed. Enjoyable and instructive from a teacher with genuine insight into life stages of a variety of organizations. I genuinely enjoyed reading it.

—Jim Ethier, former Chief Executive Officer, Bush Brothers & Company

Invent, Reinvent, Thrive is a delightfully written insight into the problems, long and short term, of entrepreneurship and family businesses. Every businessperson will find important concepts in this book. Indeed, this is a must-read for all; everyone will find important life-changing material in this book.

—James Cloonan, founder and Chairman, American Association of Individual Investors

Shefsky's new book dynamically captures the challenges and the rewards of owning and growing a business. I found the stories to be both compelling and powerful. I believe this book will serve as a wonderful resource for the next generation of entrepreneurs for many years to come.

—John W. Rogers, Jr., founder, Chairman, and Chief Investment Officer, Ariel Investments

Lloyd continues to provide special perspective and insight. *Invent, Reinvent, Thrive* includes important lessons for business and life.

—Jack Greenberg, former Chairman and Chief Executive Officer, McDonald's Corp.

Persuasive business examples in a wide range of industries definitely help you to have new and different ways of thinking and could be the most important keys for success as an entrepreneur. This enlightening book is worth reading for all businesspeople.

—Mr. Naito, President and CEO, Eisai Co., Ltd.

Invent, Reinvent, Thrive is a must-read. Having personally been able to reach out to Lloyd Shefsky for his wisdom and advice over many years, it pleases me that he is now sharing the depth of his knowledge and experience with a wider audience. Lloyd's stories embody what happens in the real world—told in a way to help, to illuminate, and to inspire generations of entrepreneurs through the challenges we have all faced.

—Bernee D. L. Strom, serial entrepreneur; Chair and CEO, WebTuner Corp. (also Gemstar, Priceline, iBiquity, InfoSpace)

A truly enlightening book that captures the essence of what drives the longevity and prosperity of businesses. The stories are powerful and the lessons profound. The book is a must-read for entrepreneurs and leaders of family businesses, who will gain important insights.

—Raphael H. Amit, Professor of Management, Wharton School, University of Pennsylvania; founder, Wharton Global Family Alliance

Lloyd Shefsky is a venerable teacher, consultant, and consigliere to entrepreneurs. His latest book is brimming with practical insights and wisdom. The author's focus on personal and organizational reinvention is reminiscent of the well-worn capital markets lament that no one has a good sell rule. Shefsky's stories are so compelling that insights cascade. This book is both interesting and illuminating.

—Stuart Greenbaum, former Dean and Bank of America Emeritus Professor of Managerial Leadership, Olin Business School, Washington University

Lloyd Shefsky's seminal book, *Entrepreneurs Are Made Not Born*, became a cornerstone in the field. Now his new book, *Invent, Reinvent, Thrive*, finds an important basis for business success. His unique insight makes this book essential. This is a very serious study of a critical issue, and no one dealing with entrepreneurship or family businesses should make the mistake of ignoring it.

—Israel Zang, Professor and former Dean of Business School and Vice Provost of Tel Aviv University

Lloyd Shefsky's new book *Invent, Reinvent, Thrive* is a must-read for every family member of every family business around the world. It is fascinating reading. Lloyd clearly brings out the fact that if you do not keep reinventing and changing the old order to yield place to new, your business slowly but surely will die.

—Subbu Murugappa, former Chairman, Murugappa Group (India)

Shefsky's book breathes optimism into all of us. The compelling and beautifully told stories and the practical tips in each chapter provide a wealth of take-home value. The lessons in *Invent, Reinvent, Thrive* are essential. This book is terrific, and a reading pleasure.

—John Ward, Clinical Professor of Family Enterprises, Kellogg School of Management

Professor Lloyd Shefsky's book is very insightful for many family entrepreneurs who are trying to introduce innovation into their continuing family businesses. The lessons in this book give them bravery and the knowledge to make it happen.

—Akihiro Okumura, Emeritus Professor, Keio University; Chairman, Japan Academy of Family Business

Many young people around the world are looking for excitement that their fathers' generation has not explored. In this regard, *Invent, Reinvent, Thrive* can serve as their handbook of success.

—Yao Yang, Professor and Dean, National School of Development, Peking University, Beijing, China

The entrepreneur is fueled by passion, vision, and persistence. She needs to go against the odds and believe in herself. And then she must constantly reinvent that vision for long-term success. Lloyd Shefsky tackles the issues many entrepreneurs face and offers practical advice to defy the odds. If you've had business success, yet need to go to the next level, read this book.

—Ginger Graham, former President and CEO, Amylin Pharmaceuticals; former faculty, Arthur Rock Center for Entrepreneurship, Harvard Business School

Invent, Reinvent, Thrive is an important addition to the entrepreneurship literature. It hits the mark. Shefsky argues that change is continuous; if you stand still you will decline. He illustrates this conclusion by recounting discussions with many entrepreneurs and owners of family-owned enterprises. The breadth of the stories is extraordinary and Shefsky is insightful in teasing out the implications of what he has heard. He has long experience in working with entrepreneurs as an attorney, mentor, teacher, and investor. His study certainly moves the bar on rigor of entrepreneurial writing.

—Donald Jacobs, Dean Emeritus, J. L. Kellogg Graduate School of Management

INVENT REINVENT THRIVE

THE KEYS TO SUCCESS FOR ANY START-UP, ENTREPRENEUR, OR FAMILY BUSINESS

LLOYD E. SHEFSKY

Mc
Graw
Hill
Education

New York   Chicago   San Francisco   Athens   London   Madrid
Mexico City   Milan   New Delhi   Singapore   Sydney   Toronto

1 2 3 4 5 6 7 8 9 0   DOC/DOC   1 2 0 9 8 7 6 5 4

ISBN   978-0-07-182300-5
MHID   0-07-182300-X

e-ISBN   978-0-07-182311-1
e-MHID   0-07-182311-5

Library of Congress Cataloging-in-Publication Data
Shefsky, Lloyd E.
    Invent, reinvent, thrive : the keys to success for any start-up, entrepreneur, or family business / Lloyd Shefsky.
        pages cm
    ISBN 978-0-07-182300-5 (hardback) — ISBN 0-07-182300-X (hardback)
1. Entrepreneurship. 2. New business enterprises—Management. 3. Small business—Management. 4. Family-owned business enterprises—Management. 5. Success in business. I. Title.
    HB615.S496 2014
    658.1'1—dc23

                                                                                    2014001656

Invent, Reinvent, Thrive™ is a Trademark of Lloyd E. Shefsky Inc.

All quoted material is taken from interviews conducted by the author from 2010 through 2014 unless otherwise noted.

McGraw-Hill Education books are available at special quantity discounts to use as premiums and sales promotions or for use in corporate training programs. To contact a representative, please visit the Contact Us pages at www.mhprofessional.com.

Dedicated to

My kids and grandkids
who make me think young and vital

My dear wife, Natalie
who makes me feel young and vital

Contents

Preface

DURING MY PROFESSIONAL CAREER I HAVE HAD THE GOOD FORtune to represent, first as a lawyer and since 1996 as a consultant, many entrepreneurs and family businesspeople. Those two areas fascinated me and became the focus of much of my research, writing, and lecturing. The combined effort has been extensive to say the least.

Example: For my previous book, *Entrepreneurs Are Made Not Born*, I interviewed nearly 300 entrepreneurs and family businesspeople. It has been published in eight languages.

Since 1995 I have taught at the Kellogg School of Management at Northwestern University, where I am a Clinical Professor of Entrepreneurship. I am also founder and codirector of the Center for Family Enterprises. I have taught and lectured in China, Japan, India, Israel, and Thailand.

I have taught, interviewed, worked with, and known thousands of entrepreneurs and family businesspeople. I represented many entrepreneurs and family businesses in the past as legal counsel, and in the past 18 years I was a consultant and coach to many more. Also I have been an entrepreneur on several occasions, as cofounder of the Chicago law firm Shefsky & Froelich, which merged earlier this year with the Taft Firm, and of several other for-profit businesses and not-for-profit organizations such as Sports Lawyers Association.

Lawyers are not naturally entrepreneurs. By a self-selection process only certain kinds of people become lawyers. Then they are trained not to think entrepreneurially. They are admonished to think in terms of precedent and the "reasonable man." Entrepreneurs, however, deplore the limitations of precedent. And they follow the dictates of George Bernard Shaw in *Maxims for Revolutionists*: "The reasonable man adapts himself to the world; the unreasonable one persists in trying to adapt the world to himself. Therefore, all progress depends upon the unreasonable man."

All those entrepreneurial stories, continually circulating through my mind, gave me what I call my "perpetual intellectual itch." There had to be a common thread that existed in the successful—entrepreneurs whose businesses grew and thrived and family businesspeople who caused their businesses to succeed through three or more generations (most family businesses don't survive to the third generation). Long ago I ceased searching for the magic formula. The mix of traits varies, and the same traits can be found in many other occupations and endeavors.

Eventually I figured it out. It wasn't that they all had a certain set of characteristics. What was fascinating was that the successful ones followed a common procedure: they continually reinvented themselves, their businesses and, when relevant, their families. And those who didn't? Some failed outright. Some had temporary success. Some sensed their inability to carry through to the end and made other arrangements. A very few got there by sheer luck (more about luck later).

As you consider the numerous issues I'll discuss in this book, I would urge you to keep a few points in mind.

Different Times Really Do Make a Difference

From Past to Present

To Sell Is to Die

In my first years after graduating from the University of Chicago Law School, I noticed that clients of my firm who sold their businesses died shortly after the sale closed. Granted, the firm's clients were hardly a significant sampling, but the anecdotal pattern I observed overall had a majority of such people dying. Eventually I realized what caused that interesting but misleading statistic.

In those days, people worked for decades building their businesses. Generally capital intensive, it took years to establish track records that could support banks' and investors' requirements. If they were successfully able to sell their businesses, they were probably already in their 60s or 70s. That approximated the U.S. male's life expectancy back then. So, nature took its course; no magic was involved.

Is Impatience Also a Virtue?

Today, young people start businesses with little capital. If they succeed, capital is available. But most capital sources are impatient and demand a cash-out within a few years or at most a decade. In addition, the obsolescence caused by technology makes every capital source leery of sticking around too long. It's difficult to argue against successful achievement, such as the development of a business that leads to a liquidity event or succession. But do those examples create expectations of quick success and cause frustration among those who take longer to succeed or who never reach a liquidity or succession event? Even worse, will it cause people with great ideas to act hastily, perhaps destroying great opportunities?

Having said that, intolerance for delay isn't all bad. Why should anyone wait for tomorrow to have what's available today? The answer to that issue is somewhat generational. Understanding that can be critical.

Today and Tomorrow

Today's impatient young people have been referred to as "the now generation" and "the immediate gratification" generation. Moreover, technology is an enabler of that attitude. In one of my classes I show a photo of a contemporary television remote with an "On Demand" button (see the accompanying figure).

Then I explain to my students that in my generation, the button would have said "On Request," not "On Demand."

The Greatest Bloodless Revolution Ever

In the final quarter of the twentieth century and so far this century, we have witnessed an unprecedented revolution, the greatest and most widely impactful in history: the technology revolution. Sure, we could debate and compare the impact of the printing press, the car, the airplane, and various earlier medical developments. But in just a few decades the computer and the Internet, the DNA helix, cellular information transmission, and space and satellite technology have had a huge impact. Other inventions and discoveries took many more decades or even centuries.

No doubt there will be more exciting inventions and discoveries that will impact society even more rapidly. But the young people today are being raised in an atmosphere where they must develop or aggregate multidimensional skills. Unlike in past generations, tomorrow's great start-ups will entail multidisciplines, such as IT and medicine, physics and genetics, or electronics and marketing.

In addition, young people may have doubts about their futures. They are being told that while every one of the past several generations could hope to achieve more and lead a better life than their parents did, this generation may not be able to do that. That may make some of the challenges discussed in this book seem more daunting to those younger readers and may mislead their parents and grandparents into dealing incorrectly with those potential leaders of the next generation.

Entrepreneurship and Family Businesses: Paradoxical Imperatives

Without a doubt, entrepreneurship continues to become increasingly important. It will bring enormous wealth to the few, but through their ingenuity, risk taking, and business acumen, an outsized share of the nation's GDP will be produced by entrepreneurs. Through their struggle to succeed, everyone can benefit. This book is meant to help those who choose the role of entrepreneur to control their own destiny.

And family businesses will continue to face the daunting process of making it through the third generation. Baby boomers who are first- or second-generation owners are beginning to hit the age when their retirement, ill health, or death will force decisions on succession or liquidity. Unless they prepare for those prospects, analyze, and choose wisely, it is possible that large numbers of them will diminish or even destroy their families' wealth.

There is so much at stake. Those who fail to reinvent are destined to repeat the immortal words of two great poets:

- "Of all sad words of tongue and pen, the saddest are these: 'It might have been.'" *John Greenleaf Whittier*
- "I coulda been a contender. I could have been somebody, instead of a bum, which is what I am." Terry (played by Marlon Brando), *On the Waterfront*

I hope that this book will awaken entrepreneurs and family businesspeople to the challenges; guide their thinking and encourage preparedness; get them to seek assistance; and teach them steps that will help them Invent, Reinvent, and Thrive.

Acknowledgments

TAKING LIBERTIES WITH THE ENGLISH PARABLE THAT SUCCESS has many fathers but failure is an orphan, I want to publicly acknowledge the many who helped me birth this book. Hopefully, it neither offends anyone nor contains any errors. If it has, the fault resides with me, and I beg forgiveness.

The most extraordinary and direct contributors to this effort are the 26 people I've interviewed (in alphabetical order): David Axelrod, former senior advisor to President Barack Obama, and director, University of Chicago Institute of Politics; Nir Barkat, founder, BRM, founding investor, Checkpoint, and currently Mayor of Jerusalem; Junior Bridgeman, former NBA player, founder, and CEO, Bridgefoods; Charles Bronfman, former co-chairman, Seagrams Corp., and Stephen Bronfman, executive chairman, Claridge Inc; Marilyn Carlson Nelson, former chief executive officer/chairperson, Diana Nelson, chairperson, and Wendy Nelson, director, Carlson Companies (Radisson Hotels; TGI Fridays); Maxine Clark, founder and former CEO, Build-A-Bear Workshop; Lester Crown, chairman, Jim Crown, president, and Steve Crown, general partner, Henry Crown & Co.; James Dan, MD, president, Advocate Medical Group; James Freeman, founder and CEO, Blue Bottle Coffee; Linda Johnson Rice, chairperson, Desiree Rogers, CEO, and Cheryl Mayberry

McKissack, COO, Johnson Publishing (*Ebony* and *Jet* magazines); Michael Krasny, founder and former CEO, CDW; Larry Levy, founder and former CEO, Levy Restaurants, and founder, CEO, and chairman, Levy Acquisitions; Gil Mandelzis, founder, former CEO, and currently executive chairman, Traiana, and Executive Committee, ICAP; John Osher, founder, Dr. John's Toothbrush (subsequently Crest SpinBrush); J.B. Pritzker, cofounder and managing partner, The Pritzker Group; Tom Pritzker, executive chairman, Hyatt Hotels Corp., and chairman and CEO, The Pritzker Organization; Howard Schultz, founder, chairman, and CEO, Starbucks; Charles Schwab, founder, former CEO, and chairman, Charles Schwab & Co.; Jim Sinegal, founder and former CEO, Costco; and Tom Stemberg, founder and former CEO, Staples, and general managing partner, Highland Consumer Fund.

These people not only gave of their precious time, they shared facts and opinions while stirring and revealing emotions and stories, often quite private. They incurred the risks of opening up for two reasons: (1) they trusted me, and (2) they are caring, giving people who hoped their experiences and thoughts, when combined with those of others, would help multitudes of people become more successful. I appreciate and am honored by their trust, and I hope I have fulfilled it and created a vehicle where the whole exceeds the sum of their wonderful individual stories.

And special thanks to all the interviewees' assistants—Claire McCombs, Hanit Mordechai, Angela Forster, Lori-Ann Moores, Cade Bittner, Amy Hyde, Beverly Smith, Christine Pak, Linda Christiansen, Jenny Klowden, Lavette Callahan, Lana McSwain, Mary Anne Coviello, Beth Schneider, Jeannine Jeskewitz, Nancy Kent, Gina Woods, Greg Gable, Stephanie Corns, Karen Paulsell and Sarah Warden. Their efficient help with communication, scheduling, and background was extremely valuable.

To round out and tell the interviewees' stories and create the lessons, I also resorted to published material and private conversations with others who wish to remain anonymous. My goal was to be fair in assessing the weight and import of all sources in coming to various conclusions.

Another group whose contributions to this book are somewhat more remote or less obvious are the many others: clients whom I represented as a lawyer or more recently as a consultant, coach, or mentor; and colleagues with whom I have partnered. They aren't named here, but my experiences with them, for which I am very grateful, expanded my understanding and skills.

Similarly, my students, primarily at the Kellogg School of Management but also elsewhere over the years, have taught me every bit as much as I did them. Likewise, my appreciation goes to the special guests in my classes who take the time to travel to Evanston, Illinois, put up with my requirements and instructions, and share with and give to my students the firsthand lessons that only they can do.

In the context of Kellogg, I'd like to thank Dean Sally Blount for her personal support and encouragement, especially for our Center for Family Enterprises and with this book. My partner at Kellogg, John Ward, has given more thought to issues involving family enterprises than any human being. He created the infrastructure of the field without which none of us could do our work so effectively. Also my appreciation to the Kellogg faculty, administration, and staff for their support and assistance. Lastly, my great appreciation to Dean Emeritus Donald Jacobs, who caused and convinced me to join the faculty and who later enticed me to found what became the Center for Family Enterprises. I had been a reluctant candidate for each, and I'm forever grateful for his foresight and confidence in me. It seems he knew me better than I knew myself. Those opportunities enabled me to reinvent myself again.

Speaking of personal reinventions, the law firm I founded, Shefsky & Froelich, has now merged with the Taft firm. My firm had embodied several of my personal reinventions. In that regard, my unique path was facilitated by Murray Simpson, with whom I founded my law firm; Cezar ("Cid") Froelich, with whom I shared the name of the firm for nearly 44 years; and by all the members and associates of the firm who provided me with support and platforms for achievement and periodic reinventions.

Assisting me with research, validation of facts, and clerical matters were Julie Swidler, Megan McEvily, Carol Zsolnay, and my two right hands, Dana Levit-Geraci and Lisa Fogt, and Bob Metz, whose guidance has been especially helpful. Thanks also to: IT guru Enzo Spinelli for invaluable assistance with interview recordings. Jeff Herman, my book agent, whose assistance and good results proved once again that a man who represents himself has a fool for a client. My editor at McGraw-Hill, Zach Gajewski, is a pro who not only helped me create a better book but listened and made the process painless. My editing supervisor at McGraw-Hill, Pattie Amoroso, who shepherded my book through the production process from manuscript through bound book. My copyeditor, Scott Amerman, who helped make the text read more smoothly. Howard Greenstein, who created the book's website and improved my social media literacy. My thanks also to two long-time friends, Bill Zimmerman and Eyal Shavit, for their special help. And a special note of thanks to Chris Froeter, the talented commercial artist whose creativity led to the design of the book's dust jacket and the website design.

A few personal words of thanks to my family. My children, Dawn, Julie, and Doug, and my grandchildren, Robbie, Emma, Jake, Joey, Brandi, Jordan, and Sam, have helped me avoid the entrapment of thinking within the boxes of my own generation. Most importantly my wife, Natalie, who keeps me grounded, convinces me to smell roses I'd otherwise overlook, and has bravely allowed me to reinvent myself repeatedly, which at times must have been frightening.

Jim Sinegal, the founder of Costco and one of my interviewees, related what Berkshire Hathaway director Charlie Munger (also a Costco director) told him: "I still have a photographic memory. I just no longer get same-day service." If my photographic memory forgot others whom I should acknowledge, my sincere apologies.

Introduction

*Change is the law of life. And those who look only
to the past or present are sure to miss the future.*
—PRESIDENT JOHN F. KENNEDY

ACCORDING TO THE TITLE OF THIS BOOK, THE ULTIMATE GOAL IN
life is to thrive. In order to thrive, one first needs to survive. The
Darwinian idea of "survival of the fittest" connotes strength and
skill. In the business arena "survival of the fittest" generally connotes power and resources (the best human resources and the
most financial resources). But actually the fittest in business may
lack power and resources. So what enables them to survive? What
has business learned from Darwin, and what more can Darwin
teach business?

Enter the chameleon: small in stature, fast for its size but not
compared to larger predators, and too weak to succeed in direct
conflict. Yet it has survived since just after the dinosaurs. One
of the traits that enable survival for that long is the chameleon's
ability to change its color, thereby adapting to whatever change in
environment it encounters. It seems to be the ultimate example of
reinventing itself to survive.

That's what this book is about. Businesspeople, in start-up, entrepreneurial, managed, and family businesses, must learn from the

chameleon. They must understand the need to reinvent themselves and their businesses frequently in order to survive and to thrive.

Reinventing Yourself to Move Up or Move On

No longer can a worker expect to work for a single employer and earn a gold watch at the end of decades of faithful service. The pact between employers and employees in which mutual loyalty bound the two sides together is history. Today that pact is riddled with employer out-clauses and fewer employee in-clauses. A far more dependable worker outcome is a pink slip when the economy slows. And often, even when the economy is stable, pink slips are in.

But there is an upside to the uncertainty. By accepting the fact that no job is secure you are free to move on. The incremental benefit of staying is clearly uncertain. But should you decide to leave, you must prepare yourself. A career change will be highly stimulating and, yes, as initially off-putting as a cold shower after the warm bath of a regular paycheck and a familiar—if boring—routine.

Reinventing can relate to what you do, not just where you do it. As we continue progressing from the Industrial Age to the Information Age, the need to reinvent people's skill sets is evident in unemployment statistics. As Alvin Toffler said, "The illiterate of the twenty-first century will not be those who cannot read and write, but those who cannot learn, unlearn, and relearn."

How do you pull this off? The answer lies in learning to reinvent yourself. With proper reinvention will come the confidence to make dramatic changes. That makes sense. For if you know you are ready and able to risk a calculated step into the unknown, you will be more willing to do so.

Some people grow up in an "atmosphere of limiting assumptions." Parents, even loving parents who want the best for their children, unwittingly influence their kids to feel limited. For some, that influence lasts a lifetime, but it needn't. If you live in that limiting state, you have a choice: (1) continue to live within that mindset or (2) reinvent yourself and become a more dynamic person with unlimited horizons.

But you're no longer a spring chicken. "How can I change now?" you might ask.

It is true. As a rule, vocational decisions are made between the ages of 17 to 22. Of course, some make the decisions much earlier; others, much later. More than you might expect never made a decision and have just drifted into what they are doing. In effect, then, the nondeciders allowed their decisions to be made for them by abdicating their right of self-determination.

"Rings of Life" Theory

Dramatic changes, such as switching from accountant to brain surgeon, become more difficult to pull off the longer you wait to do so. The following figure depicts that principle.

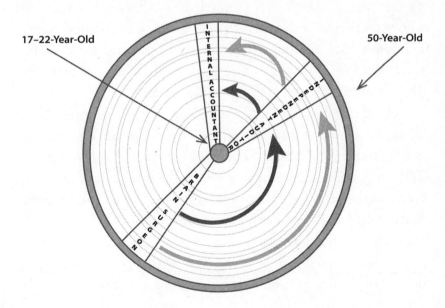

In this picture, time is measured in the same way as the cross-section of a tree, but here the greater number of rings means a greater number of vocational years. Here, the further you go from the center (the center being from a teenage 17 to a young adult 22) the greater the distance you must traverse to change vocations. Thus, the likelihood of successful career change is more problematic as one gets older. I call this my "Rings of Life" theory.

That's likely due to lost learning opportunities, including a lack of access to vocational (on-the-job) training, as employers prefer hiring younger applicants. They believe that hiring younger people gives their investment in training the employee a longer amortization prospect. Incidentally, employers may favor younger applicants for other reasons: for example, young hires tend to have more familiarity with and comfort in dealing with social media.

The employer makes a mistake if his reason is solely the longer amortization of training costs. For it is clear that the Generation Ys and Millennials have a different approach to career planning. They expect to have numerous jobs, and some will have multiple careers. They don't view themselves as beholden to employers who train them. They see on-the-job training as an opportunity to improve their skills or change their skill sets in preparation for their *next* jobs. And they don't see that as failures to perform. They are bringing value to their employers too.

Lots of people make jumps from one career to another. Such changes run along a broad spectrum. Some require a huge fundamental change as with an accountant–to–brain surgeon change. That's why such a change is rare. But at the other end of the spectrum might be an accountant who moves incrementally from independent auditor to company controller. Most of the skills are the same. Such a change is relatively easy, which is why it's so common. Changes in between those extremes require varying degrees of preparation and have varying degrees of success.

Personal Reinvention: The Confidence Factor

Indeed, your own reinvention will, in all likelihood, occur one small step at a time. Athletes don't run the marathon on day one. They begin with modest runs, and they cover ever-longer distances. Confidence grows with each interim accomplishment along the way. It is the same in career reinvention.

Generally it is easier to accomplish a partial change, which, if tailored well, can work like a charm. Then of course you can do this again and again, expanding your capabilities and your confidence as you reinvent repeatedly. That doesn't mean you must continually change employers. Reinventing yourself, even while continuing with the same employer, can enhance your skills and your career options.

As you reinvent, eventually you will reach a crossroads. So be confident and to adapt the offbeat logic of Yogi Berra, "When you arrive at a fork in the road, [be prepared to] take it."

Whether you are leaving your job to begin a new business or are about to take a leadership position where you are presently employed, remember that confidence will be a key element in the reinvention, whether of yourself or of the business you continue to work for or of the new business you find or join. That confidence can be developed through your preparations for the move.

Companies Reinvent to Survive and Thrive

Reinvention is a constant theme in this book—not just for individuals as employees or as members of families with businesses, but for the biggest, best, and the not-so-good companies everywhere. You will find examples of iconic companies that have reinvented with great success. Intel, for example, bet the farm on a switch from a commodity product to an unproven invention, with spectacular success. Similarly, Corning seems to reinvent itself periodically. It does so with such frequency as to be as good at reinventing as it is at making glass. Kodak, for its part, let its game-changing invention, a digital camera, collect dust on a shelf while its dominating film business died.

Keep in mind that reinvention is a journey, not a destination. When you reinvent yourself to start a business, it will be the first of a string of reinventions. Entrepreneurship is not a cataclysmic event; it is a constant process, if you are to be a success and not a failure. The fact that entrepreneurship consists of numerous stages is hardly a new concept. Nearly 50 years ago, Bruce Tuckman described entrepreneurial development as having four stages: Forming, Storming, Norming, and Performing. My theory differs in that I think that Tuckman's four-stage set must be repeated over and over again.

As someone who runs a business, you will be reinventing yourself and also your company, and if you decide to do an encore business, you'll have to start reinventing all over again. Then as you contemplate your personal journey ending, you must reinvent for your family.

Of course some people sell their business, perhaps knowing that they can't or choose not to go through the effort of reinventing. That's OK: just be sure you aren't committing what I refer to as "premature evacuation," where it's done for wrong reasons—because "everyone else is doing it," or because it's time to implement a plan made years or decades earlier to retire at a specific age. If you're going to retire, be sure whether you shouldn't *re-tire* instead (changing the car's tire instead of selling the car as junk).

Lessons from Captains of Industry

Whether you need to reinvent yourself or reinvent your business, there are important lessons for you in others who have done this successfully (Intel), as well as those who failed or refused to act or who acted too late (Kodak). IBM, which once dominated the mainframe computer business, represents both extremes. Big Blue lost out in the desktop computer business—it sold its once-thriving PC business—but came back strong as a giant computer consulting company a generation later.

That's what this book does. It tells the stories of companies and of people that have reinvented and those that have not reinvented. The latter usually do not survive.

The book then analyzes and compares those examples. The lessons are laid out, with advice on how to adopt the lessons and implement them. This process will enable you to build your skill set. Your enhanced skill set will give you the confidence to reinvent.

Some of the most important business decisions are directly and dramatically affected by confidence. But what comes to your mind when you read or hear the word *confidence* is probably not that to which I refer. Confidence affects our lives in many ways—such as our personal relationships. I choose to weigh confidence *in the context of a few business-related circumstances*:

- Employees feeling trapped versus making a break for it
- Entrepreneurship—pre-start-up through and past early stage
- Mature companies—"own-the-market" stage
- People reinventing themselves—to change jobs or careers, even including leaving an entrepreneurship to become an employee
- Family businesses—succession versus secession

Why You Should Read This Book

Over the years, I've observed that having the confidence to reinvent yourself and your business can do a number of things:

- It can make the difference between incremental and exponential results.
- It can make the difference between having a decent living or producing extraordinary wealth.
- It can make the difference between being one of the biggest companies and an industry leader or being an also-ran or a has-been.
- It can make the difference between being trapped in a dead-end job that lacks satisfaction or having a job you can't wait to get back to.
- In the extreme, it can make the difference between remaining unemployed or being gainfully employed.
- It can make the difference between enabling a founder's child or grandchild to take over the leadership, governance, or ownership of the family's business or causing the child to seek "greener" pastures.

If one of these alternatives sets matters to you or someone you care about, then you should read this book.

Lest you think that it's too late—that the cards have already been dealt, that your genetics, early environment, or childhood influences have sealed your fate—let me assure you that while those things may have a profound effect on where you start, they are mere potholes to those who develop confidence on their journey. Many will even exceed the success their dreams represent.

Some may find the examples inapplicable or even intimidating. True, the people I've interviewed whose stories are told here are among the greatest success stories of our time. In your current situation you may aspire to far less and feel that their example is of another realm. Your business may never achieve the success of a Starbucks, a Staples, a CDW, a Charles Schwab & Company, or a Costco. Your family business may not have the same issues as the

Pritzkers, Carlsons, Bronfmans, Johnsons, or Crowns. But their lessons can help you and your business.

Then again, who knows? You may be more like them when they were at your stage of success than you realize.

Getting Started

So how do you get started? NBA Coach Phil Jackson likes to quote the Zen philosopher Alan Watts: "The only way to make sense out of change is to plunge into it, move with it and join the dance." Reinventing certainly requires discipline, determination, and drive. That sounds a lot like "if at first you don't succeed, try, try again." But I'm sure that Coach Jackson would have told his players that practice alone doesn't make perfect. Continually practicing bad form merely perfects bad form. You must find ways, alone or with help, to improve your practice as you try again. Consider instead the words of Albert Einstein: "Doing the same thing over and over again and expecting different results is insanity."

PART 1

Reinventing Yourself as an Entrepreneur

1

Core Competencies Will Relaunch Your Career

ENTREPRENEURSHIP OFTEN INSPIRES REACTIONS LIKE THAT SEEN in the V8 vegetable juice TV commercials. The actor smacks the side of his head and says, "I could've had a V8!" So many "I could'ves," a lot of "why didn't I think of that?" even "I did think of that; why didn't I do it?" and so many "if onlys." But to me "if only" is a cop-out.

At the beginning of Successful Entrepreneurship, the course I developed and teach at the Kellogg School of Management at Northwestern University, I ask my students, "Who recently saw an entrepreneurial opportunity?" At first there are no raised hands. I don't know whether to attribute that to surprise, intimidation, or the remnants of spring break. Eventually the students begin actively participating after some of my coaxing. Since you had no spring break, what entrepreneurial opportunities have you seen recently? The point is, there are innumerable opportunities we pass by every day.

Every time you see someone struggling with a task or frustrated with the time and cost it consumes or the inefficiency it causes, there's an opportunity. Of course, once an opportunity is recognized there is much research and thinking to be done to determine viability and feasibility, as well as implementation.

Perhaps the difference between success and failure is a matter of spelling. What needs to be done to validate one's dream is "due" diligence, not just "do" diligence. Due diligence is as crucial a part of successful reinvention as it is of successful invention. Generally, success requires reinvention of your thought processes and the criteria for your diligence. That's what makes it "due" diligence, and that's what leads to an ultimate distinguishing factor of successful entrepreneurs.

For Want of a Ribbon, a Big Box Was Unwrapped

Sometimes an epiphany occurs, as it did for Tom Stemberg. Tom saw an opportunity that required a willingness to contradict the experts, and he did so with spectacular consequences.

Tom is the founder of Staples. He revolutionized the office supply industry. In the early 1980s, Tom worked for the old-line Boston-based grocery chain Star Market, a part of Chicago-based Jewel Tea. He saw that the supermarket chain sold ballpoint pens at a 100 percent markup. He was convinced that there was a way to sell the pens for a lot less and still make a profit. That was the germ of the idea for Staples.

In 1985, he was motivated to create Staples while writing a business proposal. He was unable to buy a typewriter ribbon because his stationery store closed for the Fourth of July holiday. At that time typewriter ribbons were a stock-keeping unit, like every other stationery store "SKU." (They're pronounced "skews" for the plural.) Stationery stores carried small supplies of many SKUs.

Most stationery stores were inefficient. They were closed on Sundays and for holidays even though businesspeople often worked through parts of those days. Particular SKUs were often unavailable. And those stores' prices were excessive for the small businesses that were their primary sales target.

It's the ultimate inefficiency—charging more to those who can afford it least. Even more counterproductive, the small inventories of the individual items stocked by the stationers made those stores undesirable customers for office product manufacturers. The manufacturers preferred selling large quantities to major corporations or to distributors who sold small quantities to each stationery store.

A few companies, such as Quill, attempted disruptive change with a more efficient business model. They bypassed distributors and took orders by phone or by fax, shipping the supplies to the ultimate consumers—small businesses and offices. While this approach was more efficient, shipping costs made it suitable only for large and medium-sized orders and did not solve small businesses' needs for small orders at reasonable prices. Even mail orders of individual items were simply prohibitive when the shipping expense was factored in.

An interim attempt to solve the problem was to form a co-op whereby the co-op's members were the small stationers for whom costs were too high but who in the aggregate were able to buy right. Although co-ops helped keep operating expenses lower and facilitated bulk purchases at lower prices, they left too many problems unsolved.

The industry was entrenched in antiquated thinking, some more archaic than others and none sufficiently creative. The industry had done everything possible to squeeze out unnecessary costs. What they didn't see was a way to think outside the box. They saw no alternative to the status quo.

Tom saw great opportunity in their status quo outlook. He wouldn't just think outside the box, he would reinvent the box by opening large stores now known as "big-box stores." Instead of carrying small supplies of many SKUs, his big-box stores would carry large quantities of fewer SKUs, enabling him to buy direct from manufacturers. This would allow him to earn money on competitively lower prices to the end-user customer.

It worked. Boy, did it work. Today, Staples represents nearly 40 percent of the office supplies market, with 2013 revenue at just under $25 billion. With 2,000 stores, as well as a website that generates many Internet sales, Staples employs over 50,000 people in 47 states and 25 other countries.

Tom has been quick to point out that within a few months his concept was copied by others—eventually by over 20 competitors—only a few of whom still exist. Without the protection of a barrier to entry by others, he had to count on being first to market and being best in every way.

Using Your Bean to Brew Up a Storm

Howard Schultz also had an epiphany—that Americans were ready for really good coffee in an affordable clublike atmosphere. Today, Howard Schultz, the founder of Starbucks, is a perfect example of a great entrepreneur. He didn't start out that way, but he was sufficiently confident to reinvent himself and eventually an industry and—in a very real sense—society at large. Try to imagine the United States today without a Starbucks in nearly every community, large and small.

Howard was an exceptional salesman. What I mean by that isn't that he was so slick that he could sell ice to Eskimos (although eventually he *did* sell iced drinks to Eskimos). I mean that he was sensitive to, and knew how to, satisfy the needs and wants of his customers. That's a skill he remembers learning as a kid growing up in the Brooklyn building projects with 150 diverse families living in one building with one elevator. Howard played sports all day long in the schoolyard, which he calls "a democratization of a lot of different people."

He believes that lessons learned early, "in leadership, empathy, communications, self-esteem, understanding and an intuitive sense about people" helped him understand and develop Starbucks as a "people business."

While working for Hammarplast, a manufacturer of Swedish drip coffee makers, Howard spent some time in Europe. There, he enjoyed the ambience of local coffeehouses. Howard was certain there was a need for similar coffeehouses in the United States.

As a Hammarplast salesman he noticed that one customer was buying more Hammarplast machines than any other. Partially out of curiosity as well as good sales instincts, he flew to Seattle to visit. That customer was a Hammarplast distributor, Starbucks Coffee. At the time, 1981, Starbucks was a fledging distributor of coffee-making machines and also distributed upscale coffee. But it did not own or operate a single coffeehouse.

The personal chemistry between Howard and his Seattle customer was good. Starbucks people liked him, and he liked them. He developed great rapport with the Starbucks team. They offered him a job, and he accepted. After working there for a short time, he told them about his idea for coffeehouses in the United States. They were hardly objective. They wanted Howard to keep his day job, employed by them. And they were totally focused on building their existing business. Besides, they thought Howard's idea was terrible. So they told him why the idea wouldn't work.

Most Americans hadn't been introduced to superior coffee, let alone learned to appreciate it. Nor had many Americans experienced the delight of espresso that was enjoyed in coffee-houses abroad. Keep in mind that this was in the early 1980s. There were coffeehouses in artist colonies like Greenwich Village in the United States, but they were a rarity in most communities throughout the country. For young adults, coffeehouses were where beatniks went to smoke pot and recite avant-garde poetry.

Ever the salesman, and now a man with a vision of growing clarity, Howard was convinced he could bring his bosses around to his way of thinking. But every time Howard broached his idea, his bosses would send him to meet with one of the foremost coffee experts in the country. One was a man at the largest importer of quality coffee beans in the nation.

But regardless of which expert Schultz spoke with, each one told Schultz his idea wouldn't work and went on to tell him why. The vote wasn't overwhelming; it was unanimous. They might easily have convinced a less confident man. These coffee experts were arrayed against a fellow as green in this billion-dollar industry as the leaves on a coffee tree. Eventually, his vision became a clarion call. As much as he liked the Starbucks team, he left to pursue his dream.

He wasn't just confident that he was right; he was certain. He managed to raise some capital and open a coffeehouse in Seattle. He called it Il Giornale, after a newspaper read in Italian coffee shops bearing the same name. His shop was immediately success-ful—upscale too. Howard used the best-roasted coffee beans he could buy. He soon opened a second shop and then a third one. His idea was really perking.

Incidentally, even though his former bosses had other fish to fry, Howard's superior salesmanship convinced Jerry Baldwin, one of the owners of the original Starbucks, to invest in Howard's new venture. Baldwin invested because he had respect for Howard and believed he could pull it off.

Having Jerry for credibility should have made fund-raising a snap. That's what Howard thought. Yet even after Jerry came in, 217 of the next 242 people Howard approached turned him down. Those are daunting odds, not the batting average of a champion.

So how could such a good salesman like Howard have had such difficulty convincing potential investors? The answer is really quite simple. If you ask Starbucks customers why they frequent Starbucks, you'll get many answers, such as, "I like the coffee, the ambience, the free office space, the friendly atmosphere." And "it's a cheap date site" or "they all know me at my local store."

If the customers are totally honest, they might also say they like feeling hip carrying the cardboard cup with the familiar green logo. They might say they get a feeling of belonging. Maybe they like appearing to drink a low-calorie drink, when the cup hides the caramel-based, whip cream–covered delight inside.

Of course none of these reasons existed when Schultz was seeking backers. Coffee was familiar to all, just not particularly special. Americans' reactions to coffee then were reminiscent of the two elderly women at a Catskill resort in the Woody Allen movie *Annie Hall*. One says, "Boy, the food at this place is really terrible." The other one says, "Yeah, I know; and such small portions"—the coffee back then wasn't very good, but everyone wanted the free refill.

What Howard envisioned was a nonalcoholic Cheers, a place between work and home—where everybody knows your name. What he developed was a club with secret code words like Doppio, Cappuccino, and Venti. Contrary to Groucho Marx's line, "I refuse to join any club that would have me as a member," almost everyone seems to want to join Howard's club.

Even Howard couldn't have known all that would be developed and would take place. He was selling potential investors a dream that no one could see, touch, or experience. Of course they could have done so in Italy, but at the time Howard was touting a

U.S. experiential business. No wonder he had so much difficulty and took so long raising the funds, despite the fact that he was a good salesman.

It turns out that Jerry Baldwin's respect for Howard was mutual. While Howard rejected the Starbucks owners' opinions about coffeehouses, he respected their coffee expertise and that of their employees. After a couple of years he acquired the entire company, its workers, its expertise, industry relationships, and of course, the Starbucks name. Howard believed Starbucks had great branding prospects. Starbucks would be his final employer.

Whereas Tom Stemberg was an MBA with hands-on operating experience and experience managing a store, Howard was a salesman and had never really managed anything. Although he was convinced that Americans would drink up his vision, how could he be sure he could run a coffee shop, let alone three and eventually many more? After all, being highly caffeinated can only go so far.

Far indeed. Today Starbucks has revenues of $15 billion, with 21,000 stores representing every state in the union and in 61 other countries, as well as presence in supermarkets, restaurants, and airports. In mid-2013, Howard proudly told me "last week, 71 million people went through Starbucks stores around the world." That meant that in a single month Starbucks serviced about 300 million customers, nearly as many people—adults and children—as live in the United States.

Today's global operation of Starbucks far exceeds Howard's initial vision but hasn't exceeded his skills, although clearly he has had to enhance existing skills and learn a few new skills along the way, especially the skill of attracting, hiring, and retaining excellent personnel. He has reinvented himself and his business early and often.

Interestingly, another successful entrepreneur, Ray Kroc, was similarly customer-centric. Ray sold milk-shake machines from his base in Chicago's suburbs. When he noted that a California customer was buying more machines than anyone else, he, like Howard, flew west to meet with his customer, the McDonald brothers. Again like Howard, Ray bought his customer and converted his salesman's concern for B2B customers into a concern for B2C consumers, making every detail of his McDonald's bend to that design.

Point Guard Bridgeman, Now Wendy's Shooting Star

While Junior Bridgeman was a credible NBA player, he was neither a superstar nor a household name. He did receive a good education from the University of Louisville, but he wasn't at the top of his class. His vocational experience had been limited. His parents taught him to have a great work ethic. That led to some jobs, but basketball eventually consumed all his spare time.

To conquer the business world would not be easy for an African American basketball player. But Junior started reinventing himself before he left the playing court in 1987. He has become a top point shooter in the business world.

Junior's reinventions occurred before Magic Johnson's business successes, and Junior would readily admit that he was no Magic Johnson. But he was determined. Before he became prominent with the Milwaukee Bucks, he spent three to four summers following a coach's advice, shooting 150–200,000 baskets to become a good shooter.

Junior had little business education but continually sought help wherever possible to improve and refine his skills. That is one reason he chose to be a franchisee of national brand restaurants: to benefit from the franchisors' capacities to improve his skills and to supplement them until he had learned them well. Knowing he had or would get the necessary skills made him confident he could handle first one and then more restaurants. He was confident that he could continue reinventing himself in business as deftly as he had learned to change hands while dribbling down court to a successful layup.

He doubled down, further increasing his confidence and enabling further reinventions. He went from manager, to owner of a few stores, to CEO of a firm with hundreds. Today, Junior Bridgeman, former basketball star, is one of the biggest individual owners of restaurants in the United States. Junior owns B.F. South, which has 3,300 employees and revenues of over half a billion dollars. You probably never heard of B.F. South. But it owns and operates 160 Wendy's and 118 Chili's restaurants. He has been listed as the fifth top African American CEO and his firm the fourth-largest African American–owned industrial/ service company. *Forbes* says he is worth a quarter of a billion dollars.

Understanding the thoughts and steps taken by people like Howard, Tom, and Junior can be the basis for your career change. Neither your goals nor your steps need be as big and bold as theirs. It is sufficient if you understand the essence of and principles behind what they did, so that you can follow those principles in the way that fits your circumstances.

Do as they have done and you can reinvent yourself. You can become sufficiently confident to make big changes in your life. You can achieve extraordinary success. By what you leave behind and what you strive toward, you can achieve a level of satisfaction and happiness you might be unable to imagine today. I can assure you that during their prior careers, none of them—not Tom, not Howard, not Junior—imagined that they would achieve what they have.

Freeman's Blue Bottle Formula
for a Better Cup of Coffee

People such as Howard Schultz and Tom Stemberg reinvent whole industries. Sometimes entrepreneurs' goals are more modest. For example, James Freeman had no desire to reinvent the coffee industry. In fact, he says he's thankful to Starbucks and upscale coffee maker Peet's for having made it easier for him by giving "millions and millions of people the permission . . . to buy espresso drinks . . . and pay between $4 and $5. And then a small subset of those customers wants something kind of like that but different, better, and interesting. And that's where businesses like the ones that impress me the most come in." Starbucks also softened up investors and other resources. It's like the lead cyclist creating a draft that eases the burden of a follower.

James Freeman started out as a classical clarinetist. He loved making music, as well as making and drinking exceptional coffee. As a clarinetist, he told me, "I was totally burning out. But I was really excited about coffee." He had learned to make great coffee and realized he remained excited about coffee. That's why he founded Blue Bottle Coffee.

At first he sold coffee at farmers' markets. The rent was cheap, and it afforded him the luxury of educating people who strolled by. The strollers had time to listen to his spiel and wait for James to brew their cup to order.

He selects beans that are "roasted really freshly." Often the beans are certified as "organic." And he actually has his baristas grind his superior coffee beans, put enough in an individual paper funnel, and pour the hot water over the grounds. The customer must wait for the water to filter through before she receives her coffee.

Customers weren't accustomed to individually brewed coffees. It took time. Strollers were willing to wait, but would coffee-shop customers wait for coffee they'd never tasted before? After all, without having tried it, they wouldn't know whether it was worth the wait. Besides, most people weren't strolling through life; they were racing to work, to meetings, and to the kids' schools to drive them home.

Eventually the dynamic of return customers who had tasted Freeman's Blue Bottle brand and decided it was worth the wait got traction in the marketplace by word of mouth. What makes his coffee special, he says, is his willingness to brew each cup individually as ordered by the customer. That's a high standard of perfection.

The lines of customers at the markets got longer. James decided it was time to try for success in the "real world." James opted to forgo marketing surveys. He was doubtful that the survey participants could imagine what he had in mind.

He subscribed to a thought that I've described for over four decades as, "If you're not up on it, then you have to be down on it." He would have to show it to people. They'd have to see his wait-for-a-cup-brewed-for-you idea in operation. He couldn't leave it to others' imagination.

His first real-world shop was not exactly promising. It was a kiosk in San Francisco, in what James refers to as a smelly alley. The alley was frequented by derelicts, and they were a tough crowd. But the rent was only $600 a month. The kiosk and equipment was $20,000. James paid for all this out of his limited savings. Before long the lines in the alley got longer. Eventually, the discriminating people in line crowded out the seedier element. More and more people were comfortable entering the alley.

ALPHA AND BETA TESTS AREN'T JUST FOR TECHIES

If you are going to fund your first facility, as James did, still consider alpha and beta tests (simulated and real tests with prospective users) or use immersion tests. James proved his concept at the farmers' markets, which provided inexpensive tests. Then his first facility was low cost (in the smelly alley).

James had been "discovered," and Blue Bottle became a reality. Since then Freeman has opened a few more stores in San Francisco and New York. The stores are just slightly larger than the kiosk—still minimally decorated and generally in remote, though not in smelly, locations.

He wanted to take advantage of the huge foot traffic in New York City, so he upgraded one of his locations there. Actually, he has raised capital and opened a "flagship" store in the iconic Rockefeller Center. But even there, his store is not easy to find.

SEEING IS BELIEVING

For those who have the option (available funds and low cost of start-up), there's something to be said for being able to show prospective investors an existing product or facility rather than trying to get people to see your imagination. James understood that, as did Maxine Clark, whom you'll read about shortly.

At first James was doubtful that New Yorkers, always in a rush and intolerant of even momentary delays, would wait several minutes for a cup of coffee to be brewed especially for them. But they are willing to wait. Changing New Yorkers' habits isn't easy. Most entrepreneurs adapt to the New York ways. They don't add burdens to the challenge that draws them to open in New York. After all, as Sinatra sang, they open there because, "If I can make it there, I'll make it anywhere."

Freeman isn't trying to reinvent either New York City or the coffee industry. James aimed at reinventing a small niche of the industry, so the leveraged impact on his niche was larger. Yet he remained the proverbial pimple on an elephant's hind end and wasn't a target. His number of stores is a fraction of 1 percent of the number of Starbucks stores, and his revenues are an even smaller fraction. It's doubtful his fraction will increase. Indeed, it is more likely to decrease. Interestingly, Freeman is working hard at reinventing his company as little as possible.

2

Ignoring the
Noise of Dissent

I NEVER THOUGHT I'D LIVE TO QUOTE FORMER VICE PRESIDENT Spiro Agnew, who before his disgrace and resignation referred to media critics as "nattering nabobs of negativism." That's often an apt description for naysayers. But somehow successful entrepreneurs always accentuate the positive and know when to be deaf to their nattering nabobs.

With 2,000 stores worldwide doing $25 billion in sales in 26 countries, Staples is a game changer. Tom Stemberg is worth a small fortune. Tom sold most of his Staples stock and has reinvented himself again, as a venture capitalist. He backs other star entrepreneurial companies, such as Lululemon. Some of those who provided the seed capital for Staples, like Bain Capital, earned a large fortune on their investments.

The stationery industry was well established. Others had tried to improve it and failed. Many warned Tom against trying.

Fortunately he had done his homework and he knew the naysayers' facts were dead wrong.

Junior Bridgeman's company, B.F. South, is Wendy's second largest franchisee, with nearly 200 restaurants. He is number three on the Restaurant Finance Monitor's Top 200 franchisee-owned companies. According to *Forbes* he is worth an estimated quarter billion dollars. In the days when Junior played in the NBA, jocks—and as I explain later, African American jocks for sure—didn't become businesspeople. Junior didn't pay attention to the prevalent stats on this matter.

Howard Schultz's win is, by comparison, phenomenal. Starbucks' 1992 initial public offering was one of the most successful ever for what was then a small to midsize firm. At $17 a share, Starbucks' market capitalization totaled $300 million, and the company just kept growing. In 2012, the number of Starbucks stores worldwide reached 20,891 in 62 countries, with 13,279 of those in the United States. *Forbes* says Howard was worth $2 billion in 2013. Had you put a spare $100,000 in the initial public offering and kept your shares after a two-for-one split and retained the dividends received, your Starbucks holdings would have become worth nearly $10.4 million 20 years later. That's a 26 percent annual return, which is nearly unmatchable. All the experts told Howard not to try it; they had a million reasons not to. But the naysayers' arithmetic didn't add up.

Don't Let Naysayers Block Your Reinvention

Why and, more importantly, *how* were those three entrepreneurs able to ignore the overwhelmingly negative advice and move on to great success and fortune? Given the passage of time and those extraordinary achievements, one might assume that the writing was on the wall, leaving Tom, Howard, and Junior to follow it.

But the walls were shrouded and the screams of naysayers were deafening.

What makes Starbucks' Howard Schultz, Staples' Tom Stemberg, or Wendy's Junior Bridgeman different from most of us isn't that they had an epiphany that we lacked. It was that they had the confidence to do what it took. Also they had made the effort to develop that confidence. That may sound like a riddle to you, and if it does, that's okay. Riddles can be solved. If it sounds like a Catch-22 to you, it will seem far more daunting. Just remember, however, even Catch-22s can be solved. Frequently the prerequisite to developing the confidence is negating the voices of those who say, "You can't do it."

BE HONEST WITH YOURSELF

What can you do? What can you learn to do? What areas must you get help on?

Howard Schultz and the Imported Culture

In Schultz's case, he had to overcome very loud noise—the negativism coming from industry experts who consistently said that Howard was wrong, that the United States wasn't ready for coffeehouses with superior coffee. They insisted that Schultz's Starbucks dream was illusory and that he couldn't possibly succeed with it. Of course he did succeed with it. But how?

Howard was a salesman, not a coffee expert and certainly not a restaurateur. When I asked Howard what made him think he could run a restaurant, let alone several or scores, he credited his time working for the "original Starbucks"—the company discussed in the first chapter. As mentioned, it didn't run restaurants or coffeehouses. On the other hand, some of its customers *did* run food businesses, including coffeehouses.

Once again, Howard was adding arrows to his skill set by observing those customers' behavior, which he did exceptionally well. That's because he cared, cared as only a good salesman can. He also had observed scads of coffeehouses and cafes in Europe. He converted his salesman's instinct to learn from customers into an ability to run a coffeehouse.

After all, anyone can make a cup of coffee. So how difficult can it be to make many cups of coffee? The key and the challenge was creating an atmosphere and service that customers would enjoy and crave. He needed "to create a third place in America that didn't exist between home and work." He had no desire to say, some day, "Why didn't I?" He preferred saying, "I can do that."

In reinventing himself, he merely adjusted and refined some of the arrows already in his skill set quiver. With each refinement, Howard was confronted by naysayers. Some cared about Howard and wanted to protect him from his unreasonable optimism and exuberance. Others ascribed to Howard their own circumstances and risk aversion. The innocent were equally counterproductive. You must understand the naysayers' motivations.

Those importers and wholesalers who created the noise that Howard ignored never looked beyond their own customers—wholesalers and retailers—so they couldn't see Howard's vision for serving consumers.

Howard was inspired by what he saw in Europe, his own positive reaction as a consumer, and his understanding about the American consumer, whose reaction, he was confident, would be much like his own. He also realized that the industry experts were wearing blinders. The experts' inability to get his perspective worked to his advantage. Otherwise, they might have grabbed the brass ring, too, all of which made him confident he could make his idea succeed.

Ironically, one of the experts was Faema, a leading espresso coffee machine maker in Milan, Italy. Howard had traveled to Milan with Jerry Baldwin, his employer at Starbucks and an investor in Howard's Il Giornale venture. Jerry's industry stature would surely impress Faema. Maybe so. But they still rejected Howard's idea. That was what Howard describes as "a terrible moment." Faema said Americans weren't ready for the Italian coffee experience. The irony—Italians were suddenly experts on Americans' behavior. At the same time, American potential investors had opinions about the Italian coffee experience—too pricey, too much time consumed, no wait service.

Ultimately Howard had to broker the difference between two peoples' cultures. When I mentioned the irony, Howard said, "That's a very good observation. I couldn't convince the Italians to invest in an American concept. I couldn't convince the Americans to invest in something Italian. I always thought I was a good salesman, but I guess I wasn't. I was swimming upstream—going to ask people to pay at that time $2 for coffee in a paper cup with an Italian name no one could pronounce. I had a hard time convincing people to write a check." Indeed, for Howard to satisfy his burden—to broker between two cultures (American and Italian)—the trick was not trying to impose one culture on another but instead finding a common element. In Howard's case that was achieved by adopting an idea he saw in Italy to his American customers, namely "a place between work and home."

So what did he do after Faema's rejection? Did he fly back home, tail between his legs? No. He wasn't going to waste the airfare he'd already spent. He can't even remember how he had scrounged up the money for that fare. Instead, he dragged Jerry Baldwin to visit hundreds of coffeehouses in Italy and elsewhere in Europe. In retrospect he says, those visits were "galvanizing for me because it reassured me, despite Faema's rejection, that I was absolutely on the right track."

Due diligence isn't just to satisfy investors. It also should convince the entrepreneur, one way or the other. After rejection from the 217 investors, Howard remained unfettered, while the experts were bound by antiquated practices. He believed that consumers would learn to like what he had liked. He saw the pieces of the jigsaw puzzle, together with the picture on the puzzle box cover. That enabled Howard to fit the pieces together. The naysayers saw different pictures, making it difficult for them to imagine the pieces coming together coherently as Howard knew they could.

The way that Howard dealt with the experts becomes clearer if related to a story about Herb Kohler, the CEO and chairman of Kohler Company. Manufacturing ceramic toilet fixtures is more an art than a science. In the late nineteenth and early twentieth centuries, Kohler's founders imported skilled immigrants to Kohler, the Wisconsin town named after the pioneering family. The immigrants were housed in a large "boardinghouse" built for that purpose. Years later, Kohler's employees had their own homes, so the boardinghouse was no longer needed. Herb wanted to convert the building into a hotel for a new Kohler business thrust—a kind of reinvention. Company executives didn't want to start a new business. Besides, they felt the company could use it for much-needed office space. So they had a meeting where all the executives stated their reason for conversion to office space. That building is today the famous Kohler American Club. More than just a resort hotel, it is a valuable showcase where qualified consumers spend days using new Kohler products in their hotel rooms.

Herb ended that meeting by saying: "Gentlemen, you lost by one vote—mine." Herb could silence the noise of his executives. After all, he owned the eponymous company. By contrast, Howard Schultz was merely an employee of the old Starbucks distribution company—and a new one at that. To gain the dominant power of Herb's one vote, Howard had to reinvent himself as the owner of his company.

What Do the NBA and Wendy's Have in Common?

The noise of dissent for Junior Bridgeman was totally different. Professional athletes, except for extraordinary stars like Michael Jordan, Magic Johnson, Dan Marino, Jack Nicklaus, Tiger Woods, Jimmy Connors, and the Williams sisters, have difficulty turning their stardom to commercial advantage while they are playing—let alone after they retire. They may be recognized and get a free drink or a dinner from appreciative hometown fans for a while. But they can walk down the street in another city without being recognized, although the height or girth of many retired NBA and NFL players may lead to momentary attempts at recollection.

Unfortunately, most pro athletes do not spend the time and effort to prepare themselves for second careers. Decades ago, I helped professional athlete clients do that very thing. I lectured on the subject at the annual Conferences of the Sports Lawyers Association, of which I am the founder and president emeritus.

Understandably, it was difficult for athletes to prepare during their hectic season and during their ever-shortened off-season. But then a new issue arose that virtually ended the professional athletes' interest in the subject. The athletes' compensation rose to astronomic levels, reflecting their stardom, lessening the apparent but, in my mind, the still essential need for second paying careers.

African Americans have often had difficulty accessing capital for a number of reasons, possibly including prejudice. In Bridgeman's playing days, before the astronomical NBA salaries, that lack of access to professional financing made it very difficult for African American athletes to finance second careers.

Back then, however, the unspoken noise—"an African American jock can't become a successful businessman"—was louder noise in its silence and harder to overcome than if the words were spoken. It was a deafening "sound of silence."

One day, years ago, Junior was serving customers in one of his own Wendy's stores when someone recognized him and called a TV station to lament that here was another former pro athlete who obviously had spent all his money and was forced to flip hamburgers in a fast-food restaurant. In that invalid assumption, you find the basis for the unspoken noise.

Junior was supremely confident on the basketball court. But how did he gain the confidence to become a highly successful entrepreneur and businessman? He realized that he had some useful skills, some potentially valuable arrows in his quiver, but they needed sharpening.

He was a true leader of his teams, not because he was the best player but because he instinctively understood what was needed to lead. Junior's style of leadership was evident in the way he helped NBA rookies be as good as they could be. So he didn't have to be the best to become a successful businessman. He simply had to teach his young counter employees to be the best they could be. He applied his leadership skills to a new class of followers. He went from guiding high-ego, high-performing, high-earning NBA cagers to guiding undereducated, underskilled, poor, and immature kids as to how they were to run restaurants. And he could "outsource" everything else—financial, budgeting, marketing, purchasing, and the like—to the franchisor, Wendy's. Junior chose franchising, because the franchisor was experienced in passing along skills Junior needed and could provide support and training in their areas. Indeed, that made him sufficiently confident to buy three Wendy's franchises while he was still playing professionally.

MOST PEOPLE FOCUS ON
THEIR OBVIOUS SKILLS

Most people listen to the opinions of others. Pro athletes'
gifted playing skills are obvious, and they have been applauded
for them since childhood. They become mesmerized by the
noise of fans. As a result, they seek sports-related post-pro
careers, such as coaching. Sport is familiar and comfortable
to them.

Most great entrepreneurs have three things in common: (1)
they see their vision clearly; (2) the experts in the field see even
more clearly why the entrepreneur is mistaken and will fail; and
(3) the entrepreneurs follow their visions, ignoring the experts'
noisy dissents, not out of arrogance or ignorance but because the
entrepreneurs visualize the pictures on the jigsaw puzzle box covers. They know that the experts' noise stems from seeing the puzzle pieces and not the completed puzzle pictures on the box covers.

It is axiomatic that entrepreneurs with vision face critics whose
horizons are clouded. Fred Smith got a C on his idea for an air-
borne parcel delivery service when he presented the FedEx concept to a Yale undergraduate professor. It is essential that entrepreneurs dream, indeed that they see what others do not.

Confidence to follow the dream comes from both the clarity
of the vision and the recognition that naysayers simply don't have
vision. Smith's professor was "looking" at a picture that resembled
the U.S. Postal Service—an inefficient organization whose very
existence is dependent on the backing of the U.S. government.
Contrast this with the picture Fred saw—an efficient organization with a way to send a document cross-country to be read the
next day and with a seemingly exorbitant price in order to wrest

profits from the enterprise. No wonder his earthbound professor gave Fred a C!

What gave Howard Schultz the confidence to follow a path that coffee experts agreed was a path to failure? What gave him the confidence to leave his job and follow his dream? Note that he did this while his wife was pregnant and at a time when he had almost no savings. As Howard jokingly told me, "It's a good thing the investors delivered before Sheri did."

Even if his dream was rational and the experts were wrong, how did Howard realize he had the know-how to implement successfully? After all, he had never learned key skills required for the effort and, of course, hadn't been called on to exhibit such skills in the past. How was he able to distinguish the experts' expertise in coffee from their lack of knowledge about coffeehouses?

Reinventing a "Stationary" Industry

Tom Stemberg tried his Staples idea out on every investor he could find. They all thought his idea crazy. Nobody said it, of course, but the message was: "You're nuts; you must be, since everyone in the industry disagrees with you."

Investors declined his invitation at first because they saw the high risk associated with such a drastic reinvention of the industry. Besides, they argued the conventional wisdom—that the stationery industry was inherently only marginally profitable.

Much like Howard Schultz, Tom Stemberg was sent by investment bankers and others to share his ideas and get reaction from industry experts. He talked with the late Howard Wolf, who was the CEO of United Stationers. Howard had led the company to great success. He was a respected leader in the industry. Wolf told Tom that his idea for a Staples-type store was "horrible." That might have scared off many newbies to the industry and to entrepreneurship. Tom believes that Wolf told him it was a horrible idea because "he thought if we succeeded it would be real bad for United Stationers. And he was right about that."

Tom says he knew Wolf was wrong because "Wolf's arguments didn't make any sense. They were all about the customer wanting service and hand holding when, in fact, most of these office products dealers were giving lousy service. I had talked with a lot of customers and I knew that they weren't aware how badly they were getting ripped off. But when you told them that the same dozen pens they were buying for $3.68 you could get for about a dollar, they were going to leave their loyal, great dealer in a New York minute."

Tom did his homework. He went to law firms, to friends who were lawyers there. He asked them how much they spent on office products. Few knew. After all, this was before law firms had computerized systems that could spit out such information instantly. So they'd ask their assistant or office manager, who would generally guess that they spent $200 per employee. That would have been $20,000 for their 100 employees. Tom would urge them to check, not only as a favor to him but also to themselves.

Lacking a computer system, that meant reading and adding up old invoices. That they did this attests to Tom's salesmanship. They were in fact spending over $100,000 for those 100 employees. That lawyer who managed his firm's audit for Tom was beside himself. Tom recalls asking the lawyer, "Let me ask you a question. If we could save you one-half of that, but you'd have to do some work and go to a store, would you do it?" The lawyer replied, "Are you kidding me? That'd pay for my entire family's cars and those of my partners. Where do I go? How do I do it?" Obviously, Tom was getting more accurate information than was shared by Mr. Wolf.

Tom had observed the success of Jack Miller, the founder and CEO of Quill, a major distributor of office supplies to businesses, whom Tom describes as "a wonderful guy." Jack was in fact a *true* industry leader whose innovative moves and annual messages were gospel to his peers. Jack had carried a case all the way to the U.S. Supreme Court to eliminate state sales tax charges for his company and for other similarly situated companies that chose to follow his example. Quill was charging much less than the corner stationery store, and Quill's business was already big and growing. Tom saw that the company's quick delivery served some customers well, but small orders were burdensome. Jack freely encouraged Tom in his initiative, though Tom was a potential rival. Interesting outcome—years later Staples bought Quill for about three-quarters of a billion dollars.

Tom learned important retail lessons. He saw that wholesale clubs—Costco, Price Club, BJ's, and Sam's Club—that had only a hundred relevant products in each of their stores were doing $4 to $5 million revenue per store each year. Tom knew that with nearly 5,000 items in each of his stores, nearly 50 times what the others carried, he could do very well indeed.

It's often said that the lyrics to "My Way," made famous by Frank Sinatra, should be the entrepreneur's theme song. Before you adopt that song as your theme, try to understand how other successful entrepreneurs did it their way. Adapt your way accordingly. That's what Tom Stemberg did. That's why Tom studied people such as Jack Miller of Quill and successful retailers in other fields, such as Costco, to see what worked and what didn't. And Tom applied his grocery store skills to the seemingly unrelated business of office products. That rehoned skill made Tom realize that SKU numbers were key.

So Tom looked at his research and knew that the naysayers were off base. They were using poor logic or had distorted facts or had manipulated one or both to support their naysaying in order to protect their own turf.

Make It Your Turf,
But Don't Get Buried in It

You must become *the* expert. Being *the* expert doesn't mean knowing what all the people in the industry know. It means knowing enough to understand current systems' or products' advantages and disadvantages (i.e., opportunities). This enables you to: determine the viability of your idea; convince potential investors and other stakeholders; and develop the best strategy and plans.

HOW TO BECOME *THE* EXPERT

Do in-depth homework. Learn all you can about the industry. That's what Tom did, questioning representative samples of industry stakeholders and participants. His due diligence included interviewing the stationery industry's then-current customers. Note how Tom handled the interviews: First, he contacted a lawyer friend. He focused on customer orientation, concerns, and needs as well as the extent to which those things were or weren't dealt with or being met. Always be customer-centric in such situations, but don't assume the customer really knows. Tom challenged the lawyer's "knowledge" about his office supplies expenses and landed his first customer; then he dealt with Howard Wolf. The determination as to whether "it's broke," as in "if it ain't broke, don't fix it," is often just an opinion, not necessarily a fact. If it's broken, but you don't think it's broken, you won't fix it. Tom knew what was lacking—service and price—so Wolf couldn't B.S. him. Tom was also sensitive to Wolf's prejudice. He sensed a potential competitor. Then Tom did what the industry failed to do—compare itself to the big guys like Costco. The industry just wrote off those discount operators as bit players "who didn't even carry all the SKUs."

Tom knew those operators had developed the start of a valid business model that he adopted and grew.

Eventually Boston-based Tom Stemberg obtained financing from the man who would one day be the governor of Massachusetts and the 2012 Republican candidate for president of the United States, Mitt Romney. In a speech given at the 2012 Republican National Convention, Tom endorsed Romney. That wasn't payback for the investment by Romney's company, Bain Capital. Tom agreed with many of Mitt's positions and with his insight. Mitt had immediately understood why Staples would be a success. Tom felt he understood more about Mitt than most. Indeed, Tom's story about his first meeting with Mitt, at which Bain agreed to finance Tom, told me more about Romney than all the debates leading to and including his run for president.

What innate quality enabled Tom to scorn the experts and found Staples? For that matter, why did Romney share Tom's vision and finance a dream widely regarded as foolhardy by industry experts? What put Tom and Mitt on the same entrepreneurial page? They are two very different men with two very different backgrounds, except for the fact that each attended Harvard Business School. There is ample evidence for me to argue what we all know: a Harvard MBA is neither a prerequisite for, nor a common denominator of, successful entrepreneurship.

Post-Harvard, Romney and Stemberg had divergent careers that called for significantly different skills. Yet they both had the confidence to silence the noise and leap hurdles set up by experts. Are there similarities and lessons in that confidence?

So how did Mitt Romney see Tom's vision of Staples so clearly? As Tom tells it, "Mitt Romney was one of the investors. Mitt Romney is an incredibly parsimonious person. So he could easily accept the value of saving fifty bucks on a case of copy paper which others wouldn't necessarily see." Indeed, even after Mitt agreed to invest, many others rejected the investment opportunity. It's true, Mitt Romney didn't get to be president, but his investment in Staples brought handsome profits to Romney's fund.

It might also be helpful to examine Tom's background. His mother, who was Catholic, and his father, who was Jewish but converted to Catholicism so they could marry, left Austria and moved to the United States, settling in New Jersey. There his father owned and ran a restaurant where he worked very long hours. When Tom was 11, his father died, which Tom describes as "a shock to my world." His mother moved with Tom back to Austria, uprooting him from his friends and causing him to start anew. That added shock upon shock to his world. To most 11-year-old boys, this would have been devastating. Tom told me he found it an advantage. He had learned basketball in New Jersey, where most boys learn to play and where the competition is tough. Tom doubts he could have made the team there. In Austria, however, at that time, few played basketball, so Tom made the team. Similarly, while Harvard University is deluged by applications for admission from Garden State residents, few applicants came from Austria, and Tom was admitted.

Of course, getting into Harvard was just a start. Admission was followed by another shock. Tom's education in Austria was good but uneven. In those subject areas where his education lagged, Tom was less than prepared. As he puts it, "You had to accept the fact that you're not only not the smartest person in the room, you may not be in the top ten. You have to get comfortable with that and move forward." He says that his steady successes at Harvard led to his feeling after graduation that "I may have gotten to the smartest ten in the room."

Sure, this shows Tom's personality as one that makes lemonade when life hands him lemons. (That isn't why Tom, now a venture capitalist, decided to give a running start to Lululemon company.) More relevant here is his learning early to see a whole picture, to figure out what he needed to do, such as adapting his skill set to be positioned for success. He told me "virtually every entrepreneur I've encountered was told, 'This is a dumb idea; it'll never work.'"

The C Student with A-Plus Smarts

Michael Krasny grew up in the Chicago suburb Skokie. He describes himself, "I wasn't one of the smartest kids on the block. I was not a good student, I was a C student, probably in the lower quartile." Krasny may have been a C student, likely a function of schools trying to fit a square peg in a round hole. But the way he became a billionaire through CDW, a company he founded in 1985 and sold in 2007, contradicts his self-assessment. When he put CDW on the block for billions, he proved that computers are not for dummies.

APPRECIATE YOUR TALENT

After 12 years in the classroom, grades were the only measure of Mike's talents. He assumed they were indicative of a future bereft of success. No one was grading his computer knowledge and talents, possibly because his evaluators weren't talented in that area.

While Mike didn't like school, he started using computers in 1964, working a punch-card machine, and took his first programming class in 1971 at the University of Illinois. He absolutely loved the class and computers. His fraternity brothers never asked his advice in other classes, but they all sought out Mike's assistance for computer science class.

In 1980 Mike needed a printer, and a fellow he knew helped him buy one from a wholesaler. That fellow, a Harvard valedictorian, as Mike says, "had to be smarter than me." So when Mike told him he was thinking of going into the business of selling equipment like printers, the fellow said, "It won't work; don't do it." Since the Harvard valedictorian was smarter, Mike didn't do it.

Mike was fortunate for having been born at the beginning of the largest bloodless revolution in history—the computer revolution. He was also lucky that when he didn't like other studies, which kind of left computer science as an obvious alternative for Mike, he chose schools that offered good instruction in that field.

It would be wrong, however, to attribute all of Mike's success to luck. His instincts, steeped in trade while working for his father's auto dealership and enhanced through computer education and "playing around" with computers, gave him a niche expertise. Eventually he realized that while he lacked other expertise, including seemingly critical areas of business and education in general, his computer expertise, leveraged by the computer revolution, trumped whatever he lacked. And he learned that those missing arrows—areas of basic business processes—could be gathered and honed along the way.

Around that time there was another company in Chicago, PC Network, which was the first mail-order company to sell computers. Mike wound up selling PC Network a lot of personal computers that he was brokering. That company was generating $30 million a year, and Mike thought it "was a cool business." He wanted to copy PC Network. So he went to the advertising agency that did work for his father's car dealership. He thought he could put together an ad and start doing business. But the ad exec told

Mike, "Save your money. It won't work; don't do it." Mike felt that the ad exec was the expert; he knew what such an ad could and couldn't accomplish, so he followed the expert's advice and didn't do it.

Of course the ad exec wasn't the only naysayer. Mike worked in his father's car dealership. Mike managed the dealership after his father's heart attack. His dad wanted Mike to follow in his footsteps, and his influence was substantial. So much so that when a woman from Toyota noticed that Mike was an early adopter of computers for the dealership and asked whether he was "doing something with computers," Mike replied, "No, that's a hobby. I've got to get a real job. I've still got to figure out what I'm really going to do." In the meantime, several others he respected told him not to do it.

Eventually Mike realized that the ad exec might have understood advertising in the industries he'd worked on for decades, but he didn't understand the computer industry or the people in it as well as Mike did. Mike was fortunate to take courses in computer science and to understand computers at a time when few people even owned a computer. Of course, the ad exec might have been trying to support the wishes of Mike's father, lest he lose a valued existing client. Finally Mike called the ad exec and told him to run the ad. The exec, still trying to convince Mike this endeavor was futile, said, "You've got to prepay for the ad," which Mike agreed to do.

TEST YOUR TALENTS AND SKILLS

Sometimes, instead of starting a business to see whether it works, it's sufficient to determine whether you have what it takes to pull off what's obvious. Krasny followed the advice of Mark Twain: "It ain't what you don't know that gets you in

trouble. It's what you know for sure that just ain't so." Mike did
a series of transactions, each of them successful. He saw he had
valuable skills others lacked.

Krasny claims he lacked confidence. Clearly in those early years, he lacked the confidence to start and then run his burgeoning computer distribution business. He was so scared and felt so over his head in managing the business that he tried several times to sell the company. In fact that very same naysaying Harvard valedictorian put together a group, about two years after Mike started the business, and offered him a couple of million dollars to take the business off his hands. While Mike was scared about his ability to maintain, let alone grow, the business, his passion and drive more than compensated for his fears. So he didn't sell. The money he was offered was less than one-tenth of 1 percent of his ultimate price.

At first Mike wasn't able to screen out the noise of the naysayers and overcome his insecurity. But he finally figured out that his computer knowledge made his opinion more valuable than that of the experts. His computer acumen enabled Mike to see the jigsaw puzzle box picture at a time when the pieces of this intimidating puzzle were right in front of the experts.

Along the way, he talked with and studied many businesses and businesspeople. This habit was also born out of his lack of confidence, according to Mike. He would observe companies he admired, such as Microsoft, Intel, IBM, Compaq, Hewlett-Packard, Fel-Pro, and Walmart. He learned from all of them and readily admits to copying from all of them.

Here was a self-described C student doing quality homework and learning the skills he lacked. Mike knew that while he had great instincts that helped him found and run CDW during its start-up stage, he had no experience running a large, growing business.

FIND MENTORS WHO HAVE SKILLS YOU LACK

Observe and listen to what others do well that you don't do well or even know how to do. Figure out what parts of what they do and say can help you; then ask them to be your mentors but limit their scope to the area of expertise you've selected. (Often a role model will provide a good lesson in one area, but if he or she is followed in other areas, the lessons will prove to be counterproductive.) Learn all you can about those things. Then test what you've learned—incrementally, not all at once. With each new skill you acquire, you improve your likelihood of success.

As Mike entered the mature operating stage, he sought professional managers to help him run his company. The statute of limitations had probably run out on raising his school grades. But in his own unique way, Mike seems to have learned something in school that those at the top of his class may have missed. As a result, Mike now is clearly at the economic top of his class. It would be interesting to see him at his class reunion.

For a self-described poor student, he actually proved to be a brilliant one, learning about human resources from a couple of companies, about inventory management from a friend, and about crisis management from still another friend. This incremental improvement of his management skills led him to the realization that the so-called experts were clueless when it came to his own area of expertise.

She Had Them "Build-A-Bear" to Build Her Business

Growing up in Coral Gables, Florida, Maxine Clark had a big dream—becoming a civil rights lawyer. That choice may have been influenced by her mom, who had worked as Eleanor Roosevelt's traveling secretary during World War II. Besides, Maxine believed she could be anything she wanted to be, and no one told her that she couldn't. She knew she wanted to be something that women couldn't be in an era when they were expected to marry and stay home. At the time, women were a small minority in the nation's law schools. She also knew that law school was expensive. She'd have to work to save up, so she took a job in retailing because she had enjoyed her marketing courses in college. She landed in an executive training program at the May Company in Washington, DC.

She was convinced the job would be the means to an end. After all, there were 11 law schools in the capital district. She knew she was good enough to enter law school, graduate, and then serve yet another minority as a civil rights lawyer. In short, retailing was just a temporary stop along the way.

At the May Company, she was fortunate enough to make a presentation to Stanley Goodman, May's chairman. He told her that "retailing is entertainment, and the store is a stage. When the customers have fun, they spend more money." His words made an indelible impression on Maxine. She calls that the "beginning of my reinvention: every time I got a new position, every time I moved up the ladder in the corporation, I was reinventing myself, because I was given the possibilities, new challenges, new pushing myself to places I never thought I would go."

After 25 years working at the May Company (that chain of department stores was to be acquired by Federated Department Stores—now Macy's) Maxine Clark left to become president of Payless Shoes. So she went from being an employee at a chain of huge retail stores to being an executive at a large chain of far smaller stores.

The merchandising skills gained at the May Company were readily applicable to Payless. She had enjoyed access to the top levels at the May Company in that the CEO was clearly impressed with her potential. As a result he had invited her to sit next to him at board meetings. Moreover, she reported directly to him.

At board meetings and through her professional contacts with the CEO she learned what she would need to know as a president. She figured out how to handle the responsibilities of the top job when she went to Payless. Becoming Payless's president may have been a reinvention for Maxine. But most of the reinventing occurred at May.

Maxine says, "I think the biggest change I made . . . was going from working on the [May] corporate staff to being executive vice president of a bigger division of the May Company." This made Maxine an accountable executive for the first time. She had to establish her authority and her credibility with those under her. "I was the first woman that a lot of men ever worked for."

I think both were big changes. In each position Maxine quickly adjusted her skill set and was up to the job. Ultimately Maxine's biggest reinvention of herself was when she left Payless to found Build-A-Bear. She says it was no big change. She feels it was a step back to what she initially loved about retail—customer contact. She had moved up the ladder and disconnected from the customers. That is true; she was returning to her retail roots. But she was leaving the corporate cocoon after decades. She was no longer reporting to owners; she was becoming *the* owner.

She had never been one to pass the buck, but now she was where the buck stopped. Let's face it: leaving corporate America to become an entrepreneur is to most people a daunting challenge. That trepidation is what keeps talented people in their corporate cocoon until it's too late to fly like a butterfly. Maxine agrees that most people see entrepreneurship as exponential rather than as incremental. She views it as another incremental step. And in her case it was an incremental step on the retail continuum.

She had run a company with retail stores in shopping malls. She understood the mall infrastructure. "I was in every mall in America, as the president of Payless Shoes," she says. "Even though I'd never negotiated a lease before and now had to negotiate my own, I had a sense about them. I had been in all of this. I had listened to our legal department talking about them, and I had been very curious about them. I didn't have to know everything about them, but I did need to know enough not to be dangerous." She also understood sourcing, pricing, and other retail skills.

Sure, there were steps that were new to her (raising capital, establishing a new brand, and creating a visual image to depict the brand), and of course there is a difference between selling men and women a necessity—shoes—and selling kids a luxury make-your-own stuffed animal. Also people need more than one pair of shoes. Kids don't need more than one teddy bear.

Maxine says, "I mean, nobody needed another teddy bear. That's for sure. But they might have needed a place to have personalization and customization and a feeling that they had more control over their destiny, to actually put their own story, their own creativity, their own personality into this bear."

In addition to the kids who built Maxine's bears, there were grandparents and lovers too. Elders could share an experience with grandchildren. Sweethearts could build bears with "the boyfriend or girlfriend (a more "bearable" way of "playing house"), instead of just picking a [factory] bear off the shelf," Maxine added

Clearly she had learned well from May Company chairman, Stanley Goodman. The executive in her made her understand it was much like before. She had to determine what she did and didn't know and hire or retain great people, such as the extremely creative and successful brand designer Adrienne Weiss, to do what she couldn't do. As for finding capital, she was fortunate. She had enough money to open one store, and she knew she could get more from family, friends, and acquaintances. As it turned out, she didn't have to seek capital. Capital sought out Maxine.

When Maxine opened her first Build-A-Bear store in her hometown, St. Louis, a man who had heard about it came by the store and liked what he saw. On the spot, he offered to invest what she needed to open more stores.

THE MAGIC OF A TANGIBLE VISION

Maxine had the funds to build a first store. Her angel investor saw it and invested. Who knows whether he would have invested if all he'd had was Maxine's explanation of her vision and no store? It was a lot like James Freeman's coffee store in the smelly alley, mentioned in Chapter 1. It was unlike Howard Schultz's burden, selling just a vision until he'd opened a few coffeehouses that people could see, touch, and smell.

Not everyone was as supportive of Maxine as her first investor was. She says that "there were a lot of naysayers, because they couldn't visualize what I was talking about. And many people, particularly adults, said, 'Why would anybody want to make their own stuffed animal, if they could buy it already? People want speed. They don't want to stay longer in the mall; they want to stay shorter in the mall.' I didn't really believe that, because I really believed that people wanted to engage with products."

Besides, what did adults really know about teddy bears? Maxine's source of validation was her 10-year-old friend, Katie.

Katie Burkhardt, the daughter of Maxine's closest friend in St. Louis, although only 10 years old at the time, became a close friend in her own right. Maxine would pick up Katie and her brother, Jack, after school occasionally.

KNOW WHOM TO LISTEN TO
AND WHAT INFLUENCES THEM

Right away, Maxine knew that she had two sets of relevant customers: (1) those who wanted the bear and the experiences of making it (kids) and (2) those who wanted to please kids and share in their experiences (parents, grandparents, aunts, uncles, and so on). She understood that kids' reactions would be purer, while adults' would be comparing her concept to other experiences or observations, such as unrelated businesses.

They'd go on shopping adventures with Maxine, seeking Beanie Babies that were missing from their collections. On one of those outings, Katie observed the simplicity of construction of Beanie Babies and told Maxine that they could make them at home. Maxine says that was her "aha! moment." She immediately started checking out sources, factories that could make what she needed.

When Maxine was just beginning her initial investigations, her first propositions to factories were invitations to partner with her on her exciting new adventure. She was rebuffed repeatedly. Here were people already in the business of making teddy bears. They were incapable of seeing the assembled jigsaw puzzle that Maxine saw. They subscribed to the "if it ain't broke, don't fix it" syndrome.

After all, they were doing fine, and besides, what did this shoe lady know about teddy bears or any kids' products for that matter? No one was asking them to drop what they were doing. They could have done both. Indeed they were uniquely situated to do both. But they didn't get it. In fact, they weren't up on it, so they had to be down on it.

DON'T ASSUME OTHERS KNOW WHAT YOU KNOW

The reactions of the bear manufacturers were not unlike the reactions Howard Schultz got from coffee experts. Maxine knew she wasn't going to be in the stuffed animal business. She was entering the "retail is entertainment" business, à la Goodman of May Company. Build-A-Bear was going to be focused on entertainment. The important thing was hands-on bear-building entertainment, not manufacturing teddy bears.

Maxine had to be dejected. Then she talked with Katie. Katie got it. She was up on it and urged Maxine to do it.

Over the years, Maxine continued to listen to kids who had all kinds of suggestions and wishes. They told her they wanted animals other than bears; they suggested accessories; they urged her to open on specific sites; and they shared insights regarding operations. These were, of course, kids. So they didn't submit expensive McKinsey Consulting reports. They talked about what they liked and didn't like. And Maxine listened.

Certainly, kids weren't the only ones with opinions. Adults were full of them. Some advised Maxine, "Maybe make the store really small and try it first. Don't put so much of your own money into it." But Maxine knew she had to go with her vision if it was to work.

WHEN FRIENDS REBUT, LISTEN TO YOUR GUT

Maxine's friends wanted to protect her from her own passion. They urged her to build a smaller store and not put in her own money. In the case of Blue Bottle Coffee, mentioned in Chapter 1, that approach worked. There, the customer's experience is in the limited space near the counter. For Build-A-Bear's customers, the experience required more ample space. Maxine knew what was needed.

Maxine tuned out the naysayers. She gained confidence from kids she talked with. She understands now that part of entrepreneurship is, to quote her, "when you cross over from sanity to insanity, when no one can talk you out of it, no matter what they say, [do it]. I could see the vision. And every kid I talked to could tell me every animal they could see in their Build-A-Bear store."

As did Starbucks' Howard Schultz and Costco founder Jim Sinegal, Maxine agreed with my analogy—that entrepreneurs must ignore the naysayers who see only the jigsaw puzzle pieces and not the fleshed-out picture on the box cover.

It turns out that with Build-A-Bear, kids saw the puzzle box cover's picture, just as Maxine did. By choosing which "critics" to listen to, namely Katie and other kids rather than the naysaying adults, Maxine proved to be a wise entrepreneur who was free to reinvent herself.

Recently, Maxine resigned as CEO of Build-A-Bear, having recruited Sharon Price John from the children's division of Stride Rite, ironically another shoe company. Now Maxine's longtime part-time commitment to help improve education will be her full-time pursuit, as she reinvents herself yet again.

PART 2

Reinventing Your Business

3

In Business, Reinventing Isn't Everything; It's the Constant Thing

Present Obama in his second inauguration speech spoke of what he sees for Americans: "limitless possibilities," particularly for those with "endless capacity for risk and a gift for reinvention."

Reinvention is what this book is about. Our rapidly changing world offers limitless possibilities for those who reinvent themselves and their businesses as change is thrust upon them. For those who master the art of reinvention, there is nothing to fear. As the president suggests, they are meant for this moment and must seize it.

You may think the odds are stacked against you. They really are not. Actually the risks are quite reasonable, unless you're one of those entrepreneurs who don't have a clue as to what they are undertaking and don't take advice on how to improve their chances for success.

Risk is a relative concept. While I think I always knew that, nothing taught me the lesson better than having students in my course who served in the U.S. armed forces in Afghanistan and Iraq. They were studying Successful Entrepreneurship, my course about starting a business. I've also taught and lectured Israeli students who experienced the risks of war.

Unlike most other students, they had faced risks with far greater consequences than entrepreneurial risks. Clearly the percentage of soldiers who are killed and wounded is less than that of entrepreneurs who fail. It's just that the consequences are so much worse and we value each of the soldiers so much. While I respect them and appreciate their having taken the ultimate risk, I had to get these students to realize that the risk of an entrepreneurial venture failing isn't much more prevalent than the risk of injury or death in a war, even though a business failure is not as lethal.

Studies revealing the risks inherent in starting a new business are daunting and well known. The statistic most frequently reported is that 9 of every 10 business start-ups will fail. Who in their right mind would accept such odds? Certainly those war heroes in my classes wouldn't have accepted those odds in war.

Human beings tolerate risk throughout life, but they aren't crazy. They try to avoid risks as bad as 9 to 1. Why then do so many people start new businesses? Obviously, there's more to those odds than meets the eye. The possible reasons include (1) the odds are misreported and are, in fact, lower; (2) they rationalize that the 90 percent are mostly incompetent or inappropriate entrepreneurs who aren't "as qualified as I am, so I'll fare better"; and (3) many new businesses are in endeavors with too much competition or they are undercapitalized so they run out of cash. In other words, either the stats are wrong or "my situation isn't like all those others, and so the odds of success are markedly better for me!"

In any case, getting a new business up and running is difficult but nowhere near as difficult as it may seem. Completing all the necessary steps may seem overwhelming, but they are often quite doable.

After you get the "perfect idea" and after you do smart research, you'll have learned such things as (1) whether others have tried and (2) whether there are existing patents that would block your goals. And, if others have tried, you'll find out (1) why they failed and/or (2) whether competition exists from similar products or, alternatively, from solutions to the problems solved by your product or service. Also you'll know (1) how, where, and at what cost and volumes you can produce the product; (2) what price would be necessary to assure profit; (3) to what extent that price would be acceptable to customers; (4) what marketing plan, business model, and distribution channel would work best; and—this is critically important—(5) how much cash it would take to pull this together.

Then you determine (1) the best way to gather a great sales force and at what cost; (2) how you form the rest of the team needed and at what cost; (3) how you convince investors that your dream is viable; (4) how you prove you have what it takes to make it happen; and (5) how you can make it happen with the cash being invested. Otherwise you'll soon face a desperate need to raise capital, which is an overwhelming distraction. This will be followed by possible "cram-downs," wherein subsequent round investors demand substantially better terms to invest in your now-desperate business. The cram-downs will dilute your holdings and those of your partners. So you must be certain your projections are sound, that you are not fooling yourself, and that you're realistically optimistic.

Last, but certainly not least, you must convince yourself and those close to you that you can achieve success before you consume your nest egg and wear out the patience of spouse, kids, and long-suffering relatives and friends.

That is a lot to accomplish. If you do all that successfully, you should be home free, right? You should have beaten those nine-to-one odds, right?

Well, that seems sensible, and for some fortunate few it may even be true. However, it isn't accurate. This isn't necessarily bad news. Actually, it is good news. The truth is that nine out of ten new businesses *don't* fail during the first stage of the enterprise, when all the steps described in the preceding paragraphs will have occurred. For entrepreneurs, that's great news.

The Kaufmann Foundation, the largest research facility analyzing entrepreneurship, conducted a study of new businesses and concluded that the failures take place over a relatively long period of time, namely 10 years or so (see the following figure).

When Do Entrepreneurs Fail?

Percent Failing	By Which Year
23.7	2
51.7	4
67.7	6
80.0	10

Compilation of research by Jeffery Timmons and other sources.

What can be read from this analysis? Several possibilities exist:

- At first, you survive because you are a nonthreat. But with growing success, competitors will focus on you.
- Early passion overcomes many obstacles, but over time, it is hard to sustain passion, in yourself and your team. (It's not very different from a marriage.)
- Managing an established business requires a different skill set than that required for starting a business.

So a rather large percentage of entrepreneurs make it through the early entrepreneurial stages successfully. It's the subsequent stages—running, not starting, a business—that pose the greater risks.

Operating requires different skills than founding. Those entrepreneurs who succeed either have the operating skills or acquire them. They can get each necessary skill directly, by improving their skill sets, or they can hire professional managers. Either way, they can beat the odds.

So can you. Entrepreneurship is not just a game of chance. You can change the odds by improving the skills you bring to the table. But as a founder if you don't have and can't acquire the skills you need to run the operation, it will be time to turn over management to others or to sell to someone with operating skills. The guys with the operating skills probably lack founding skills, which is fine. That may be why they are available.

"It Ain't Over 'Til It's Over"—Yogi Berra

While all of the skills previously mentioned are relevant, I find that in many situations the key lies in the absence of the entrepreneur's willingness and ability to *periodically reinvent* the business or allow someone else to do it, someone who has the necessary skills.

Reinvention sounds doable. What could be so hard about reinventing a business when it is necessary to do so? Well, first of all, the necessity isn't always obvious. In fact, the need to reinvent is very rarely clear. Fortunately, it needn't be obvious to everyone. It's sufficient if one person sees it, assuming he or she can make the case to the people who need convincing and then lead the people who need to be on board to get it done. That usually describes the one who first got the company up and running; the one who originally convinced the various stakeholders of the company; the one who originally led the team to its early successes. Given that great fortune, there shouldn't be anything to worry about.

But there is. You're not just asking entrepreneurs to reinvent a business; you're asking them to alter something nearly as personal as their own children. You're appealing to entrepreneurs to modify a concept that they had to believe in to their core. Otherwise, they wouldn't have been able to do and sacrifice all that they have. You're urging them to disavow a belief without which they couldn't have convinced the difficult-to-convince stakeholders. For entrepreneurs, that's a cross between heresy and treason.

My philosophy in addressing this problem is: never argue with a person's beliefs; argue instead with their knowledge, because most people believe far more than they know. That's what Stemberg did when he asked his lawyer friend to determine how much his firm spent on office products.

You probably think business reinvention is almost never necessary. After all, if each of those enumerated steps were a fork in the road and if you chose all the right forks, you would have reached your destination. But serial reinvention is almost always necessary. Most people think that once you've chosen the right product and model, then with good execution your results will be excellent, as illustrated by the proverbial hockey stick seen in the following graph:

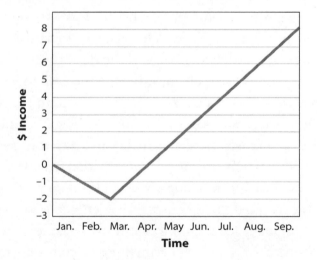

If that were true, then every company that passed the start-up stage would emerge a winner, so long as each start-up successfully managed and implemented execution. (That result is inconsistent with the Kaufman Foundation report.) Indeed, under that theory, with continual effective execution, such a company would continually succeed and would last forever. Businesses, however, are not inherently "built to last." While the title of the popular book *Built to Last* may lead you to the conclusion that businesses can in fact exist forever, the book really focused on just a few businesses. Out of thousands and thousands, those few represented the exceptions that had done what was necessary to make their businesses last. At best, it might be said that successful businesses, ones that can last, are (1) built to be susceptible and amenable to, and capable of, being reinvented as often as necessary and (2) built by people who remain ready, willing, able, and confident enough to reinvent the business, as well as themselves, or to allow others to do so if they can't do it themselves. This kind of situation is better illustrated by the curve shown here.

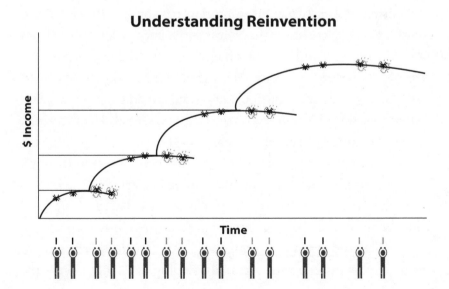

(Those of you viewing this electronically can see that the graph is created somewhat like the form of the arcade game *Space Invaders*. In that game, one shoots projectiles upward to blast invaders above. Go to the following website, www.inventreinventthrive.com, and click on "Reinvention Curve" to see the graph in motion.)

For our purposes, the projectiles in the graph are things that happen and that would adversely affect a business (much like Shakespeare's "slings and arrows of outrageous fortune"). If the business were left as is, the projectiles would be effective and would destroy the business. If, however, the businesses are reinvented (represented by the next successive curve), they will move out of the projectiles' range and be protected against those projectiles. The business will successfully grow, until the next time a challenge arises, such as when competitors improve, laws change, or raw material costs (or availability) become problematic.

Each reinvention will be imperfect. Although a timely reinvention may save the day, at some point weariness, competition, or changes in customer demand will cause the entrepreneurial momentum to peak and begin a decline.

Curiously as it turns out, each reformation is both easier and harder to complete successfully. It is easier because one starts from a base wherein fundamentals have been created and as a result an infrastructure is in place. Yet it is harder because it entails letting go of the existing business one sired. In addition, it requires reigniting spirit. Passion always wells up more easily the first time, much the same as in a romantic relationship.

So my graphic of a successful entrepreneurship, seen through an even stronger lens, is more like a roller coaster. On the incline of each curve, the rider has the tracks and car between him and the upcoming missiles, but on the descent there is no protection. The "slings and arrows of outrageous fortune" cause each curve to begin its downward slope, eventually ending in the oblivion of the nine out of ten entrepreneurial ventures that fail. But a few survivors are protected from the slings and arrows by the reinventions moving them out of range.

Reinvention isn't always enough. For example, Studebaker, founded by several brothers who emigrated from Germany, made horse carriages until the turn of the twentieth century. Over one hundred years ago the horseless carriage arrived with a new kind of clatter. Buggy-whip manufacturers lost their snap. They were doomed. On the other hand, some horse-drawn carriage makers such as Studebaker reinvented themselves as automobile manufacturers. Long after Studebaker Company turned out its last automobile in 1966, the sign painted on the old brick factory building in South Bend, Indiana, still read "Studebaker Carriages."

It's curious—Studebaker was able to adapt by reinventing itself in the face of the revolutionary change from horse-drawn carriages to automobiles. But the company eventually couldn't successfully reinvent itself again to continue competing with the Big Three automakers. One innovative Raymond Loewy redesign of the Studebaker body late in the game caused people to say they couldn't tell whether it should be driven forward or backward.

Perhaps the design was indicative of a bigger corporate paradox. Clearly Studebaker needed an overhaul. The new dramatic design of its car was meant to attract attention and customers. With volume the company could have lowered cost, enabling price reductions to be competitive or to increase profit per unit. The car that seemed to go backward did increase attention, but that didn't translate into sales. Backward didn't prove to be the new forward. As a result, in the mid-1960s, Studebaker drove backward into history.

Interestingly, in 1957, when Ford came out with the Edsel design, that vehicle too was a dismal failure, but it wasn't a bet-the-company wager. Ford had many models and other products to offset Edsel's impact. At worst the car was an embarrassment, since the Edsel was named after Edsel Ford, who had died in 1943 and was the son of Ford founder, Henry Ford. In the Ford Motor Company's case, it was safer to try and fail than not to try at all.

The best businesses are able to reinvent themselves continually and as a result last indefinitely. But they are exceptions, not the rule. You are not required to reinvent yourself or your business. But if you don't, your business is likely to remain just as it is and be a sitting duck for the "slings and arrows of outrageous fortune." Or you'll lose out on new possibilities for the growth and success of the company. If you want to experience real success or dynamic growth, you must figure out how to reinvent. To do so you must fix your skill set, including your mind-set (confidence, determination, and passion).

Several entrepreneurs I've interviewed have exciting stories relating to the reinventions of their businesses. Some, such as Howard Schultz of Starbucks, Chuck Schwab of Charles Schwab & Co., and Jim Sinegal of Costco, are extremely well known. I will share their stories shortly, but first, the story of an entrepreneur you may not know—Gil Mandelzis, who is an interesting example of timely reinvention. (The story of another relatively unknown entrepreneur, Larry Levy, follows in Chapter 4.)

Gil Mandelzis—If at First You Don't Succeed . . .

Gil Mandelzis is a study of reinvention at multiple points in time. He reinvented himself from an Israeli management consultant and after-hours bar owner to an investment banker who arrived in the United States to work on Wall Street. From there he became an entrepreneur. That was anything but the end of the story. Over the next seven years, he was forced to reinvent his company— Traiana, where he served as entrepreneur and CEO—repeatedly in order to survive and ultimately to thrive.

Founding Traiana in 2000 was not easy. His prior attempt to be an entrepreneur, as a bar owner, was a disaster. It was so bad that he promised his wife, Sima (and truth be told, also himself), that he would never again try entrepreneurship. He loved Sima and valued his marriage, but he had a vision and was convinced he could convert it to reality. Besides, how long could it possibly take? In typical entrepreneurial excess optimism, he was sure that the burden would be over before it could impact his family.

At first Traiana aimed at establishing a form of trading exchange. Gil saw a need for this exchange and the way to fulfill it, but he had difficulty getting others to understand it. I watched extremely smart investors spend considerable time trying to get their arms around whatever it was Gil said he had. They passed on the investment because they just didn't understand it—it wasn't clicking.

It's dangerous for an entrepreneur to argue with his or her potential investors, telling them they don't get it. Entrepreneurs are generally better advised to accept the blame for failing to explain well enough. In Gil's case it was the inherent difficulty of the field: derivatives. This was years before financial writers were seeking to understand the causes of the 2008 crash. It likely was also a problem for Gil, because his plans and business models were not totally clear in his own mind as yet. Besides, he was forced to change plans and models as various events unfolded.

BLAME YOURSELF FIRST

Don't blame potential investors if they are not getting it. Blame yourself first for not explaining it well. Gil figured that out. Howard Schultz also figured it out, just in the nick of time.

Along the way, however, Gil was able to sell his idea to several of the most respected venture capital firms in the world, including investors such as Evergreen Venture Capital and Gemini Capital Fund Management.

Gil was certain that his business concept was valid—still, the market said otherwise. He was nearly destroyed by the dot-com debacle, when pioneering Internet companies went bust with a resulting market swoon in 2000.

Rather than close up shop, Gil reinvented Traiana. He didn't need a magnifying glass to read the writing on the wall. Nor did he hesitate to adopt a brilliant model when one was conceived by someone else. The model reinvention was not Gil's idea. It was the brainchild of Joe Buthorn, a Traiana executive. Before joining Traiana, Joe had run the foreign exchange prime broker-age business (FX Prime Brokerage) for Deutsche Bank. Now, Joe's new model could leverage the technology and capabilities of the company.

FX prime brokerage consists of a bundle of services that invest-ment banks provide to hedge funds and other large investors such as commodity trading advisors. FX prime brokerage services include not only facilitating and processing trades but also provid-ing credit lines to traders doing business with other banks. The hedge fund manager who wants to trade approaches any bank the fund wants to trade with (executing bank) to execute the trade. After the trade is done, the trade is "given up" to the FX prime broker. As a result, the prime broker executes the trade with an executing broker. The FX prime broker thus engages in two trades—one with the client and one with the executing broker. Gil explained this setup as being similar to a transaction any of us would do using a credit card—we buy a shirt at the store (execut-ing bank) and the store settles with our issuer of the credit card (prime broker).

The hedge fund benefits from this arrangement because it often is able to piggyback on the prime brokerage's higher credit rating with the securities dealer and as a result gets better terms. The hedge fund also reduces its operational costs by having one account to manage, optimizing the credit utilization, one statement, and so on, just as we all do using credit cards.

Investment banks began offering FX prime brokerage services in the late 1990s in response to explosive growth in hedge fund numbers. In 1997 four banks offered FX prime brokerage services to fewer than 10 clients each. But by 2005, 20 banks offered FX prime brokerage services to an estimated 450 to 600 hedge funds and other major clients.

Gil realized that indeed there was a need for a financial infrastructure that would provide market efficiency in this field. So Traiana developed software that facilitated tri-party foreign exchange trading, which it referred to as "Foreign Exchange Prime Broker in a Box."

The Traiana team was on board. It was not immediately clear to Gil that the new model would work in the FX brokerage business. Still, Gil supported his team, who were eager to press ahead. Fortunately, he lacked the false bravado of some entrepreneurs who insist that they themselves come up with every idea that moves the company forward. Such an attitude—"not invented here" (NIH)—prevents many critical reinventions, but it is generally less prevalent when a company faces desperate circumstances. Traiana's circumstances were indeed desperate.

Imagine the audacity of this young entrepreneur. He listened to his team and boldly reconfigured his ship. He reinvented his business, and captain and crew sailed into the vast unknown again.

During this transitional period, the ever-optimistic Gil Mandelzis continued in his efforts to attract additional investors. That's because he knew he'd need more capital to further fund and scale the concept. After a discouraging string of rejections, Gil scored again: that's when Silicon Valley–based Sequoia Capital of Israel, the A-list venture capitalist, agreed to become an investor. Sequoia was expert in the high-tech world of Silicon Valley, where it is based, having provided venture capital to an impressive list of heavyweight U.S. companies, including Google, Apple, Oracle, and Yahoo! With Sequoia's imprimatur behind it, Traiana thought it would never again have to beg investors for cash.

EVERY REJECTION IS A LESSON

Gil had over 100 rejections before getting Sequoia to invest. What counts is not just how many rejections you receive but how well you improve the product or your presentations after each rejection to reflect valid criticism along the way. Often it is a matter of stepping out of your shoes and into your customers'. You see the forest, while others are still struggling with the trees. You see the puzzle box picture, while they see 1,000 seemingly unrelated jigsaw puzzle pieces.

Deutsche Bank became convinced that Traiana's software could be applied to its FX Prime Brokerage unit. Traiana licensed Deutsche and soon added a second client. Others quickly followed, and eventually Traiana's customer list became a who's who in banking. Its client list would include Bank of America, Deutsche Bank, JPMorgan Chase, AIG, Citibank, Credit Suisse, and many other household names.

The time was mid-2002. The FX prime brokerage business was expanding rapidly, and this time Traiana was in the right place at the right time—a most convenient state of affairs.

"NOT INVENTED HERE" IS HAZARDOUS TO BUSINESS

The arrogance of the "not invented here" mentality deprives leaders of opportunities. Gil was quite willing to listen to and adopt ideas conceived by his executives and his customers. He was also willing to support and give credit to those executives. That is how you build an atmosphere that promotes more good ideas. (See the discussion about Larry Levy in Chapter 4.) It's good for Gil and his colleagues that he did.

Traiana's software was more than adequate for the task. Indeed, the company successfully sold it to top trading institutions. The product was sound, and Traiana's customers paid recurring fees. In effect they paid rent to use the software. So Traiana could have run in place forever. But once Gil signed up the handful of institutions that made up the majority of the market, the prospects for growth were limited.

The company hit a wall. Again. Five years into its existence, Traiana was still losing a lot of money. So much for not having to beg for capital. Of course the company could scale down its costs dramatically and just run the existing business with limited to no growth. However, neither Gil nor his investors were interested in running in place. Despite having Sequoia as an investor, Gil was rejected by others, until finally Pitango Venture Capital, a newcomer to Traiana, provided $10 million in additional funds.

Mandelzis realized the business model used in this business was flawed. The prospects for growth were not customers like those he had—prime brokers. Those were limited. Scale would be based on the growth of foreign exchange prime brokerage transactions, as this form of service and execution takes a larger share of the market. In addition, there had to be a way to tie Traiana's growth to those brokers' counterparties, the executing banks, as well as the prime brokers' customers.

Luckily, in addition to its main software business, Traiana had a little network—Traiana Harmony—that it had put together to connect its clients. Traiana Harmony was nothing more than a marketing facilitator sold for very little and run by fewer than 10 people on the Traiana team. Even though the product enjoyed little attention, Gil realized the volume of existing clients' transactions on Harmony was growing steadily, in addition to new clients joining. After serious thinking he decided to bet Traiana's future on Harmony and redirect all the efforts that way, charging clients a fee for each transaction.

Traiana switched from a software company as such to a network, paid on a fee-per-transaction business model. It was far from easy, but Traiana's team, led by Gil, reinvented the company's business. They had to change their product—from a software product to a service provider as a hub—which necessitated changing their relationships with customers so that they could charge a fee for each trade. The foreign exchange prime brokerage market was growing exponentially, and now Traiana could serve as a hub for that growth. Traiana would expand its list of clients to include second- and third-tier investment banks, investment fund managers, and hedge funds. Traiana was ideally positioned to take full advantage of its tie to the burgeoning prime brokerage industry. Its makeover was complete. Scaling achieved!

Gil repeatedly stressed during my interview with him that the success was not attributable to him alone but to his team. Even so, this success was clearly entrepreneurial derring-do. First, Gil had to convince his investors that the business they had invested in was wrong and that they should trust the entrepreneur who had touted that business to them to change it to a different business. Then, Mandelzis and his team had to make the new, totally unfamiliar business sufficiently valuable to an existing sophisticated clientele as well as to a new clientele who had not dealt with Traiana on that basis before. The new direction meant the company had to be rebuilt from the ground up. Within weeks, 30 percent of the 140 employees had to be let go, which was distressing. Even so, within a few months, nearly all of the remaining 70 percent were working in Harmony. Soon things really started to hum.

Now Traiana got paid every time the network was used, every time the brokers' customers made a trade. The new Traiana package of services in a prime brokerage network, including trade processing, loss and profit limit monitoring, reporting and reconciling trade activities, were each measured and priced based on transaction volume. Traiana was the hub of a wheel, with the prime brokerage clients connected to the Traiana network forming the spokes. That hub was the new processing arena that Gil and his team had created for Traiana.

So how did Traiana build a new customer base for its new products? Did it replace those laid off with a team of super salespeople? That was not necessary. You see, the power of a network is the existence of networkers. Every user asked their partners, those on the other sides of the hub, to join Traiana's network. Think of a simple phone network. Once you join it, you would push to have your friends and family join. Otherwise you have no one to talk with. That's the phenomenon that created the growth at PayPal and likely at all social media companies.

By charging a fee for each transaction handled, Traiana's revenue stream grew with the increased usage by FX prime brokers, its clientele. Of course, the business model reinvention was *not* a no-brainer. Gil was betting that the number of transactions would continue to increase and that the large institutional customers needed Traiana's processing arena so much that they wouldn't simply walk away. There have been many instances where big companies have taken extraordinary measures to crush a small, pesky start-up that they considered too big for its britches. In this case, however, the large institutional customers liked the Traiana network as well as the tenacity and positioning of the team that formed this new space. Indeed they "partnered" with Traiana to make it work. Furthermore, usage did escalate.

With the latest reinvention, Traiana was unique. It was the leading such network provider without any strong competition. Over the next two years, fiscal 2006 and 2007, Traiana's network revenues began to take off. Losses declined with volume.

After having shrunk its employment base during the transition, Traiana grew again—to 125 employees in 2006. The build took time. Traiana was still losing money, although by 2007 losses started to decline. Projections called for further loss reductions in 2008 and a turn to profitability by 2009.

Mandelzis began getting calls from investors around the world clamoring for a piece of the action. The future had never looked brighter. In 2006, a mere 12 months after the latest turnaround, as the company began to take off, one of the players in the industry contacted Gil about his interest in selling the company. Negotiations with the interested acquirer became serious over the next several months and resulted in the potential buyer offering $165 million for Traiana.

This suitor was not the only company in the financial industry to reach out to Mandelzis. Several others had also contacted him expressing an interest in buying Traiana, but Gil didn't meet with them, focusing instead on the firm with which he was already negotiating.

In that the idea of selling the company had been initiated by the potential buyer and not Traiana, Mandelzis's management team had not made any prior effort to value the business. At the same time, venture capitalists were continuing to ask about investment opportunities in Traiana. Gil estimated that, if necessary, Traiana could have raised private venture capital funds at a $150 to $160 million pre-money valuation.

As Mandelzis and the management team began discussing the offer on the table, they realized their decision depended upon the extent of their faith in the company's future. Expectations were high. If growth continued as it had—Traiana's transaction volume was rising 5 to 10 percent a month—the company's value would be substantially larger two or three years out. In that case the $165 million offer seemed far too low.

If, on the other hand, the company did not perform as well as expected (after all, how long could that growth level be sustained?) and if there was a reversal, what impact might that have? The Traiana team would be walking away from a chance to sell at a huge profit that might never be available to them again.

As the FX prime brokerage industry began to take off, demand for electronic automation had grown because it was seen as being able to deliver greater efficiency, more transparency, faster speed, and lower costs. Global markets could be linked far more easily than before, and trades across exchanges worldwide could easily be linked and tracked. Traiana's network was the ideal solution for the various market players seeking greater automation.

The industry's growth outlook was another factor weighing in favor of rejection. With industry volumes approaching $3 trillion a day in 2007, Traiana's FX business appeared to be most promising.

Clearly, $165 million was a great deal of money. The offer seemed quite good for a company that had yet to turn a profit. Gil's institutional investors would have realized a serious gain from a deal that they once may have feared would be a total write-off. And for Gil, it would have been a game changer, a life-altering result.

Yet Mandelzis and his investors could still remember the optimism surrounding the old concept, just before it fell apart. No one wanted to hear, "Don't you ever learn?" And financial uncertainty also weighed in favor of taking the offer. You never knew what lay around the next corner.

Traiana's board was great. Board members were available to Gil virtually on an as-needed basis. He tried to respect their busy calendars, but they became a highly functional team. They became critical as matters progressed. After extensive negotiations the offer by the suitor was upped to $235 million. The deal was heading to final documents and closing.

Gil Bets the Traiana Farm

All the terms had been set. Gil was in charge on two fronts. Not only was he negotiating the terms of the deal, he was also in the process of reinventing Traiana once again. And this time it was the biggest reinvention of all—moving Traiana from a small, independent entrepreneurial venture into a subsidiary of a major financial institution. Gil's board would disappear; governance would be imposed from above, from the financial institution. Gil and his team would have to live with them, and Gil needed to know what kind of people, what kind of bosses, they would be.

Sure, Gil and his investors would walk away with loads of money. But the Traiana team would be saddled with the acquirer. Gil felt responsible for the team's well-being as well as the long-term fate of the company he started.

Months before, the acquirer's executives and legal counsel had agreed to a series of suggested terms. Now, as the deal was approaching closure, Gil and his board felt the acquirer was back-tracking on fundamental terms that his company would not have agreed to in the first place. Further, the acquirer introduced new terms unacceptable to Traiana and its investors. Changing positions would be costly for Traiana. The deal still could have been relatively handsome, but now material risks would be created by the change. Gil explained to the acquirer's executives that it would be hard for Traiana and its investors to swallow the new terms and asked the acquirer to live with Traiana doing what it had originally agreed to. However, the acquirer's counsel strongly argued against it, and the executives refused to override.

The institution had imposed a standstill period in the agreement, meaning Gil couldn't talk to other potential acquirers for a certain time. That's typical in such transactions, as it assures continued good-faith discussions, since the seller doesn't know whether there are alternatives and leans toward the "bird in hand" philosophy. For example, a seller who reacts negatively to an acquirer's change of terms, say as a result of findings during due diligence, might like to determine whether there are viable alternatives to the acquirer. The standstill provision precludes checking with others, so the seller is more likely to continue working with the acquirer rather than giving up the existing prospect and chancing the uncertainties elsewhere.

Gil was in a spot. He had lost confidence in the acquirer. He didn't want to cause his team to live with people he was not sure he could trust. He felt that the two organizations' cultures were incompatible. But—all that money, and no way to know if alternatives existed! It wasn't just not knowing if others would pay as much, but would Traiana be deemed "spoiled goods" because of this transaction's failure?

Gil and his board deliberated. Board members, made up of investors' general partners, wouldn't have to live with the acquirer. Upon closing of a transaction, they would receive bundles of cash and move on. Of course, the board was somewhat concerned about whether people who acted as the acquirer had would close the deal. And of course, they couldn't be sure if Gil would proceed and stay on with the company, despite the prospect of him becoming wealthy. No deal could occur without Gil.

The board supported Gil, who notified the acquirer that the deal was off. Fortunately, the first people Gil called after the no-shop period were at ICAP, the world's largest interdealer broker, who reacted quickly and positively. They bought Traiana for slightly over $250 million, a bit more than the prior offer.

CONSTANT COMMUNICATION IS A GOOD INVESTMENT

Throughout all seven years Gil constantly kept his investors informed, telling them of both good and bad news and of his thought processes in dealing with events. At times that was burdensome, not only to Gil, but likely also to his investors. But when Gil needed them most—when the ultimate reinvention was on the line—they trusted him and followed him.

As mentioned, this was far from the first example of Gil's ability to take the risks needed to reinvent himself and his company. When examining Gil's past, there is a temptation to attribute his success at reinventions to his unique background. Gil was born and raised in Israel, which is referred to as "The Start-Up Nation" in a book by that name authored by Dan Senor and Saul Singer.

Gil's father, like virtually all Israelis, served in the Israel Defense Forces. However, Gil's father gave his life, in 1973, when Gil was five years old, during the Yom Kippur War. One who has lost a parent to war might grow up feeling risk taking is in his blood. How could his risk even compare to that taken by his father? But this is a country where nearly everyone, Gil included, serves in the military. Everyone grows up under threat by terrorists and threats by countries with far larger populations and wealth. In these terms entrepreneurial risk can seem minimal.

But I have counseled, mentored, and partnered with many entrepreneurs, in Israel, the United States, and elsewhere. Israeli entrepreneurs are somewhat bolder in their willingness to take on risk (perhaps more style than substance), but often they are more stubborn in resisting reinvention.

Gil could be stubborn and could resist pressure to do something he wasn't willing and ready to do. In addition to stubbornness, Gil had a single-minded deliberative focus. Contrary to a popular image of entrepreneurs, he was not a gambler. He didn't make emotional, snap decisions. If the task at hand was recruiting a new executive, Gil was quite comfortable taking a year to find the right person. Then deliberations and decisions moved quickly.

THE WORLD CHANGES; KNOW WHAT IS CONSTANT

Technology and new financial instruments were in a state of superfast flux in Gil's world. But some principles and concepts—the values that were the backbone of Traiana's culture—were steady, even as others seemed to spin out of control. Gil was able to keep his eye on the constants while reinventing to adapt to extraordinary change.

In Gil, I saw something unique, even in a unique country. He was able to think like his customers, to visualize what was likely to happen. He saw the picture on the jigsaw puzzle box cover. Even more daunting, for the less imaginative, the picture on Gil's puzzle box kept changing. But each time, he was able to see the puzzle box pieces all together. He could get beyond the din of doubt.

AVOID SCALING LIMITATIONS

While Traiana was doing well, it had a small customer base to grow from. It had a compelling story but lacked the mass to create a meaningful growth paradigm. The purchase by a much larger company solved this problem. Similarly, Chuck Schwab had agreed to live with the limitations and restrictions of Bank of America (BofA). For Chuck to solve his problems, he had to buy back Schwab. Only his buyback shattered the BofA shackles (see Chapter 8). For Traiana, ICAP proved the perfect partner. People at ICAP shared the same values, were very entrepreneurial, fostered innovation, and saw great value in growing Traiana.

When Gil Mandelzis sold Traiana, he and his team entered into long employment agreements with ICAP, the buyer. Such arrangements are customary. They foster continuity with stakeholders such as employees and customers. They tie up the entrepreneurs for years, to keep them from reinventing as entrepreneurs and competing. These are rarely healthy relationships. The entrepreneur, who by definition is unemployable, feels imprisoned having to answer to a boss. Indeed, avoiding the need to serve a boss is likely one of the factors that originally led the seller to entrepreneurship.

Besides, the entrepreneurs have just come into substantial liquid assets, and they are tempted to try new toys, new hobbies, and even new spouses. Two-thirds of the time, the entrepreneurs leave employment with the acquirer early, having endured all they can, forfeiting the salaries, which aren't so important given their newfound wealth.

The ICAP/Traiana situation exceeds all expectations. At a time when most large financial institutions are valued much lower than in 2007, Traiana recently received a minority investment from eight investment banking firms at a higher valuation than the acquirer's price. Similarly, Gil's situation is different than the typical scenario. He is now the executive chairman of Traiana. He has been added to the executive committee of ICAP, where he is running other (and larger) parts of ICAP. He is happy with his job and looks forward to helping ICAP grow in different directions.

In effect Gil has reinvented himself again. This time he's gone from entrepreneur to executive through the sale of Traiana to the right buyer. He has provided himself with a higher platform. In much the same way that the pricing of the sale had to take into account the higher base of the buyer, so too will the higher platform provide Gil with leverage he never had. He is no longer what Jim Sinegal referred to as "king" (see Chapter 4) but is instead prince of a bigger realm.

Gil was able to adapt to this new venue and role by adding a few skills. He may have modified those of his skills that he demonstrated while relating to his board and venture capitalist shareholders to fit his new relationship with his ICAP bosses. Or he may have reached back to his days as an employee of Deutsche Bank, or both. Either way, it is an example of another way to reinvent—entrepreneur to executive of the acquiring company—and so gain the advantage of a higher platform. And he is still happily married to Sima.

Although we will explore examples of reinvention to higher platforms later, the technique seldom works in acquisitions. Some entrepreneurs are incapable of accepting change. And sometimes the acquirer fails to provide a welcome mat the way ICAP has to Gil. Today when Gil thinks back, he may want to thank that lawyer and the executives who backed him.

4

Sleeping with the Enemy

WHATEVER THEIR MOTIVES, THE NAYSAYERS OF SCHULTZ, Stemberg, Bridgeman, Krasny, and Clark were their "enemies." Had the naysayers prevailed, those great entrepreneurs might never have made their businesses the iconic brands they've become. There are, however, situations where one should not ignore but instead embrace the naysayers. If that sounds confusing, remember Gil Mandelzis having listened to his employee who told him to abandon his existing business model. Larry Levy ignored an external naysayer until his colleagues convinced him to "sleep with that enemy."

Larry Levy's story is at once remarkably different from, yet startlingly similar to that of Gil Mandelzis. For both, the ideas that prompted the reinventions were not theirs but recommendations from key employees. Neither was burdened by an arrogance that rejects others' ideas automatically (an extreme form of "NIH," or "not invented here"). Rather, they willingly embraced the ideas.

Both are open to "aha moments" of others. In addition, each had rejected a crucial idea. Levy rejected an unrelated businessman's urging that Levy enter the stadium catering business. Mandelzis rejected his board's initial decision regarding the price at which to sell the business.

Larry Levy's first real job after military service as a Green Beret and obtaining his MBA was in the real estate industry. "I have never stopped being in the real estate business," says he. To this day he continues to erect buildings, to buy and sell them, and to do other entrepreneurial things in real estate.

Yet to think of his enterprise, the Levy Organization, as a real estate business per se would miss its essence. You'd also miss a fascinating story, and you'd deprive yourself of important lessons to be derived from understanding the business's progression.

Don't Ignore Naysayers; Take Advantage of Them

Starting in the industrial real estate market as a broker and later as a speculator, Levy accumulated 5,500 acres of land in Chicago's collar counties (the counties abutting Cook County, where Chicago is situated). There he switched to office buildings, first as part of the Hawthorne Group, where he became president at age 28, and then, in 1978, as founder of the Levy Organization. He had that organization buy the land for the Woodfield Office campus. The office campus ultimately housed a million square feet of offices and three hotels.

Later, Larry acquired a valuable piece of land at the corner of Michigan Avenue and Oak Street in Chicago. This property is at the preferred end of that stretch of Michigan Avenue known as "The Magnificent Mile," which runs from the Chicago River to Lake Michigan's Oak Street Beach. That mile-long stretch of

Michigan Avenue houses the best shopping in Chicago, and the choice property that Larry acquired became the One Magnificent Mile Building, housing offices, condo apartments, retail stores, and restaurants. It was generally referred to as "One Mag Mile."

Around the same time, Larry decided to invite his brother, Mark, to join him in opening a restaurant, D.B. Kaplan's, a Jewish-style delicatessen, which they opened with an operating partner.

Restaurant operators almost always seek street-level locations. But Levy opened the restaurant on the top retail floor—the seventh—of Water Tower Place, a unique new vertical mall on Michigan Avenue. It was developed by a former U.S. secretary of commerce, Philip Klutznick.

Levy's operating partner "did everything wrong," according to Larry. So they fired him and bought back his stock. Larry brought his mother to Chicago to manage the restaurant and do the cooking. She did a great job. The deli soon became profitable. Even the peculiar seventh-floor location turned into an asset. It became the "in thing" to ride the glass-enclosed elevator to the top floor and then ride the escalator down, floor by floor, to see what new stores had opened since the last visit.

Water Tower Place became Chicago's number one tourist attraction. The Levy team gamble had paid off. The Levy Organization was rewarded for its willingness to take risks. The firm was granted the right to open four more restaurants in the building. Larry's firm thrived.

The success of his highly visible and busy restaurants in Water Tower Place along with the groundbreaking for his spectacular new building, One Mag Mile, made Larry a Chicago luminary. It is hard to say if the firm's primary business was real estate or restaurants back then, but for a while it sure seemed the restaurant business was the far less troublesome for Larry.

Cyclicality and Vulnerability—Huge Distractions

I was coaching Israeli entrepreneurs from a safe office in Chicago during Hezbollah's shelling of northern Israel. I marveled at those entrepreneurs sending me e-mails regarding pending business projects from their bomb shelters. They assured me that their first priority was getting into the shelters, after which they shifted to longer-term concerns.

Similarly, when the "missiles of outrageous fortune" are launched, the call "incoming" does its job—causing entrepreneurs to hunker down and stay safe. After that momentary reaction they must expand their concern to longer-term issues. Focusing solely on staying safe or assuming that staying safe is the same as succeeding may be just what causes a failure to survive. That's what almost happened to Larry Levy when he assumed that the enemy that hadn't been able to touch him never could.

The time was 1978–1979. To build One Mag Mile, Larry had borrowed $100 million at an interest rate of prime plus one—1 percent above the prime rate. The prime is the rate big banks charge their best customers. That meant that as the prime rate rose, so did the interest rate on Levy's building loan. In the opinion of then Federal Reserve Bank chairman Paul Volcker, increasing interest rates was the best way to fight inflation. Eventually, the prime rate went to 20 percent, so Larry's rate was 21 percent. In addition, the high rates made it difficult for people to get mortgages needed to buy condos and for businesses to afford new leases. You might be thinking that there had to be days during this period when Larry wished he was solely in the restaurant business.

But normalcy returned, and One Mag Mile filled up. Of course, the dismal economy hadn't been good for restaurants either. And as the economy improved, new multiuse buildings on Michigan Avenue attracted tourists and local folks too, all of them craning their necks to see the newest iterations of retail outlets and restaurants. These were all competition for Larry's Water Tower eateries. Essentially, the restaurant business was broke.

I tell my students that I believe in luck but don't rely on it, preferring to make my own luck and to be ready to pounce when luck appears. More about that shortly. At just the perfect time, Larry was approached by Jerry Reinsdorf, a successful former real estate developer.

Reinsdorf and some of Chicago's most prominent people bought the Chicago White Sox baseball team. Later, Reinsdorf also bought the Chicago Bulls basketball team, shortly before Michael Jordan became the Jordan we all know. How's that for luck?

They bought the White Sox in 1981 from Bill Veeck, a P. T. Barnum of baseball, who once put a little person at bat for Cleveland knowing the pitcher couldn't strike him out, given his reduced strike zone. A true baseball fan, Reinsdorf had grown up in the shadow of the Brooklyn Dodgers' Ebbets Field. He knew that the White Sox team and its home, Comiskey Park, would have to be reinvented. He wanted to retain the loyal blue-collar neighborhood fans, including Mayor Daley's family, who lived in Bridgeport, near the park. But he also wanted to attract the downtown and suburban executives and professionals—the "big spenders."

Catering to two markets would cost more, in both infrastructure and operations, which would have to wait, as the Reinsdorf Group dealt with debt service from acquisition loans. To meet those obligations, the purchase price debt service, the Reinsdorf Group built 17 "sky boxes," as they were called then. Reinsdorf asked the Levy Organization if its people would cater the sky boxes with food prepared in the group's Water Tower Place restaurants the day before each game. The day-old food was to be taken to the park in panel trucks with built-in heaters for the food that was to be served to sky-box patrons.

To that Levy replied, "No, we don't do that. We're not an institutional food service provider." Larry felt the organization should only do what it was good at. Besides, rewarmed, day-old food wasn't acceptable in the group's restaurants. Therefore, it wouldn't be tolerated by people paying small fortunes to rent sky boxes for what he saw as insular indoor seats that deprived them of a true ballpark experience.

Larry was baffled that fans would pay so much to rent sky boxes. What was their reward? Watching a second-rate team that hadn't won a World Series since 1917.

Reinsdorf continued to pursue the Levy Organization, explaining that the new team owners were committed to spending big money on good players. They would bring the World Series to Chicago, and Larry would have front-row seats. Finally, Larry gave in. He agreed to cater the sky boxes with day-old food transported in vans with reheaters.

(Note: Jerry Reinsdorf was correct. He did bring Chicago a World Series, but it didn't happen until 24 years later. Unfortunately, Larry was out of the country on vacation, and so he wasn't sitting in those front-row seats.)

At the Ballpark, Day-Old Food Is a Gourmet Treat

The following year, the White Sox built 17 *more* sky boxes, and of course Reinsdorf asked Levy to cater those too. By then, the Levy Organization realized that it had made a significant profit on the sky-box catering business. With 34 boxes, the profits were over a quarter million dollars. What's more, the fans were raving about the food. "You people are geniuses. The food is great, sensational," was what they heard in the media and on the street. It was still day-old food, rewarmed and transported in vans with reheaters, and the Levys knew it wasn't up to their restaurant standards. But they came to realize that the reason for the rave reviews was the fans' low-level expectations for ballpark food.

The Levy Organization held a management retreat that year, at which the internal financial people said the cost of building a restaurant was $1.5 million. If the restaurant worked really well, it could yield $.5 million a year. And if it didn't work well, the $1.5 million build-out, plus net operating losses while open, would be lost to Levy and/or the Levy investors.

What the managers realized was that one bad restaurant offset the profit of more than two good ones. And the restaurant industry is known for having far more losers than successes. On the other hand, they noted that the alternative—catering sports and entertainment venues—entailed very little investment while yielding very large profits.

Some members of the Levy Organization executive team made a simple but compelling analysis: "Look what you've done with the White Sox with no investment. And when you build restaurants, which require serious capital investments, some are good, some are not."

At the same time, still more Chicago buildings were erected. The buildings' new restaurants even more adversely affected the sales at Levy's Water Tower Place restaurants. Larry and Mark followed their executives' lead and began exploring possibilities in the sports arena business.

A PIECE OF THE ACTION

Invite and reward good ideas. Don't be afraid to admit you didn't think of it. Some companies run retreats so that leaders can motivate employees and recognize good efforts. Levy's retreat was to invite new, even contrary ideas and to listen to those executives who had suggestions. Levy listened and realized his executives were making sense. He wasn't afraid to tell them they were right, that he had missed it. Levy made a number of his executives rich when the company was sold. And Larry is quick to say they deserved it. They contributed valuably to Larry's benefit. There is nothing quite like "owning a piece of the rock."

Between 1982 and 1987 in addition to Comiskey Park, the Levy Organization won the catering contracts for Wrigley Field and McCormick Place (the Chicago convention center), Arlington Race Track, the Lincoln Park Zoo, and Ravinia, a suburban Chicago concert facility.

Levy began serving Ravinia in 1982, when he bought Hillman's, a catering company that owned the Ravinia catering contract at the time. Levy really bought Hillman's for its downtown Chicago real estate, which had housed Hillman's retail store for over 50 years. For another one of Chicago's premier real estate figures, the Hillman property became a real estate nightmare. But Levy had acquired a far more valuable asset, the Ravinia catering contract, for $1 more.

"We made a concerted effort," Larry said, "to win what became a new wave of sports facilities being built around the country." They opened the first three in 1994, and then "there was just an incredible wave of others," Larry said. "We wound up in a very short period of time in Cleveland, Kansas City, St. Louis, Portland, Orlando, Los Angeles, Atlanta, Denver, Miami. . . . We even thought about going public. We got to 20 percent market share very quickly. And we got to 50 percent market share before I sold the company. And now it's even more."

Coincidentally, the Disney Company decided that it could improve its food offerings by letting restaurant companies bid for the right to own and operate their own restaurants in Disney World. The Levy Organization won the competition and eventually built three restaurants there. The three were, according to Larry, "wildly successful and wildly profitable." The Levys of course realized belatedly that they had entered a totally new type of business.

It was obvious to Larry that the stand-alone restaurant business was high risk: competing with the likes of Rich Melman, the owner of Lettuce Entertain You, a highly successful restaurant owner. Instead of relying solely on their ability to attract patrons to restaurants they owned, they relied on others—sports teams and theme parks—to provide the customers. They did so with consistency and predictability. The sports teams and theme parks increased revenues and decreased costs.

One of the reasons for the high profitability was that Disney "had many of the same characteristics as the sports business," according to Levy. "And another reason was that our service entailed Chicago hospitality. We really care about the guests, where we win one customer at a time, and where you don't treat the customer like a captive audience."

The history of others' poor results in catering hot dogs at sports venues and the resulting low expectations meant that Levy could really change the paradigm of a sports team owner's expectations. In addition to the improved financial results for the Levy Organization, customers were happier. As one might expect, each new arena and stadium elevated expectations. Yet Levy was able to far exceed even those expectations.

The sports venues would have seemed daunting to some—Levy was competing against six well-established food companies, including Aramark, Volume Services, Service America, and Delaware North. Yet the risks were actually low. The competitors, according to Levy, were not concerned with food and service quality. Larry feels "they were all old businesses; they were all run by hacks at the time. They knew how to count the beer cups so that nobody would steal, and they knew how to make a warm hot dog, not a hot hot dog. And the buns were served right before they went stale. And basically, over the period of a year we learned that this was a huge opportunity." Around that time, the name of the company was changed from "The Levy Organization" to "Levy Restaurants," a clear indication of which side the group's bread was buttered on as well as a better brand for its growing facilities catering business.

Levy notes that as a land developer he benefited from his understanding of the economics of real estate. And the economics of a new baseball stadium was about specific real estate—the premium (club and sky-box) seats and special restaurants that served them. Those old catering companies, the old establishment of the industry, were not capable of providing competitive food and service.

According to Levy, "They didn't have people that they called chefs. They had sort of an army of logistics people. And we had chefs, and we had recipes, and we had my mother. And we could really promote those people. So the big companies conceded the sky boxes to us. They said, 'We don't want to embarrass ourselves, and we're not going to make any money doing that anyway.'

"We learned that the demand created totally elastic pricing. You could charge just below gouging. And in this sky-box business, the person paying for it is not present. The people in the box, in almost all cases, were the best customers of the company that leased the box. The most important person in making a sale, a presale of lots of food and beverage, was the secretary to the lessee's CEO."

"It's just a different kind of business," continued Levy. "And we really understood it and gathered a lot of data and had a lot of the same customers in different cities. Then we invented the dessert cart, which became the talk of the industry."

KNOW WHO YOUR CUSTOMER IS

Larry knew that his customer wasn't the corporate CEO who rented the sky box. It was the stadium owner. Sure, that owner wanted happy sky-box tenants, but the added value Levy provided was in helping the stadium owner finance, build, and maintain his stadium food sections and sky boxes better and more profitably.

The dessert carts, with their attractive presentations, decadent taste, and sizable portions, actually added another element—entertainment—that could be enjoyed by even non-sports fans, bringing another demographic to the ballpark. Elsewhere I share other stories about people who understood that a key to retail success is entertainment.

"Another thing that happened," Larry added, "is that the new stadiums got the All-Star games and many times got the good teams. So the owners of other teams began to see what we were doing as they were pursuing buildings."

RETAIL IS ENTERTAINMENT

The beautiful, enticing dessert carts with oversized servings likely fattened many sports fans, but the carts also fattened the wallets of stadium owners and Levy Restaurants.

Denise Gaffney: Executive Reinvents as Partner

When TV host David Letterman was called for jury duty he told his TV audience that he was pleased and well suited to serve because he could determine who was guilty just by looking at him. Likewise, all too often entrepreneurs believe they can determine who will be a capable executive just by seeing the person or his or her résumé. The employee who performs well at a lesser level is assumed to have passed a test, thereby qualifying that person to do so at the next level. That ignores what's known as "the Peter Principle," which says that every employee will get promoted to his or her level of incompetence. The best example of that principle is the company that promotes its best salesman to sales manager, despite his lack of management skills, leaving the company with a bad manager and without the good salesperson. It also ignores an employee's ability to reinvent some of his or her skills and adapt them to a new opportunity. Larry Levy spotted Denise Gaffney's ability to rearrange the skills in her quiver and become an integral part of Levy's future success and thus become his partner.

"I had an executive, Denise Gaffney, who was in charge of finishing the condominiums on behalf of the condo unit buyers at the One Magnificent Mile building. Since I had decided not to continue building condo high rises, I put her in charge of building the sky boxes and club seats. She was thankful for the new opportunity, and I was thankful to have her. She specified the equipment, found ways to save money, because we found that sports architects didn't know anything about food service. They were just used to beer and hot dogs.

"Denise Gaffney has very winning ways about her. She didn't go to college and has one of those 'I have something to prove' attitudes. She truly became an expert on sports venues' equipment for food service and efficiency. And she became *the* expert in the industry. She has now done 50 projects, and she is still with the company, a senior vice president. When I decided I wasn't going to build any more residential properties, she had to decide if she was going to stay with the company.

"We liked each other, and she believed in me. One of our strategies was: if you win one of these accounts, it's a minimum of $10 million in sales and up to $25 million. (One of the things about sports, by the way: we've never had one that lost money. We've had a lot of restaurants lose money.)

"A key part of the strategy became, you get Denise for free. We'd say, 'No obligation. Why don't you see what Denise can do to help you—work with your architects?' So three years before the opening day, we were already working on the project. And by the time the bids came out, there was no advantage that anybody else could have like what Denise gave us.

"It helped that we understood real estate and the value of an income stream. We would make the presentation that, if the food tastes good and it's served by nice people, we'll sell a lot more food, we'll sell a lot more beverages, we'll certainly sell a lot more desserts. We started getting industry statistics, and we were doing twice the per capita sales of the other people doing it.

"I'm talking about the sky boxes. We had great data from our experience, so we could guarantee revenue. We just started winning that way."

What Levy is saying is that Levy people no longer had to win bids by giving owners a larger share of the food revenue. They could avoid giving away such a large part of the income because they were able to determine projected revenue more accurately and thus could give the owners a guarantee of minimum revenue without much risk to Levy Restaurants. As a realtor, Larry understood that the guaranteed income minimum was bankable by the owners and could facilitate stadium financing. Therefore, the owners were willing to forgo higher income sharing.

"We were the insurgent," said Levy, "we came out of nowhere, and really had a disruptive approach to the business, with the simplest approach you could possibly have—we're going to give you better service and better food.

"So Denise became an amazingly valuable asset. Because of her, we could save the stadium owners two, three, four million dollars. And, as a result, we were getting these contracts, and instead of a restaurant that would do $3 million if it was really good, we were getting the Staples Center, home to the Los Angeles Kings, where in just the sky boxes and club seats, we did $25 million in sales in the first year, and that was starting in 1998. So we had a period, you know, all starting from that transition, where we went to $100 million in sales to $200 million in sales, and for a very unusual reason."

That reason was that Levy Restaurants figured out how to modify and apply its real estate skills to its catering business. It had reinvented itself without any seemingly big jumps; it was done with small incremental steps.

People at Levy Restaurants honed their restaurant skills into catering skills; they set aside their site selection skills and their marketing skills; and they applied their real estate development skills to the real estate needs of stadium developers. They merely rearranged and slightly modified the skills in their quiver. As a result, they dramatically reinvented their business.

HEDGE YOUR BETS VERSUS FOCUS

Everyone, including me, tells entrepreneurs to focus on their main business. "Play to your strengths" is a constant refrain. Many years ago, the comedian Jonathan Winters developed a routine for his familiar character Maude Frickert, as the founder of The World's Oldest Airline and Siding Company, making fun

of the airlines' inability to focus on their main business, resulting in confusion and worse. Levy stretched his bandwidth to
accommodate both of his commercial interests—real estate
and restaurants. Only because he had expertise in both was he
the perfect fit for the sky-box catering challenges.

It's not insignificant that Larry Levy recognized that in reinventing his business he could also benefit by reinventing a key
employee—Denise Gaffney. It would have been easy to let her
go after the condo project ended. Instead, Larry saw valuable
skills and knew it wouldn't take much to modify her skill set just
slightly, thereby keeping a winning player whose modified skills
could be applied to Levy Restaurants' reinvented business.

The company was making lots of money, but Larry Levy
didn't have any money, largely because he had bought out his
brother to resolve their differences. A risk at the time, it enabled
Larry to build the company according to his vision. The downside was that Larry used a substantial amount of money to buy
out Mark and had to service debt incurred. That left Larry as a
cash-poor owner of a profitable and growing business. In addition, the growing business needed capital to grow, leaving nothing available for extra distributions to owners. So he sold half
the company, took some money out, and took out all his investors. The other reason for selling half the company was that every
sport went on strike. Baseball went on strike twice, and there
was a contract coming up. Hockey lost a season; there were two
National Basketball Association strikes; and football had a strike,
with substitute players.

Levy is very proud of what else occurred when half the company was sold: "I did something that was revolutionary at the
time. I arranged for my management team to share in the appreciation. When we sold half, the value far exceeded what we told

them it was worth. One of my proudest things is, when I sold the company, Denise was one of the people that got a lot of money."

Reinvention Doesn't Come with a Lifetime Warranty

Larry, you'll recall, had brought his mother, Edith (Eadie) Levy, up from St. Louis to substitute her recipes and do the cooking for their faltering first restaurant, D.B. Kaplan's, the deli in Water Tower Place. She turned around Kaplan's in just a couple of weeks and later was actively involved, providing recipes, giving guidance, and even acting as hostess, as their other four Water Tower restaurants were opened. A life-size cardboard picture of Eadie greeted patrons to Mrs. Levy's Delicatessen in what was then Sears Tower. People actually stopped to have their pictures taken with the cardboard statue. Along the way, Eadie worked with kitchen staff as they catered Grammy Awards, U.S. Open, and Super Bowl events. She became the beloved substitute mother for much of Levy Restaurants' staff and worked for Levy Restaurants until shortly before her death in 2013, at the age of 92. I doubt that Larry could have guessed all that would come from bringing her to Chicago to help with the emergency that necessitated reinvention at Kaplan's.

Not everything went smoothly. As Larry told me, "We wanted to stay under the radar of the big companies. They were conceding the sky boxes to us. We got to approximately 40 percent market share. The competitors were paying ridiculous rents for their spaces [for hot dogs and traditional stadium food fare], making small amounts of money on high volume. And they figured out that we were making a lot of money. They said 'We're now going to get good at what they do.' And so Aramark [a giant catering company that sells uniforms and boots and food], told the California Angels 'to consolidate all catering into one company rather than have two contracts—one for good food and one for hot dogs, etc.'

"We said 'We agree.' We competed, and we lost. It was laziness on our part. We just thought that all we had to do was serve good food and we'd keep winning. And so at that moment we said, 'We're going to go after their business.' We took over the Dodgers' general concessions, the Staples Center general concessions (Staples Center is now $75 million in sales), and the Cubs general concessions. (We went from doing $2 million in the sky boxes to doing $48 million in sales.)"

Larry didn't just ignore the naysayers' noise. He realized that their noise was actually a signal that they weren't paying attention and didn't understand the ramifications of letting in a competitor. The naysayers in the industry were big companies. They thought of Levy as more of a nuisance than a menace. As a result, they left a hole big enough to drive a food reheating van through, and that's exactly what Levy did.

SLEEPING WITH THE ENEMY SHOULD BE A MATTER OF LOGIC, NOT PASSION

The same type of logic Stemberg used—learning what customers wanted and realizing that the naysayers from the industry didn't get it—is what guided Levy to embrace the naysayer, Reinsdorf, after Larry's executives stated their case logically.

Late last year Larry Levy evidenced further reinvention. A new company, Levy Acquisition Corp., which he founded with his son and stepson, successfully completed its initial public offering, raising $150 million to buy other companies. Larry not only reinvented himself as an entrepreneur, he reinvented himself and his family as a family business.

BELIEVE IN LUCK, BUT DON'T RELY ON IT

Remember my message to my students—that I am a firm believer in luck; I simply don't want to rely on it. I generally follow that by telling my students a somewhat personal story.

One of my uncles had a chain of six stores in very small towns in the southern United States. In 1940, he had bought an excessive amount of inventory, which sat in a warehouse. The problem was that he didn't have the funds to take down the inventory and sell it to his customers. His attempts at obtaining bank financing failed, as these were still Great Depression days. One day two men in suits, hats, and ties walked into one of the stores and asked for my uncle. They showed him badges, which announced they were from the federal government, and told him they wanted to discuss his warehoused inventory. Even though my uncle was an American who had served in World War I, his European background probably had him fearing these feds were going to send him to debtors' prison. The feds broke the silence by asking my uncle how much he wanted for the inventory. He named the biggest price he could utter with a straight face. His asking price was clearly insufficient, because they said they would buy it. As it turns out, the inventory consisted of boots and raincoats. The feds wanted them for U.S. troops they believed would shortly be joining World War II. My uncle's business was saved. Indeed, his future retirement was assured, where two days earlier he was convinced he would have to go bankrupt or even go to jail.

So I believe in luck. When it appears, however, you need the skill to spot it, grab it, and turn it into something meaningful, as my uncle did. Or you accept and run with it, as Levy did, or you hang tough, as Mandelzis did. It's OK to believe in luck. Just don't rely on it. Leave that to Dirty Harry ("You've got to ask yourself one question: 'Do I feel lucky?'").

Knowing What to Change and What Not to Change

When Jim Sinegal, the founder of Costco, was a sophomore at San Diego Junior College, he was hired by Fed Mart, later known as Price Club, to work over Christmas vacation. He worked "for a buck and a quarter an hour," Jim proudly recalled. He was there for 23 years but no longer at a buck and a quarter an hour.

While at that one employer, Jim worked his way up from the bottom rung of the ladder. His start was inauspicious: "I schlepped mattresses and tied them onto the tops of cars. I loaded warehouses. Then I got involved selling furniture on the floor, and then became a buyer, along the way taking on greater responsibilities." And Jim wound up being the executive vice president, the number two person in the company.

Knowing Jim's ultimate success and stature may trigger one or two thoughts: (1) His ascension may seem preordained or automatic (Jim accepted each new responsibility even though he says, "In hindsight I look at it and I think, 'Gee, how unprepared I was to go into some of those things.'" Each change was a reinvention of Jim, which he gladly accepted because it was "an exhilarating experience."), and (2) his longevity at Price Club doesn't make sense. Why didn't he leave earlier? To answer that, you must understand Jim's feelings about Sol Price.

Jim attributes his success to his lifelong mentor, Sol Price, the founder of Price Club, who Jim calls "the smartest man I've ever known, and he taught me everything that I know." Jim believes that Sol enabled him to refine and improve his skill set to be ready for the new challenges in his next promotion. As Jim's boss, Sol not only allowed but required Jim to take the time to step back and think, which proved to be an invaluable lesson, or as Jim puts it, "You can't go in and send everybody out for a long pass. There's got to be a plan."

Talking with Jim, one cannot but sense respect, indeed veneration. It seems Jim was totally dependent on Sol. Jim believes that without him, each reinvention would have been impossible. In fact, Jim was smart, hardworking, and a quick study. Jim had confidence in himself, but not in his ability to do what Sol had done ("I never had illusions that I would be smarter than Sol").

Still, if he believed that he was dependent on Sol, how was he able to leave Price Club and go out on his own? He had confidence that he had learned leadership from Sol, that he could attract five to six key people, and that as a team they could pull it off.

And so, in 1979, Jim left Price Club, with the intent of starting a new business. The best-laid plans, however, were thwarted, due to the high interest rates in the Carter administration years, which precluded his raising the necessary capital. Jim had to work to feed his family, so he decided to become a broker, finding products for retailers. This was totally different than anything Jim had ever done. He was able to do that because he had been "able to observe what other people were doing." He'd had trepidations leaving the cocoon he was in at Price Club and becoming a broker. It's never easy starting a venture in an area that's totally new to you. But Jim had adjusted his skills by observing other brokers, and that seemed to suffice.

Jim wound up being very successful as a broker, because he worked harder and was more creative than many others. He was making more than he ever made being the number two guy at Price Club. Yet he knew that this wasn't what he wanted to do.

When the opportunity came to start Costco, he took a big cut in pay to do it.

BE PREPARED

Jim says that having savings, living frugally, and being able to take a cut in pay enabled him to found Costco.

In *Entrepreneurs Are Made Not Born* I told the story of the late Joe Sullivan, a successful entrepreneur and extraordinary hands-on philanthropist who told me that he drove a seven-year-old Volvo, which he used as a symbol of the frugality that enabled him to grab entrepreneurial opportunities. When the book came out, Joe was kind enough to invite me to lunch so we could celebrate. Immediately after we were seated, he said the words no author wants to hear: "Lloyd, your book has a mistake in it." Then he continued, "You said I drove a seven-year-old Volvo, but now it's over ten years old." That tells you how long the gestation period was for that book. It also demonstrates how disciplined Joe was. It enabled him to grab the brass ring when he spotted a great opportunity and with Sam Zell acquired Vigoro. Jim Sinegal had similar discipline.

Starting Costco meant going up against "*the* smartest man I ever knew, the man who taught me everything I knew." He believes he was able to do so only because he could find and attract a handful of "really good people."

As entrepreneurs generally do before going out to raise capital, Jim and his team prepared a business plan. They projected that they would "eventually grow to 12 Costco stores and they would make it a $1 billion company. Clearly, Jim was a better businessman than business forecaster. Today Costco has about 650 stores, in a dozen countries, and sales exceed $100 billion. The market capitalization of Costco (the aggregate value of all its stock) is over $50 billion. Along the way, the company was reinvented several times, each in a different way.

Everybody loves to shop at Costco, whether you like the quantities or the tasting samples, themselves a form of retail entertainment. Those who like the produce, meat, seafood, and baked goods love the quality consistency. They say, "It's always been great." You'd get a similar reaction from those who fill their prescriptions or their gas tanks at Costco. But originally Costco did not sell any of those products. Today those products occupy a significant part of the Costco store. Talk about a reinvention! What caused it? Why was Sinegal willing to chance it?

Although Costco experienced smooth sailing opening the first three stores, Jim says that with their fourth store "we fell flat on our faces." They even had to close a couple of stores. He considered that a touch of reality, to know that "not everything was going to be a home run, and you better be prepared as you expand the business [to deal with] setbacks." He knew they had to figure out how to deal with different marketplaces. Clearly there was *necessity*.

Around that same time, Jim discovered that Price Club, his old employer, also experienced a couple of failures. Therein was the *opportunity*. (Necessity and opportunity collaborated to teach Jim a lesson: brand recognition was a requisite to success in new markets.)

Knowing that, one might conclude that it was an invitation to Jim to take advantage of a Price Club mistake and close the gap between them. But Jim didn't read it that way. He wouldn't have seen Price Club's failures as an opportunity for Costco to catch up to it. Remember, Price Club wasn't just a competitor in Jim's mind. It was the company run by the "smartest man in the world." There would have to be overwhelming evidence for Jim to bet that Sol had erred. However, the word from Price Club was that it attributed its setbacks to its business model being stale. Jim took that to mean that he'd better reinvent Costco, at least partially, from time to time, lest his stores, like those of Price Club, became uninteresting. He decided to add new items periodically.

So over the years Jim added fresh meat and seafood, bakery goods, gas stations, produce, optical departments, and pharmacies. He constantly reminded himself and his colleagues, "There's no annuity [here]. You've got to continually add stuff that's new and exciting. Otherwise you become boring."

WHEN YOU REINVENT, "MAKE NO LITTLE PLANS"

That quote is from Daniel Burnham, as he prepared in 1892 to reinvent Chicago's then-desolate south lakefront area with a world's fair. His attitude was similar to Jim's willingness to reinvent Costco. Jim could comfortably add food, fuel, and pharmaceuticals, changing one-third of the store, a major renovation. And he would reinvent Costco "early and often." But he kept the values of the organization. It's a recurring theme— Retail Is Entertainment—similar to Starbucks, Build-A-Bear, and the Levy Organization.

At first I found that inconsistent with a fundamental aspect of the Costco business plan, that it would carry no more than about 4,000 stock-keeping units (SKUs) and sell larger quantities of each SKU, packaged together. Now it was taking on additional SKUs in each of those departments. And a steak or a pie surely wasn't the same as a package of dozens of rolls of toilet paper.

Jim explained, "We weren't going to be butcher shops that would sell one New York steak at a time. We were going to sell about four or five New York steaks at a time. We were going to create the same type of efficiencies [such as bulk packaging] as in the rest of the warehouse."

He went on, "But we still wanted to keep our SKU count in the 4,000 range. Gee, there are easily 50 SKUs that we can discontinue over all the existing departments to bring in the meat department. Same thing with the bakery."

The immediate result was great. Having those new departments brought in new members who actually spent $2 on the other departments' merchandise for every $1 they spent on fresh foods.

"Wow," said Jim. "You don't have to be a Phi Beta Kappa to figure out that this is a good result." So Costco rolled out fresh food departments in all its warehouse stores. That's what I call "adjustable single-mindedness."

Jim says that taught him a lesson, that adding those departments—fresh foods, pharmacies, and so on—"enhanced the shopping experience for our customers. It renews you. I mean, you are indeed renewing yourself at that point."

It also demonstrated to him two things, which you should remember: (1) the removal or reinvention needn't be total, and (2) don't change the fundamentals. Packaging efficiencies and a lower number of SKUs did not change; quality would, of course, continue to be unconditionally guaranteed.

Sure, Costo had to reach into the collective history of its executives, to times when those people worked elsewhere, where they had handled fresh meat, bakery goods, and so on. And when necessary, managers brought on new employees who had skills that they lacked. But overall, not many skills were changed or required, just enough to partially reinvent Costco and add the changes into its current operation.

For Jim Sinegal, there were only a few basic Costco principles. One was the consistent markup. This meant that customers knew they were getting the best possible deal.

Perhaps what I refer to as Jim's "adjustable single-mindedness" can be better comprehended if you understand Jim's feelings about the importance of building and maintaining a brand. And keep in mind: brand isn't just a company or a product name, logo, and design.

Jim has a video clip from a newscast where the reporter asks a man sitting in his car in line for a gas pump, "Why are you here?" "I'm here to buy gas," the man replies. "Can anyone buy gas here?" "No," comes the reply, "you have to be a Costco member." "Well, why do you come here to buy gas?" Again the reply, "Because it's cheaper." And to the final question—"How much does the gas cost here?" The Costco member replies, nonplussed, "I don't know." That, Jim says, is when you know you have a valuable brand.

Jim shared this second story with the students in my Successful Entrepreneurship course. Costco carried a medicine that was priced at about $300 at Walgreen's and CVS. Costco charged $15 for the same medicine. One of my students wondered why Costco didn't charge $115, making an extra $100 and still killing the competition. Sinegal explained that by staying true to his rule—always marking up products by the same percentage, so that if product costs drop, the savings will be passed on to the customer—Costco can always be trusted by the customer.

That's what causes a Costco customer to sit in line at the gas pump knowing he'll save money even if he doesn't know the price he will be charged.

Those two examples explain how Costco maintains brand. It can dramatically change product lines, thus reinventing the business; yet by maintaining a few simple principles and values, the company obtains the benefits of the successfully built brand while adding successful new lines.

TO REINVENT SUCCESSFULLY, EARN THE TRUST OF CUSTOMERS

Jim sacrificed income and incurred inordinate extra work for himself and his employees by steadfastly maintaining his promise that customers, not Costco, would benefit from cost reductions. That thinking enabled him to reinvent the business several times. Customers accepted the reinventions because of their trust in Costco.

Sometimes the change seemed to necessitate learning a new business. Jim takes great pride in the fact that Costco has never changed the $1.50 price for a hot dog and a Coke at the fast-food counter near each store's exit. What the customers don't realize is that in order to do so, Costco had to stop buying the hot dogs. Instead, Costco built its own plant and produced the hot dogs. So Costco had to reinvent itself from mere retailer to both retailer and manufacturer in order to keep things the same. Does it pay?

"Well," says Jim, "they still make money on the hot dog." And if that doesn't convince you, Jim told me that when he announced his retirement in 2012, President Barack Obama called to congratulate him on his retirement.

You may recall that Jim had addressed the 2012 Democratic National Convention, endorsing the president's candidacy for reelection. After a few minutes of chatting, the president said, "Tell me one thing, Jim. Does this mean the price on that hot dog is going to go up?" The answer was no, of course.

SOMETIMES THE GOALS OF REINVENTIONS ARE TO STAY THE SAME

Jim reinvented Costco from retailer to manufacturer and retailer of hot dogs. Again we see a reinvention to stay the same, not to become something new. He did it to retain the hot dog–and–Coke combination that pleased all his customers, not just the U.S. president.

As time went on, Jim became more confident about the reinventions the company undertook. But how did he muster the confidence to effect the earlier reinventions? You might think it stemmed from his extensive experience as a retailer.

Actually, Jim would refer to that as arrogance, which he defines as saying, "We're so great we can do anything we want." That was not his style. Instead, he always tested new concepts in one or two Costco stores. Then, if it worked, if it made the Costco team confident, they would roll it out.

Costco's reinventions didn't stop with introductions of additional product lines. As Jim said, "Going to private label was a real departure." That reinvention has several advantages: (1) manufacturing at lower cost than purchasing products of the same quality, (2) being able to introduce higher-quality products, such as tuna, which was so much better than the canned tuna that Costco had been buying from suppliers that Costco actually had to increase the price, and (3) leveraging themselves with suppliers ("General Mills is smart enough to figure out that we're only going to have 4,000 SKUs," says Jim. "If something is coming in through private label, something else is going to leave. And they want to be sure it isn't them." So General Mills becomes more accommodating by adjusting or retaining price, packaging in larger containers, assuring timely deliveries).

Some might say that Costco's largest reinvention occurred on December 31, 2012, the day that Jim Sinegal, Costco's founder, retired as CEO. Jim is candid about the impact on him personally—"It's good to be King. Not many people remember the ex-champ. When you're gone, you're gone. You have to be adult and recognize that. But there's always going to be that time, and it is better to have left with the business in good shape."

Of course that reinvention of Costco was less than total. His handpicked successor, longtime colleague Craig Jelinek, asked Jim to remain on the board and be available to him. They made the succession seem seamless.

Again, we find a big reinvention with the goal of continuity. I'll bet that, if the First Lady allows it, President Obama will be able to get his hot dog and Coke at Costco for a long time to come.

Spinning Your Way Through
Serial Entrepreneurship

By definition, a serial entrepreneur is one who starts at least two, and generally more, businesses, usually over an extended period of time. John Osher certainly fits that definition. Actually he takes it to an extreme. John is now in his late 60s, but he started his entrepreneurial series before he entered first grade.

When he was five years old, his parents were taking an art class where they painted pictures of nude models. To shelter their children and to avoid shocking neighbors, they hid the paintings in the attic. But John quickly found them.

Instinctively, he realized the paintings could do more than satisfy his curiosity. For if he was curious, so would be his young friends. Therefore he charged each of them 5 cents to come up to the attic and see the nudes. A nickel here, a nickel there, John was soon better off than his peers.

By the time he was 19 and a freshman at the University of Wisconsin, a "hip school," says John, "where trends were started," he noticed that the coeds were getting their ears pierced and buying earrings.

When he transferred to the University of Cincinnati in 1967, ear piercing was just getting started. He assumed it would catch on quickly. So he decided to start an earring business. He'd need some capital. His father didn't believe John would succeed, so he refused to back him. He had better luck with his mother, who "invested" $1,000. She accompanied John on a purchasing trip to New York. They visited numerous earring wholesalers—all found on low-rent second floors—where they bought loads of costume jewelry earrings for 19 cents a pair.

Back at school, John found a tiny former shoeshine stall, which he set up as an earring store. Because the store was tiny, his inventory appeared greater than it was. He hung his earrings from a wall against black velvet. The earrings looked great. Rent was extremely low. John sold his 19-cent earrings for $4.99 a pair. That's a 96 percent profit margin—a massive profit by any standard, but of course, it was 4 percent less profit than John earned in his first business. (Since the nude picture viewing business was cost-free, he enjoyed a 100 percent profit margin.)

John recalls that there was a Kresge's store, part of a then-huge national chain, a couple of doors away. They sold *identical* earrings at 39 cents a pair—obviously a more traditional markup. Some might have been inclined to lower the price from $4.99 to something closer to Kresge's. Not John. He saw that while his earrings were flying off the shelf, Kresge's earrings were not selling at all.

In conversations with his customers, John learned that the girls were afraid of the "cheap" earrings, concerned that faulty materials might infect their earlobes.

Hardly. Precious metals were cheap then. All the earring earpieces were gold plated. John did so well he was able to buy Kresge's entire inventory at Kresge's full price and sell them at *his* price in his hole-in-the-wall store. John might have been scared by Kresge's failure to sell earrings like the ones he sold. Instead, his filter let him see opportunity to buy Kresge's inventory. In time, he sold that business. On the proceeds he took an extended trip abroad and bought a coveted MG sports car, which he drove around triumphantly. He began to look for a new venture after he transferred to Boston University.

He moved to Beantown and studied for his degree. Soon he started an antique dress business in Harvard Square in nearby Cambridge. This was in the 1960s, and Barbra Streisand had popularized similar old dresses.

John said, "These were velvet dresses, and I mean all these great things were from the 1920s and 1930s." He found them in old warehouses. Nobody recognized the value. "You couldn't give them away," he said. "They cost me 30 to 40 cents apiece, and I sold them for $59 each. You knew there was never a question of my taking a loss on all this inventory. You sell one dress and you paid for the whole truckload." This was another highly successful venture.

Osher would never experience such exceptional operating profits again. But he continued to grow as an entrepreneur. Thereafter, John entered the home air circulation business. In the 1970s, John's company, Conserve Inc., the products of which saved householders fuel, was doing so well that it was listed in *Inc.* magazine as one of "the nation's fastest growing businesses."

Note that a company with a $2.5 million sales base might double that for a 100 percent gain at $5 million in a single year.

Obviously, a company with $2.5 billion in sales rarely doubles revenue in a year on such a large base.

After that Osher moved in a new direction—baby stuff—with "Crawl Space," a portable protected area where infants could move about safely with minimum supervision in otherwise dangerous home environments like kitchens.

Going from the energy conservation business to the baby product business may seem like passing over a big divide. But skills John developed in the energy business were refined and adapted to great effect in the baby product business. For example, he had sensed the positive impact of taping a photograph of the enclosed product to the box of his air circulation units. This made it possible for people to visualize the product as they walked through crowded aisles of shelves loaded with goods. Now he did the same thing with Crawl Space, which helped build sales volumes.

Shortly after that he developed Rainbow Toy Bars, a rod with toys hanging from it. It was the predecessor of a similar toy, developed by John out of polypropylene tubing he became acquainted with while working as a plumber. This was one of John's proudest entrepreneurial coups.

Rainbow Toy Bars hung from the top of cribs. In time they would be known to millions of babies. Rainbow Toy Bars had been the biggest seller at Toys"R"Us. John sold the business to Gerber. Hired by Gerber as part of the package, John was left in an office with nothing to do. Gerber dropped the ball. Yet the concept was so successful Fisher-Price and others did hugely successful knock-offs. Gerber's failure to apply resources to promoting the product allowed the copycats to eat away Gerber's volume and margins.

Some entrepreneurs can't cope with the idea of professional managers taking charge of their best ideas. That's like loaning a cherished old car to a friend who doesn't take care of it. But in John's case, he never loaned the "car" to a "friend." He sold it to strangers, without any remaining stake in or lingering emotional tie to it. He simply left in disgust to pursue a new idea.

· SELLING YOUR BUSINESS IS NOT YOUR MOST RECENT DECISION; IT'S THE PREDECESSOR OF YOUR NEXT MOVE

Prof. Daniel Kahneman, the only noneconomist to have won the Nobel Prize in Economics, uses creative experiments to prove that people will go to extreme lengths to validate their most recent decisions. John Osher overcame that urge by not brooding over what buyers did with his "babies." Instead, the rejection freed him to move on to his next opportunity.

Osher's new diversion served older children. He developed Arcade Basketball, a set that could be hung from the top of any door. Soon, John was on a toy roll again. Stretch Armstrong was a short, muscular action figure that could be stretched from inches to five feet. In typical imaginative Osher fashion, he referenced band aids. If a kid tore an Armstrong figure when stretching it, a band aid repaired it. Stretch added robust sales to the enterprise. John's toy company would grow to $125 million in sales.

Spinning Stories of Reinvention

Along John Osher's yellow brick road to profit, he met an inventor who showed him a lollipop device that would spin in a person's mouth. It was a clumsy attempt. But John had always spun lollipops in his mouth—turning the stick manually. Moreover, he'd seen other kids do the same.

So John had his toymakers fix this awkward spinning lollipop. Using the skills developed on John's other toys, they streamlined the device. Perfected, it became Spin Pop. Over a hundred million Spin

Pops were sold before John's company was sold to Hasbro, then and now one of the world's biggest toy manufacturing companies.

John knew his team had special skills and the ability to reinvent his company by refining those skills, as they had exhibited in engineering Spin Pop. Now he decided they should further hone and supplement those skills and reinvent themselves in a totally different industry. John wanted to create an inexpensive, disposable electric toothbrush. There were already electrics on the market, but they were expensive, costing in excess of $100.

By contrast, manual toothbrushes sold for very little and were giveaways at dentists' offices. (For years dentists had given away lollipops, which made it seem they were trying to increase cavities.) John was convinced the team that created Spin Pop could create a spin brush. Of course, battery life would have to be longer. Moreover, teeth-brushing mechanisms had to comply with dental hygiene standards. And the retail price had to come in at about $10 to $15—a major challenge. John's team went at it. They used their existing skills—creating spinning products at very low cost and with decent battery life. They designed a package for sale in large retail chains. They also developed some new skills in creating oscillating brushes and seal proofing that could meet exacting dental hygiene standards.

John's market research lacked focus groups, even a budget. It consisted of reconnaissance at a couple of the local drugstores to see what was already available and how the successful electrics on the shelves were packaged. That was followed by one or two conversations with discreet friends at big chain-store companies to determine what was selling and what was not. That was it.

Many successful entrepreneurs I know have little patience with formal research and resent spending the capital needed to pay for it. These savvy operators prefer to go with their gut instincts. Sometimes their gut reflects years of experience in the particular field. Other times, they have learned how to ask good questions in other fields and simply apply it to their new product. One complained to my class that when the MBAs come in they tend to gather tons of data and loads of analyses that only a giant like Procter & Gamble can use. Entrepreneurs are more adept, and they move quickly. They are the speedboat that outmaneuvers the aircraft carrier.

CHOOSE YOUR INVESTORS

If John had accepted money from institutional investors, he couldn't have made his seemingly rash decision on pricing the disposable electric toothbrush.

Typically, John Osher was successful in his quest for a practical, low-cost electric toothbrush. The resulting product was called Dr. John's SpinBrush. Osher is not a doctor, nor does he play one on TV. By odd coincidence, however, almost all of the team's principal engineers were, like Osher, named John. Dr. John's SpinBrush was an immediate success. Sold to Procter & Gamble for well over half a billion dollars, it became the Crest SpinBrush. Subsequently the SpinBrush was resold to Church & Dwight and is now called the Arm & Hammer Spinbrush.

Each reinvention—from energy device to baby products, to toys, to edible lollipop, to dental product—seems like a huge leap. However, they were, in fact, a series of incremental changes—not monumental shifts but slight pivots. Basically, John was refining existing skills and learning a few new skills. Then off to the races. Was this "reinvention for dummies"? Absolutely not!

Since that home run, John has continued to explore and start new businesses—inexpensive electric razors, dog leashes with lights, news transmission. I'm sure he'll reinvent again. I don't know what his next big thing will be, but I'd bet that some of his new businesses will be something that expands on his teams' existing skills—requiring only modifications of those—and supplemented by a few new skills called for by the product.

CHANGE THE FILTERS ON YOUR LENS

There are just too many opportunities that come into the sight of someone skilled at seeing them. Osher added a filter to his lens, so the only opportunities that came through were those that would in some way require skills similar to those he had used before. His skills developed with Crawl Space easily progressed to Rainbow Toy Bars, which led to related products, including lollipops. After Spin Pops, a spinning toothbrush penetrated his filter.

The "Reinventrepreneur"

You needn't be like John, who reinvents as Chicago voters vote: early and often. He does that because that's who he is. He is clearly a "reinventrepreneur." He has mastered the art of finding a way to adapt his skills, to only slightly modify his and his teams' skills, making the jump a short one. And because he's a reinventrepreneur, he has learned to jump almost continually, as if barely lifting his feet over a jump rope rather than traversing chasms.

You may do it once, taking some of the skills you learned on your job, refining and adapting some of those, and adding a few new ones. In other words, you needn't totally reinvent yourself or your business to be reinvented, and you needn't do it repeatedly as a reinventrepreneur.

Captains of Industry: Don't Just Grandstand—Do Something

5

Maturity Is No Excuse: Reinvent or Atrophy

PARTS 1 AND 2 OF THIS BOOK DEAL WITH REINVENTIONS OF INDI-
viduals, the realignment of their skill sets to change from employees to entrepreneurs despite the forces of naysayers who urge
otherwise. Part 3 deals with businesses—well-established, even
gigantic companies—as evidence that the need for reinvention is
perpetual and critical at all stages. This brief review will form the
base for consideration of grown entrepreneurial and family businesses I have interviewed.

Creative Destruction Is the DNA of Business: Survival Is Hard Won, Not Automatic

Austrian-American economist Joseph Schumpeter wrote his book
Capitalism, Socialism and Democracy, published in 1942, 15 years
before Bill Gates was born. Schumpeter used the term "creative
destruction" to describe a "process of industrial mutation that

incessantly revolutionizes the economic structure from within, *incessantly* destroying the old one, *incessantly* creating a new one." He went so far as to call this concept "the essential fact of capitalism."

At one time, IBM was the 800-pound gorilla. Indeed, that understates it; IBM was *the* gorilla. At a critical point, it could have taken one step to perpetuate that status, but why take a step to assure what was perceived as certain? If IBM were the only company to have suffered terrible consequences of failing to reinvent as a result of excessive confidence, it would be an interesting but noninstructive story. However, IBM is not alone. Similar stories can be told about many overconfident companies. It wasn't as though Microsoft came on the scene with a solid patent that froze out IBM. Nor did Howard Schultz have a patent on coffeehouses that prevented his employer, the old Starbucks company, from beating him to the punch. And McDonald's founder Ray Kroc didn't patent the hamburger and fries. Wimpy's and even drive-ins with skating waitresses had been selling those for years.

No, dominant players are rarely insulated by patents. They are mostly overwhelmed by the creativity of new rivals with fresher ideas. Schumpeter's theory wasn't "licensed destruction," it was "creative destruction."

There are many high-profile corporate lapses—Sears, Borders, Motorola. There are even some lapses by whole industries— buggy-whip makers, silent-movie production companies, black-and-white television manufacturers, railroads, and TV networks.

Digital photography was an example of creative destruction of a product—film photography. But Kodak was *not* just an example of creative destruction but an example of bad business judgment, a matter of failing to eat your lunch before someone else does. The losers were overly confident and suffered. Kodak might be seen as paranoid. That's not unreasonable, but if so, its approach at dealing with its challenges was based on overconfidence. Either way, the company suffered terribly. Some losers survived but with drastically less power and market share.

Why is this kind of overconfidence so self-destructive—so different than the actions of Andy Grove also motivated by paranoia, so unlike Howard Schultz's, Tom Stemberg's, and Bill Gates's creative confidence? Is it a difference in degree or in kind, and what can we learn from that?

More importantly, why is it relevant to this book? We have been exploring the reinvention of businesspeople and their businesses. One of the major enablers of reinvention is embedded in the creative destruction and strategic blunders of competitors. Then, of course, reinvention is best deployed pursuant to a well-conceived strategic plan. Understanding all this can help you spot, analyze, and take advantage of competitors' mistakes.

Intel: There Was More Than Paranoia Inside

Andy Grove, the founder and CEO of Intel, the pioneering microchip company, tells one of the most remarkable stories of a successful reinvention in business history. Of course, some business reinventions are more spectacular than others, but Intel's was truly monumental.

The reinvention was described beautifully by Grove in his bestselling book *Only the Paranoid Survive*. Intel, the large, highly successful manufacturer of memory chips, decided to abandon the very soul of its business, the product that was *the source of virtually all of its revenue*. Intel's old stalwart memory chip was becoming a commodity. Prices were starting to swoon in reflection of fierce competition, largely from the Far East. Intel might have continued to compete in memory chips. However, Intel's founders, who still managed the company, saw the writing on the wall and were too smart to ignore the coming cataclysm. They decided that Intel would instead *start over* as a manufacturer of microprocessors. They wisely followed an old Yiddish proverb: "You can't control the wind, but you can adjust your sails."

These microchips were tiny computers on a chip on which Intel secured patents. A microchip "computer" was barely visible to the naked eye, yet it could perform highly useful tasks. Each of us today carries a tiny microchip in a cell phone, one of the countless tiny electronic items now commonplace via Intel's patented computer on a chip.

While Andy Grove's book was excellent, whoever picked his title—which is a grabber, of course—misled the public. First of all, it's hardly paranoia when there is a real threat. That, despite the joke: "Even paranoids have real enemies." But "paranoia" attracts attention. And Andy Grove is too humble to flaunt his prescience, confidence, and bravery. All of those attributes are what account for Intel still being a viable company and for there not being an empty building bearing a fading sign "Intel Memory Chips." In addition to paranoia, Grove and his colleagues had the guts to take a huge gamble and the leadership skills to secure needed support. What made them so confident? Could you be so confident? I think so.

In Chapter 4 I wrote about Jim Sinegal and Joe Sullivan having been prepared to grab their brass rings. Businesses also must be prepared. If Intel hadn't been financially sound, it couldn't have afforded to make such a bold move, and Grove's paranoia would have been a mere psychological condition and not the driver of a great business reinvention. Back then, no one—not Grove nor his brilliant, lifetime career partners, Bob Noyce and Gordon Moore— knew if Intel could create a business around this unique item.

To some it may appear that successful reinvention requires seeing around corners or having a crystal ball. After all, isn't that what Andy Grove did? That's how it may appear to an outsider. As stated earlier, that's how it may be for someone just starting a new business. But to someone involved in a business and industry, you generally needn't see what's on the other side of the wall if you take the time to read the writing on your side of the wall.

One way to do that is to avoid assuming that the future will be bound by the restrictions of today's realities. For example, if in 1980 you tried to predict the potential for the cell phone industry, you might have concluded it was a passing fad. The handsets were large and difficult to use, the costs of infrastructure were excessive, and the bandwidth was inadequate. In fact that's what the venerable consulting firm McKinsey & Company concluded. AT&T relied on McKinsey's report and dropped its cell phone business. McKinsey and AT&T assumed the future would be restricted by the constraints of 1980s' realities as to costs, equipment, and bandwidths. The resulting lost opportunities are immeasurable.

Intel was convinced its existing business was no longer viable. So in making a change, its downside was limited. But unless there was a viable upside, its investment of capital and human resources in the new business would be attacked as a violation of its duties to shareholders and would be a black mark on the company's fine reputation. Andy and his colleagues couldn't have moved forward on paranoia alone; they had to be confident.

I'm unable to determine whether these people were paranoid, but three paranoid men could not turn around Intel on their own. They needed their whole team plus numerous outside stakeholders and supporters. They needed to get all of those people to trust their leadership in this endeavor. They also had to "be sure" they were right.

Today, they are rightfully applauded for their foresight, brilliance, timing, and implementation of the reinvention. And for their unadulterated chutzpah! This was done on a humongous scale, against all advice and opinion. Talk about "bet the company" decisions! This one takes the cake, because Intel was already a huge, successful company, a paragon of the high-tech world. Could Intel reinvent as a "chip off the old stock"? Intel faced desperate conditions.

Not every reinvention is a *desperate* bet-the-company situation, although many more would be desperate if matters were allowed to continue down old pathways.

Four Motivators of Reinvention

This is how I categorize the motivations behind reinventions: (1) desperation, (2) necessity, (3) opportunity, and (4) addiction. *Desperation* takes place when all else has failed. It is best symbolized by the "Hail Mary pass" in the final seconds of an American football game. *Necessity* is a more calculated gamble, not a last-ditch effort. It is undertaken despite costs or odds because it is needed, maybe even compelling, and worth trying. *Opportunity* occurs without relation to a company's current conditions, although such conditions may determine the wisdom of reaching for the opportunity. *Addiction* is a condition of certain entrepreneurs who feel the need to start new businesses on a near-continual basis.

Yes, Intel was in a stage of desperation. Status quo was a death march. Intel's taking the fork in the road was indeed a case of nothing to lose and everything to gain.

One might think that delaying the inflection point until it is proximate-to-critical makes it easier—that is, that it will require less confidence or that consensus confidence will be easier to obtain then. Indeed it may be easier to convince others in an everything-to-gain, nothing-to-lose spot, the proverbial burning platform situation. However, by that point, implementation may be more difficult, and key people may already have left or put a foot (and their soul) out the door

Intel emerged as a giant multinational semiconductor chip maker headquartered in Santa Clara, California. Intel's reinvention has made it the world's largest and highest valued semiconductor chip maker, based on revenue.

As evidence of the repetitive need to reinvent, Intel now faces new challenges. The computer industry is rapidly moving from desktop and even laptop computers to tablets and other mobile devices and to "the Internet of things" applications, most of which use Quark chips, which are made by companies other than Intel. As a result, Intel's chip sales are declining and its fabs (chip fabrication factories) are underutilized, thus decreasing Intel's margins. To offset those declines, Intel must consider allowing competitors to use Intel fabs to make competitive products. Once again, Intel faces potentially dire consequences and must consider extreme reinventions.

Other companies, whose situations are less dire, may find the choice more difficult. Of course, seeing the need for reinvention and determining which category—desperation, necessity, opportunity, or addiction—confronts your company is a challenge best handled by wise, experienced leaders and certainly not by the faint of heart.

6

Kodak and IBM:
The Goliath Factor

EASTMAN KODAK AND IBM WERE JUGGERNAUTS IN THEIR respective fields. Film giant Eastman Kodak gave us the "Kodak Moment," which persists as the quintessential photographic experience even though Kodak in decline is not a major factor in the digital camera age. IBM (Big Blue) was so pervasive in mainframe computers that purchasing agents bought Big Blue computers knowing they would never be fired for making this choice. Both companies were supremely confident, making decisions that presumed the past was an appropriate guide to the future. They did so even as the world was changing dramatically. The seeds of their downfall are echoed in Schumpeter's creative destruction idea whereby changes in customers' taste, technologies, and global economic circumstance destroy the Kodaks and hobble the IBMs.

Creative destruction is like a virus that enters the body economic. Real viruses, such as the common cold, are managed and can be overcome by otherwise healthy, well-rested bodies. More virulent viruses, such as cancer or AIDS, may be kept at bay temporarily, but ultimately they tend to prevail. As with some virulent real viruses, the introduction of new strategies, models, financing, and talent—the "medicines" of business—can overpower or slow down the progress of the business viruses.

We're about to consider two companies that failed to take their medicine. Whether because they felt immune or thought the virus less potent than it actually was, they each paid a price. What happened is well worth consideration and study by all companies. At your company, the economic virus may be different, but the effect may be more deadly because you may not have as robust an immune system.

The Kodak Moment Enters the Dark Room of History

Another company that was a leader, until it wasn't, was the Rochester, New York, behemoth Kodak. It was rock-solid and the dominant company in the photography industry until creative destruction turned granite to sand. To me, there has never been a more iconic company than Kodak. Coke may have been the "pause that refreshes," but it shared the platform with Pepsi. McDonald's arches were alluring to billions of customers in every crossroad of the world. But direct competitors like Burger King and Wendy's and indirect rivals like KFC, Subway, and Pizza Hut made McDonald's one of a select crowd.

By contrast Eastman Kodak thundered along for decades with little or no competition, during which nearly every snapshot that mattered was "a Kodak moment."

Kodak—What the Hell Were They Thinking?

Yes, Kodak was once a truly great company. It brought photography out of the studio and into everyday life by making it affordable to the average family. It was an exception to the razor/razor-blade analyses, where companies were said to willingly give away the one-time purchase equivalent of the razor free in order to gain recurring razor-blade sales. (Gillette's use of that model has been refuted by some scholars but continues to serve as an iconic basis for business decisions.) But Kodak managed to make money selling cameras too, although its film and film-processing businesses generated the bulk of its profits. Its customers weren't just average consumers. Kodak sold film and equipment to hospitals, clinics, dentists, and podiatrists for x-ray pictures, which required higher quality and thus higher-priced film than that for the everyday consumer.

There had been competitors from time to time—Ansco, Agfa, and Polaroid. Each posed a threat until Kodak reacted forcefully through the power of its market share and financial strength. Besides, Kodak's distribution channels were loyal. These consisted of camera stores and corner drugstores that knew better than to bite the hand that fed them. Those retail outlets were given steady recurring revenue through handling charges for film processing.

They forwarded the film to local or regional Kodak processing centers. So long as they did that, they were allowed to keep the bright yellow sign in their window proclaiming that consumers could get trustworthy development of their precious pictures. Brand mattered. People really cared about their pictures—often the first thing they would grab while exiting in an emergency like a house fire.

Kodak was totally focused on its film business. That was the goose that laid golden eggs, all day, every day.

When Polaroid came onto the scene, Kodak improved the technology of its cameras, projectors, film, and processing equipment. And it priced aggressively to turn Polaroid into a luxury item, leaving Kodak as the primary source for photographs that could be savored for years.

Relationships with retail camera stores and pharmacies, effectively tying together the camera, film, and processing, enabling the retailers to maintain and increase profitability over decades, assured that "upstarts" like Agfa and Ansco were a less-recommended and less-preferred alternative.

It wasn't until the 1980s and 1990s that Fuji made serious inroads. But this thrust was countered by Kodak's successful entrée into global markets—even China's.

George Fisher Enters Kodak's Hallowed Ground

When George Fisher, Motorola's highly capable CEO during that company's heyday, became the CEO of Kodak, he faced a daunting challenge. The culture in century-old Kodak was deeply embedded. Employee tenure was marked in decades, not years. Employees had witnessed numerous challengers, all of which had been unable to scale the outer walls of Fortress Kodak.

Still, at this point, Eastman Kodak faced a formidable opponent in Fuji. Fuji was a thriving Japanese film manufacturer. Fisher had made Motorola the clear leader in cell phones, so bringing George on board would seem to be just what Kodak needed to retain its dominant lead.

Fisher was able to accomplish some things right away. He managed to outmaneuver Fuji in China, which everyone believed would become a game-changing market for the industry. The deal he struck with China called for a level of exclusivity for decades, depriving Fuji of its closest large potential market. This adroit feat was universally applauded in Rochester, Kodak's home, and on Wall Street. Why not? It saved thousands of jobs and perhaps the company itself.

When the conquering crusader returned to Rochester, New York, he set out to fix other problems. The company was fat. Changes were needed to make it more competitive. But Fisher met resistance at every turn: He was an outsider. He didn't understand Kodak culture. Message: "You can't just adopt new ways. That's not how we do things here." Around that time, Fisher expressed his frustration to me.

He had successfully moved Kodak—and indeed the United States—into China's capitalistic answer to its stultifying purely Communist economy, only to face resistance at Kodak, a key bastion of the American capitalist system. This was the "not invented here" syndrome, wherein a company rejects any idea invented elsewhere, on steroids. The Kodak culture effectively decreed: no Kodak "outsider," even if he was the company CEO, was going to tell hidebound Kodakers how to change. But George Fisher was not only a top corporate manager, he succeeded as a diplomat. In effect he secured an international "corporate treaty" with the largest country in the world at a time when others had failed to do so. I've always regretted that George never got the chance to achieve what he told my class was his ultimate dream—to be the U.S. ambassador to China. I'm confident that he would have served the United States in admirable fashion. Yet he was unable to make any headway against the deeply embedded Kodak culture. Kodak, like its customers posing for snapshots, stood still instead of reinventing itself. As if standing still wasn't enough, circumstances at Kodak got much worse.

Life Seen Through a Glass, Darkly

Nearly a hundred years after its founding, Kodak still reigned supreme on film, its number one moneymaker, although foreign companies were capturing serious market share in cameras and other equipment. It was as though Kodak was happier to have competitive cameras out there. It lowered costs and improved the technology, thus making camera ownership and film use more widespread. After all, cameras were like razors, and Kodak was selling all the blades—the film and the film processing.

Had it become more price competitive against Fuji and rival camera manufacturers Kodak might well have staved off the invasion, but it hadn't done so. Its judgment was flawed at best. Having beat out all competitors, its confidence had morphed into arrogance. In retrospect, Kodak had survived on momentum and power of market share—not on ability to stem the tide of competition.

When focus causes you to wear blinders, you are far more likely to be blindsided, and that's exactly what happened to Kodak. It was blindsided by cataclysmic change and became the poster child for Schumpeter's creative destruction theory. In very few years, this century-plus-old company allowed a virus to prevail.

Could Kodak have saved itself from ignominy? Was there a time and a way to reinvent Kodak to remain viable? Surely there were paths available. Kodak could have been resurrected, perhaps not to the position of dominance it held for nearly a century. But it had a history of finding new products, inventions, and business models. All it needed was time to capture opportunities again.

Given Kodak's reliance on film, the company's fall as a result of the turn to filmless photography was predictable. If that were the whole picture, the analysis would lead to a company failing to reinvent itself when it should have. But the colossal irony goes much deeper than that.

In 1975, Steve Sasson, a Kodak engineer, created a digital camera. In such devices, as you know, images are stored on a silicon chip. Film is unnecessary. Sasson not only created the digital camera, he also applied for and later received a patent for the underlying technology. That was the genesis of creative destruction of film and the cameras that used it.

That patent could have been the basis for a Kodak reinvention of a magnitude that rivaled Intel's. Had that happened, you might well have read a book by Walter Fallon—who was Kodak's CEO then—rather than Andy Grove's. Clearly, Kodak's digital camera patent provided the potential for one of the most exciting corporate reinventions of the century. So how did Kodak reinvent itself? Well, it didn't: not at all. Instead, this once-great company that had made a stellar city of its hometown, Rochester, hid its digital camera on a shelf, deep in the bowels of company headquarters.

A Deer in Headlights Doesn't Reinvent

Kodak sat on the key to what would become a new industry of epic proportions—digital photography. Is it possible that none of Kodak, Fallon, and Sasson understood that they had entered the doorway to a new industry with his invention? Were they blind to its potential or fearful that digital photography would adversely affect their precious film business? After all, film did contribute most of Kodak's revenue and profit.

That Kodak patented and then hid the digital camera is fascinating. It's difficult to recall where such an approach (hiding an invention) has succeeded. Granted, some have taken that approach and succeeded, but not in cases in which the new technology was so valuable that it could topple a giant. And certainly not in this age of omnipresent, instantaneous information and communication that has virtually (pun intended) obliterated the now-quaint concept of secrecy.

The mantra of the late 1990s, "eat your lunch before someone else does," suggested to brick-and-mortar stores that they open parallel e-commerce facilities, even though the online facilities would steal market share from their brick and-mortar operations. Otherwise, independent e-commerce companies would serve the online market and steal market share from the brick-and-mortars. Think: Amazon.com. In other words, it would be better to move profit from one pocket to another before someone *picks* your pocket.

A patent is an exclusive license granted by the government. Patents are granted in order to afford the inventor limited protection from competition. This justifies the inventor's investment of time and capital to develop the protected technology. Patents are also granted in order to entice the inventor to publicize the underlying technology (which occurs when the patent application is published), enabling others to use the underlying technology for unrelated inventions and products.

Given all that, if a company decides, rightly or wrongly, to keep its invention secret, why would it share its secret technology with the world? So why did Kodak file for a patent, knowing that would result in publication of its secret, while trying to keep the technology a secret?

It's possible that a company in Kodak's situation might try to hedge its bet by securing a patent, perhaps followed by securing a minefield of related patents, to buy and extend time to reinvent the company strategy, including its product line. Otherwise it seems like a strategy conceived by a committee that never met. I can't imagine them being oblivious to the potential of digital photography—both its advantages and its impact on film.   However conceived, it is a poor attempt to hedge the bet and indicates a dramatic departure from the discipline that governed Kodak's century-long thoughts and actions.

Whether this inaction represented company confidence bordering on arrogance or a total lack of confidence, it clouded Kodak's lens, resulting in an inability to reinvent Kodak. The result has been devastating, leaving Kodak as a nonplayer in a new industry it could have owned. Kodak was left with the old industry—film and film processing—that was virtually nonexistent. And now so is Kodak, having come through bankruptcy reorganization, a form of involuntary reinvention, as an intellectual property and patent owner, no longer as an operating company.

The photographic film business as we knew it is dead. If you doubt that, think about the last time you bought photographic film. Okay, so you bought a cardboard camera and sent a dozen negatives to a drugstore processor. That's an infinitesimally small market to build a business on. Even dentists, not the fastest adopters of new technology, are using digital devices for photographic x-ray.

But while the film market has dissolved, Kodak could have survived. The iconic phrase "a Kodak moment" remains in use. Unfortunately, because Kodak didn't reinvent itself, today's Kodak moments are recorded on smartphones, made by just about everyone but Kodak. And "Kodak" will likely become the wrong answer in a future trivia game asking for the name of a TV detective who was bald and sucked lollipops (Kojak).

IBM—Most Admired, Not Inspired

If Intel is the quintessential example of superb reinvention and if Kodak is at the opposite end of the spectrum, then IBM is the extraordinary example of being in second place at both ends of the spectrum. Although a rare example, it is well worth noting.

Why do some extremely confident companies fail to reinvent on a timely basis? Desperation is, of course, a great motivator of reinvention. When you have little to lose, you are more willing and more likely to risk it all and reinvent. As literary giant Samuel Johnson put it in a related context, the prospect of being hanged focuses the mind wonderfully. However, as we just saw, Kodak focused too hard and missed the big picture.

Of course, desperation isn't just the actual measure of a situation. It's also the measure of the recognition of and a perception of and even a belief about a situation. Though your circumstances are dire, it only matters as a motivator if you truly believe your circumstances are dire.

Like Kodak, IBM was an industrial giant. Both were companies that were in every conservative investment manager's portfolio and whose stocks were among the 30 that constituted the preeminent indicator of the stock market's health, the Dow Jones Industrial Average (DJIA). Both large companies failed to reinvent themselves, and they have suffered accordingly, albeit for different reasons. Also the extent of their sufferings has been different. There are lessons in the similarities and the differences.

A Culture of Arrogance

Sometimes it is the very confidence that enabled a company founder to block out the noise, reinvent himself, challenge the world, and make his dream child an industry leader that becomes the enemy. Confidence becomes arrogance, and arrogance results in the company's slide or even its destruction. Often, decades or even an entire century after its founding a company will develop a culture of arrogance. This may not be tied so much to its founding or even to its founder. Instead it may be born out of its successes. The arrogance can be unrelated to the founder's confidence. This destructive arrogance can take hold long after the founder is gone.

Such arrogance can prevent a company's reinvention when that step is essential. Having dominant market share can cause one to "ignore the kid with the slingshot" and to decide that there is no need to reinvent. Kodak and IBM are prime examples of this, although in Kodak's case it was both David and Goliath. Unfortunately, these examples are not unique; fortunately, however, the failings of these two companies are not the norm.

IBM was a rarity in its earlier years. There weren't many companies that could be characterized as computer companies. Indeed, there weren't that many computers. In the 1950s and 1960s, a computer was a gigantic contraption that filled a 40- by 40-foot room, and the room required air conditioning 24/7, though that phrase was invented decades later. Few Americans knew how to use these computers. Computers, though large in size, were puny in function by today's standards. They only did limited computing and data crunching. A major institution was fortunate to have one computer. There were many universities that had none.

In the late 1950s and early 1960s, I was a student, employed part-time by my school. My boss was a brilliant woman working on her PhD at the University of Chicago. Part of my job was to work on the statistical analyses for her thesis. The deadlines were tight. We had to have our work finalized in time for her to run the data during the one hour per month when she was afforded access to the college's one computer.

In a world with so few users and so few manufacturers of computers, IBM couldn't afford to make any mistakes. The company was an amazingly well-organized and disciplined one, from training, to sales techniques, even to dress code. Its rules were geared to prevent the necessity for its people to think about unnecessary matters, so they could focus on important problems and "keep their eye on the ball." I mention this because I want to dispose of any notions of arrogance in the usual sense. This was a company that owned a huge piece of the market, but certainly not all of it. It had competition from UNIVAC, which was much smaller. IBM was more like an oligopoly than a monopoly. Not that it would likely have been attacked as a monopoly, since the government was one of the company's most eager customers. There were continual developments in the industry, and IBMers were committed to being at the cutting edge of those developments. By and large, they were. Their commitment to their rules, their dedication to their discipline, made them confident, but they were still diligent. Changes in their products, which today seem infinitesimal, were monumental back then. Yet even then, those changes would not have been described as reinventing the company.

So IBM was the leader, at the cutting edge of technology in its field and confident in all it did. But at one important point in time, it wasn't at the cutting edge, yet IBMers were still confident. That was a day in 1980 when they met a young man with a vision: Bill Gates.

Remember, this was before Gates was the richest man in America, before the Microsoft tune that plays every time you start the Microsoft system challenged (and likely has beaten) "Happy Birthday" as the most frequently played tune ever. At that time the name Microsoft was virtually unknown. It would more likely suggest a laundry additive to assure softer underwear and socks.

Bill Gates and Paul Allen were a pair of college dropouts, without the trappings of success, who claimed to have a better vision of the future in the computer world than that held by the world leader, IBM. IBMers thought of themselves as a hardware company. After all, they did fill those very large rooms with a lot of hardware. Yet IBMers were anything but foolish. They were mulling entry into the field of smaller computers, but they needed an operating system.

Gates proclaimed to IBM that software, not hardware, was the future. Someday soon, people would no longer vie for a few minutes a month on the house computer, assuming there was one. Gates argued that individuals would have *personal* computers sitting on their desks. He might as well have said that people would build a car that could operate without gasoline. The ubiquitous iPhone of today was as realistic then as the Dick Tracy wrist radio.

At that time it would have been sheer fantasy to think that today's smartphones would outnumber the members of the population and that each one would have more computer power than IBM's biggest computer back then.

So it was understandable then that IBM sloughed off the importance of Gates's operating system. After all, the hardware was what mattered, and the software would be like any other component. IBM ignored the value of Gates's approach, though Big Blue took a license for the Microsoft software. In a huge lapse, however, it allowed Gates to sell the operating system to others too.

That they were oblivious to the potential, that they didn't grasp the importance of Bill Gates's operating program, was bad, but not as bad as Kodak, which actually owned the patent.

IBM should have reinvented itself. Gates's operating system would have allowed the company to do so. IBM could have made its license of the Microsoft software exclusive. God knows, IBM could have afforded it back then. But then, a serious industry leader can't listen to every ragtag group of kids that comes along.

IBM didn't get to be Big Blue by making uneducated or ill-advised assumptions. Granted, it was the 800-pound gorilla lurking in the computer industry jungle. But how could they have been so supremely confident as to ignore Austrian-American economist Joseph Schumpeter's signal contribution to economics: creative destruction?

IBM's Reinvention After the Fact—a Very Rare Feat

Fortunately for IBMers, they eventually realized that the world was turning and they'd better fasten their safety belts. Around 1993 they reinvented IBM as a consulting company, basically, and in that guise, the company has done exceedingly well. Their recent moves through the application of Thomas Watson technology, its supercomputer, to healthcare is evidence of the future greatness potential of IBM.

That IBM could make such a catastrophic mistake and survive attests to its size and the power of its brand as well as IBMers' skills. That's different than Ford's survival after Edsel, which was the result of Edsel being but one of many models and products. In any event, this gave IBM the luxury of a subsequent reinvention.

But not many companies are so well endowed. IBM may have been too big to fail; Kodak erroneously thought it was too big to fail; and you likely aren't.

After listing several recent disruptions, such as GPSs disrupting Rand McNally atlases, the *Wall Street Journal* suggested that perhaps disruption has become the new normal. More likely, that perception stems from the nature of the new technologies where incremental changes, which occur more frequently, are sufficient to enable new products. For example, a new app for the iPhone can disrupt an entire industry (when did you last use the Yellow Pages?). And remember when Facebook was a new disruption? Now Facebook is hastily reinventing itself for better use on mobile devices. And Google continues reinventing itself to dominate the "Internet of things," such as its billion-dollars-plus purchase of Nest, the thermostat company. Certainly there will continue to be cataclysmic changes like digital photography and operating systems. They'll simply occur less frequently.

Clearly, you will want to be a survivor, not a failure; you will want to sing along with the Bee Gees and "Stay Alive." No, reinventing your business is not easy. But its implementation at your level is likely easier than reinventing an Intel or a Kodak. Given the alternatives—survival or failure—reinvention is a necessity.

You devoted all the time and effort needed to start your company and make it a success. So when the business needs you to take new risks—to spend the time, effort, and money to extend its life, how can you decide not to? How can you let your entrepreneurial baby gasp for breath and die? Here too it is not just knowing how to reinvent your business. It's also ignoring the inevitable naysayers who insist it can't be done. The naysayers may well be within the company. They may be shortsightedly protecting current paychecks (or, as we see in the case of family businesses, protecting dividend distributions). Such people aren't visionaries.

If they were, they well might have left the company to become entrepreneurs.

Ultimately, it's doing your homework to understand the risks and rewards and then conducting thoughtful risk/reward analyses. It is training yourself to be sensitive and to knowing in advance how you'll react when the "what ifs" occur. It is going with your educated instincts and then having the guts to follow through on a sound business proposition.

PART 4

Entrepreneurs Morph to Corporate Chiefs

7

Moving to a Higher Platform

MY GRANDMOTHER USED TO SAY, "MAN PLANS, AND GOD laughs." Businesspeople are the ultimate planners. But life makes lots of unpredictable interventions that create a web of ambiguities with unexpected consequences. Our ability to deal with these ambiguities helps determine the limits of our opportunities and fortune. Indeed in entrepreneurship classes, we say that to be an entrepreneur one must have a "tolerance for ambiguity." Some say it's the ability to "go with the flow." If you've ever gone white-water rafting, you know that going with the flow can be dangerous. Unexpected rocks in the water can do you in. Only experts with comprehensive knowledge of the river can successfully go with the flow.

As an entrepreneur you'll not wake up one day with the knowledge to avoid disaster. But if you know you're "going rafting" and work on improving or gaining new skills, then perhaps you'll steer through the rapids successfully. In business the "rocks" are formidable, such as a pricing fumble that hurts the bottom line, an unexpected tax that cuts into profits, or a changing business environment that forces a business leader with one skill set to segue as cautiously as time permits in acquiring a new skill set.

We'll consider a few who successfully reinvented themselves from entrepreneur to something else. These include Dr. Jim Dan (entrepreneur to corporate executive), David Axelrod (entrepreneur to White House staff), and Hon. Nir Barkat (entrepreneur to the mayor of Jerusalem). In addition we'll explore the impact of pricing (a possible form of reinvention) and the need to finance your entrepreneurial business to enable reinventions.

Proof That Practice Doesn't Always Make Perfect Sense

Moving from being a practicing physician to a corporate executive seems like a monumental change and difficult to navigate successfully. It would seem like a violation of my "Rings of Life" theory. In fact it's a map of how to maneuver the Rings of Life. That's the transition that Dr. Jim Dan was to experience. But he accomplished this through a series of incremental steps that made the difficult feasible. He demonstrates the smart way to achieve fundamental reinvention—with incremental steps that changed only the skills that needed to be changed at given times.

Dr. Jim Dan was a popular physician who gave up his patients to run the group practice he had joined. That group grew into the largest independent practice in the Chicago area. Eventually, he left to join the biggest healthcare system in Illinois and soon became CEO of a key division.

Jim Dan had always wanted to be a physician. His course selections and performance were consistent with his decision. He was a primary care physician for 28 years. And Jim was good at what he did; he enjoyed doing it. His patients adored him—proof that he was well suited for his chosen profession. In the early days of his practice, his involvement in business matters was limited to his staff's payroll; purchases of furniture, equipment, and supplies; and involvement in minor tax matters. Office staff and the outside accountant routinely handled the mundane business chores. That left Dr. Dan free to treat patients.

But as the years progressed, increases in his practice and the growing intrusions by insurance and government necessitated his involvement in business matters. A sole practitioner, Dr. Dan lacked negotiating power with insurers, with Medicare and other providers like hospitals and specialists. He lacked sophisticated staff to deal with business issues and with rules and regulations.

So in 1995 he joined with a score of other physicians to establish a new entity. They merged their practices to create Mid America Health Partners, which could afford professional business staff. As a substantial professional organization they had clout with payers and providers. Dr. Dan thought he would be free to do what he enjoyed most: treating patients.

But he actively participated in the formation of the firm, attending the meetings with lawyers and accountants. He was developing business capabilities that, while unsophisticated at that point, were better than those of his new colleagues. He also seemed to take to the business issues naturally, learning them easily and well. Most important, he understood the impact of the issues on the practice and was able to translate them into common language. Thus, he gained the confidence of his partners as a good businessman and as a fair and just leader.

The doctors in his firm quickly realized the importance of having a physician lead them. After a series of starts and stops, Dr. Dan was elected president of the group, the name of which later evolved to DuPage Medical Group.

While Dr. Dan continued to practice, more and more of his time was devoted to his role as manager. Professionals handled the day-to-day management issues. But the group continued to grow rapidly, indeed soaring over time from 50 doctors to several hundred. The group practitioners now included more than primary care physicians. DuPage had become a multispecialty group. Each specialty had unique business considerations. Dr. Dan's oversight responsibilities caused him to increase his knowledge of the specialists' side of the business. For example, specialists received referrals from the DuPage primary care physicians. Inevitably, then, Dr. Dan gained special knowledge on the business side of all the practices—specialists as well as primary care physicians.

Eventually, DuPage Medical Group became the largest independent physician group in the most rapidly growing Chicago collar county—DuPage County. (Chicago's collar counties were so designated as they formed a geographic "collar" around downtown Chicago.) By the time this had happened, Dr. Dan's management and leadership duties had eclipsed his medical practice.

Over a period of years he had effectively reinvented himself from full-time physician with a small amount of managerial/business work to an executive with an MD who spent limited time with patients. The progression was slow. Each step was deliberate. After all, managing an organization of several hundred doctors may be the ultimate example of "herding cats." His progression was not preordained. There was no set plan that dictated the steps Dr. Dan was taking to greater management and business expertise.

Instead of the end justifying the means, the end was the result stemming from the means he employed to get there. Each time he solved a problem, he added skill arrows to his quiver. There likely was no strategic plan for the long term. But the cumulative effect of successful tactical solutions led to a valuable and satisfying end result.

WHICH CAME FIRST:
THE END OR THE MEANS?

In Dr. Dan's case, the development of the means actually determined the end. That's the opposite of Desiree Rogers and Cheryl Mayberry McKissack (see Chapter 11), who set their goals (Desiree to be a CEO and Cheryl to be an entrepreneur) and selected jobs to add needed arrows to their skill quivers.

Then in 2007 Dr. Dan left DuPage Medical and became the president of the Advocate Medical Group with the largest health system in Chicago. This group now has approximately 1,200 physicians and 150 advance practice clinicians in 50 medical and surgical specialties with 150 neighborhood branches offering a wide menu of services. This was an example of an entrepreneur who, having developed new skills, changed to an executive employee who happened to have a medical degree.

If one looks at Dr. Dan's skill set in 1995 and compares it with Dr. Dan's skill set today, one imagines a huge jump over a giant chasm. That would have been daunting and extremely difficult to achieve, even for someone as talented as Dr. Dan.

If instead, each step is viewed as a small, separate reinvention, then it seems achievable. But how did Dr. Dan get the confidence to make these mini-reinventions? After all, even small jumps entailed "Rings of Life" changes many years out from the center of the tree of life.

To understand how Dr. Dan had the confidence to make these mini-reinventions, we must reflect on his background and his progression from that perspective. Each move involved a decision and his having the confidence to make the decision.

Books such as *Blink*, by Malcolm Gladwell, and *Thinking, Fast and Slow*, by Nobel laureate Daniel Kahneman, have treated how decisions are made through the study of behavioral science. Each reinvention involves important and sometimes even monumental decisions. Yet most of those people I have interviewed made their reinvention decisions without consciously reflecting on them in advance. They believe they followed their instincts applied at that moment. Of course, the best people don't just have periodic unrelated reactions; they learn from each decision by learning just how right or how wrong they were. They store that lesson, and it fleshes out the basis for the next decision and all successive decisions. At the time of each decision, they aren't thinking of the learning process. They are who they are at that specific moment in time. Their then-cumulative being decides.

LADDER RUNGS ARE SET CLOSE TOGETHER PURPOSELY

Dr. Dan likely couldn't have jumped successfully from being a sole practitioner physician to the president of a major medical system. By following his intellectual curiosity and changing needs, he took small steps, often years apart. In-between, he listened and watched, learning the new skills he'd need to move up. This is similar to Maxine Clark observing how mall space leases were negotiated and Howard Schultz watching how customers operated their coffee shops (see Chapter 2).

To demonstrate the decision process, I present a couple of stories where changes, such as pricing, have taken place while seemingly adjunct factors have, in fact, effected the reinventions of the business.

Reinvention: When Price Is *the* Object

Most of us have watched the TV salesman Ron Popeil of Ronco. Ron's father, Sam Popeil, invented kitchen devices that he sold in stores. Ron was one of his pitch artists who stood in store aisles hawking his dad's new products, mesmerizing customers into believing they were witnessing the best new product ever created. That's where Ron learned the skills witnessed on TV. Ron became an infomercial giant on TV, ultimately calling himself, none too modestly and perhaps a bit too proudly, "The Salesman of the Century."

Sam invented numerous kitchen gadgets that were bought by millions but used by many fewer than that, proving that Ron could sell a solution looking for a need. In 1972, Sam invented a new product, "The Pocket Fisherman," a fishing pole that could be folded to fit in your pocket. He got the idea when a boy with a fishing pole nearly poked out Sam's eye at Chicago's O'Hare Airport. Millions of Pocket Fisherman poles have been sold by the Popeils, at the retail price of $19.95 each. It would seem that the product was very attractive to buyers, and one must assume the product was also priced perfectly.

You might assume that the price of the Pocket Fisherman was determined by some scientific methodology. After all, business schools teach courses on pricing. Books have been written about pricing. Pricing has been the subject of many scholarly papers and business articles. Pricing consultants charge handsomely for their advice. Pricing decisions can affect customer targets, marketing techniques, channels of distribution, types of employees hired, and company financing. With such changes in business models and plans, they can effect reinventions of businesses.

What really happened in the case of the Pocket Fisherman? There was no precedent. There had never been an identical product. How was the price of that unique product determined? Sam Popeil's patent lawyer, Jack Dominik, told me that while Sam was developing the Pocket Fisherman, he frequently went to the Golf Road Trout Farm. This facility in suburban Chicago featured several artificial ponds stocked with trout. There, the inventor practiced casting the Pocket Fisherman. He took extensive notes. A perfectionist, Sam Popeil went there frequently, to be sure to get it right.

One day Jack Dominik needed a meeting with Sam and agreed to see him at the Golf Road Trout Farm. Sam brought his daughter, Elizabeth, then a precocious five-year-old girl who now practices law in California. After settling his patent queries with Sam, Jack asked Sam what price he was using for the Pocket Fisherman. Without hesitation Sam said, "$14.95."

Jack asked, "How did you come to that decision?" Sam mentioned the Popeil pricing guideline, one that followed an info-mercial industry practice: price should approximate seven times product cost. But Jack knew: that rule merely established the floor prerequisite. Since one never knows if product cost is as low as it should be, the industry practice is insufficient. One still must determine whether the price would fly with consumers.

Although Sam was the expert in such matters, Jack's engineering and legal background caused him to suggest a more "scientific" approach. He had Sam hand Elizabeth a Pocket Fisherman and instructed her to walk around the pond asking each fisherman what he would pay for it. Elizabeth returned from her "focus group" and reported that pond fishermen mostly said they'd pay $19.95, or $5 more than the $14.95 Sam had planned to use.

Expert or not, Sam changed his mind and used the higher $19.95 price. Millions of Pocket Fishermans were sold, each at an additional $5. Needless to say, all the millions of $5 premiums went straight to the bottom line. That's because Sam, the expert, was nobody's fool and was eager to benefit from Elizabeth's "scientific" research.

That decision resulted in sufficient extra cash to finance several new products. That's one kind of decision that enables you to reinvent yourself or your business.

Would you have felt comfortable raising the price by $5, based on an "around-the-pond" market survey conducted by a five-year-old? Remember, a mistake on price could have jeopardized the product you worked on seemingly forever and might adversely affect the company's ability to thrive or even survive.

Why was Sam so quick to do that? His willingness to change the pocket fisherman's price that way was neither based on whim nor was it rash. It was an example of best-selling author Gladwell's "Blink" concept. Blink has been described by Gladwell as "thinking without thinking." It is expertise accumulated over years of practice, through thousands of prior decisions that allow one to develop a unique ability to make a "blink-of-the-eye" decision.

The Pocket Fisherman pricing decision was but the very last part of a decision that actually started decades earlier, long before Sam was almost poked in the eye with a fishing pole at O'Hare Airport. The process continued through the uncounted interim decisions and ended with his instant reaction to Elizabeth's announcement. Therefore, it wasn't an instantaneous decision but one that had been, in effect, carefully considered over the years, and executed instantaneously. It's much like the movie actor who, after a 15- to 20-year career, suddenly becomes a hit and is described as "an overnight success."

Decisions such as Sam's can only be made in certain environments, and it's important to understand that concept before you start your business. It's likely impossible to do so if you have institutional investors, such as venture capitalists, who will want to understand the risks and balance them against possible rewards.

They will likely want to see more than your hunch. So if you are prone to making decisions in that manner, think about the kinds of investors you invite into your company and certainly discuss it with them beforehand.

John Osher's Target Price

A second story to help you understand the decision-making process I have referred to involves John Osher, the serial entrepreneur who developed what was originally known as Dr. John's SpinBrush and which, when sold to Procter & Gamble, became the Crest Spinbrush. John, whom you met in Chapter 4 and who isn't a doctor, hadn't had any experience with the toothbrush industry. But he and his team were experts at developing spinning products such as the spinning lollipop. He produced his devices very efficiently and at low cost.

Those spinning products sold well. He was able, with all of his spin products in their turn, to produce and sell them at a significant profit. There were electric toothbrushes on the market, but they were expensive, costing over $100. Of course nonelectric toothbrushes had been around forever and sold at low prices. What John saw was an opportunity to develop an electric toothbrush at a much lower price.

Rather than convene a focus group or conduct expensive market research, John told me that he and his then-wife visited a couple of stores to check out electric toothbrushes and how they were packaged and priced. That was followed by conversations with friends at major retailers to determine what was selling. Then, based on years of experience pricing new products, John made a near-instantaneous determination of the pricing goal. He then challenged his team to develop a product at a cost sufficiently below the target level to allow suitable profit. Mission accomplished.

John had not reinvented the wheel, but he had created a special kind of wheel that turned the toothbrush bristles. The point is that he had put an *affordable* electric toothbrush in the hands of everyday folks. Much like Sam Popeil's willingness to raise the price on the Pocket Fisherman, John Osher's easy resolution of the price for the SpinBrush was possible due to his team's prior work with spin technology. This experience paved the way for a low price. More importantly, Sam's move from his field of expertise, kitchen products, and John's move from lollipops and other toys to a dental hygiene product sound like monumental reinventions.

But the way they dealt with *unrelated* products based on *related* experiences provides lessons for all businesspeople—you too can reinvent by moving to unrelated products using related experiences even though you may lack the levels of experience they had.

Incidentally, they both knew themselves well enough that they self-funded rather than weigh themselves and their projects down with burdensome deliberations with outside investors. Besides, they knew that such tedious approaches wouldn't be as accurate as their own. Lest you think pricing fits a simple formula, compare Jim Sinegal's commitment to the $1.50 hot dog and Coke, where he built a plant to be able to retain the price, with his bringing in better tuna even though it required raising the price (see Chapter 4).

The Highest Platform Dive: From Running After News to Running Those Making It

There are rare occasions when there is no higher platform. Perhaps you have overachieved to reach the highest platform you can attain. Or there may simply be no higher platform—anywhere.

Consider David Axelrod, managing the presidential campaigns of Barack Obama to become the first African American president,

followed by serving in the White House. Axelrod chose to reinvent and move on, reaching his apex at the White House and as
Obama's reelection campaign manager.

When one thinks of Axelrod, it likely is not in the context
of entrepreneurship. It is probably as the White House political
advisor to the president of the United States or the campaign
strategist who masterminded the two successful campaigns of
the first African American president. But before his presidential
campaign and glamorous White House positions, David Axelrod
was a reporter for the *Chicago Tribune*, where he reinvented himself to become a political strategist. And after the successful 2012
presidential campaign, he reinvented himself again to become an
employee at the Institute of Politics at the University of Chicago.

David grew up in New York. His father was a psychologist and
his mother was a journalist. He arrived in Chicago, in 1972, and
enrolled as a freshman at the University of Chicago. He was not
a journalism major. But journalism coursed through his blood, as
did politics. As a kid, he watched his mother maneuver politically
through organizations, learning from both her achievements and
her inability to achieve what he thought she could.

After his freshman year, he went back to New York to seek summer employment at a newspaper. He recalls knocking on 70 to 75
doors without success. Finally, he persuaded *The Villager*, a small
newspaper in Greenwich Village, to give him a chance. He loved
the job and stayed for six months, taking a quarter off at college.
He was paid $50 a week. Most important, the paper let him try
and "do everything" in what he describes as "a tremendous learning experience." It was the start of an eminent journalism career.

Upon graduating from the University of Chicago, having
developed a precise and pleasant writing style, as well as the well-
known U of C brand of intellectual rigor, he accepted a job at
the *Chicago Tribune*. He started two days after graduation and

spent two and a half years working the night shift. Occasionally, he worked days to write about political campaigns. It wasn't long before his bosses recognized his superior talent for covering political news.

Thus in 1979, at the age of 24, David became the youngest political reporter in the newspaper's long history. As such he came into contact with many Illinois politicians, most of whom caused him to hold his political nose, but not the savvy Jane Byrne, a Democratic reformer. David was assigned to cover Jane, who was running for mayor of Chicago. She won in 1979, and a colleague left the paper to work for her. That opened a slot that David got to fill.

While still a reporter, covering the Chicago mayoral campaign of a former congressman, Harold Washington, he watched the efforts of media consultants for the three candidates—Jayne Byrne, Richard M. Daley Jr., and Harold Washington—all three of whom were ultimately elected mayor of Chicago.

David was especially impressed with the talent of Harold Washington's media consultant, Bill Zimmerman, who had grown up in Chicago and graduated with a PhD from the University of Chicago. But by then Bill lived in California. He was in Chicago to help Harold Washington prepare for a press conference.

At the end of the press conference, David complimented Zimmerman and said, "I sure wish I could do what you're doing instead of what I'm doing." Zimmerman said he'd be happy to have dinner with David and teach him a thing or two. Over the dinner, Bill was forthcoming about what was involved with the job, and David left with an understanding of what the position entailed and some of the skills he had to refine if he were to embark on that new career.

Meanwhile, he had bills to pay and mouths to feed, a wife and the first of their three children. So he continued working for the *Tribune*. But his disillusion with that paper, indeed with the entire newspaper industry, continued to grow. He saw news agencies like the Associated Press providing content that decreased his opportunities at the *Tribune*. He sensed huge changes coming to the industry. He couldn't possibly know the impact the Internet would have, but he felt an apocalypse was coming that could deprive him of the opportunity to do what he loved doing. In other words, the writer didn't have to see the other side of the wall. It sufficed that he could read the writing on his side of the wall. Later he had a chance to work on the campaign of Paul Simon, who had gained notoriety as a 21-year-old newspaper publisher in downstate Illinois. Simon had quickly established a reputation for integrity and honesty. In fact, he had reinvented himself into that rarest of breeds, an elegant and honest Illinois public servant. By the end of Paul Simon's campaign, David was confident that he could do it all, that he had sufficient skills to run a campaign. He reinvented himself, opening his own political consulting firm.

Eventually, David met a new politician who was serving in the Illinois State Legislature: Barack Obama. Axelrod and Obama hit it off, and there is no doubt that David's efforts and talent are at least somewhat (and likely largely) responsible for Obama becoming the first African American president of the United States.

David was invited by Barack Obama to serve in the White House as the president's political advisor. That title and its responsibilities constituted a significant reinvention. The job is in fact different than that of running a campaign. It is certainly different than running one's own consulting firm or being a newspaper reporter. After a couple years, and as expected, he left the White House, returned to his campaign management firm, and helped guide his candidate, President Obama, to reelection.

Certainly, he could have gone back to the White House. If you decline work at the White House, it's difficult to imagine where you find a higher platform. David chose to return to the

University of Chicago, this time not as a student but as the head of the university's Institute of Politics, which he founded. Thus David notched another reinvention, as entrepreneur of a not-for-profit organization, while seeking a "higher" plane where no higher plane was conceivable.

Soldier to Entrepreneur to Value-Added Investor to Politician

Nir Barkat is currently the mayor of Jerusalem. In the Middle East, politics has frequently been a family business. In my opinion the Arab Spring was predictable: the result of failures to properly plan for succession in what the fathers considered to be the family business—running a nation. (Even in the United States, politics continues to be a family business for the Daleys, Cuomos, Jacksons, Bushs, Clintons, Kennedys, and a handful of other families.)

As for Israel, no one in the Barkat family was involved in politics. And Nir's move from military leader to owner/manager of an antivirus software firm, to a value-added investor, and ultimately to the mayor of Jerusalem may seem like a series of cross-chasm leaps. However, to Nir Barkat each move, each reinvention, seemed to be mere refinements and adaptations of his skills to a new endeavor.

Nir developed two of the skills in the army: leadership and smart risk management. Both were developed through numerous battle experiences. Not only were these two skills helpful to an army commander, they were also helpful in the software and value-added investor businesses that he eventually entered and excelled at.

The software business, BRM Technologies, was founded in 1988 by Nir, his brother Eli Barkat, Yuval Rakavy, and Omri

Man, all computer students at Hebrew University in Jerusalem. This was a moonlighting effort. All four had unrelated day jobs. They developed BRM by committing their free time to it during the evenings, and often they worked into the night.

BRM evolved naturally from their school experience. Viruses had attacked school computers, and the four students resolved the problem. They were convinced computer viruses would become a serious threat to computer users generally. So they created algorithms that addressed the issues. Soon they formed BRM, with Nir as the leader of the business.

BRM had no capital and no income, and it was in debt. The company faced a threat of bankruptcy. Nir had to hold the group together and keep spirits up. He says this experience was similar to one he faced during Israel's 1982 war in Lebanon. Nir and his company commander were standing next to each other when both were hit by enemy fire. The commander was killed, and Nir, though wounded, had to assume command.

In 1990 BRM finally had a hot prospect for its antivirus software: a Baton Rouge, Louisiana, company, Fifth Generation Systems. The company was owned by a preacher who had never met an Israeli. The company was seeking an antivirus product to sell. The preacher explained how he had fruitlessly sought a high-quality product with excellent capabilities. BRM's product provided a fix for the preacher's company. It also fixed BRM by generating a million dollars of revenue. That sum was a bonanza, sufficient to allow the four partners to quit their day jobs and focus on BRM.

Before long, an additional fix was required. Fifth Generation needed a product to facilitate customers' backup, and not surprisingly the preacher called BRM. Nir and his partners met with the client on a Friday. The Nir team told the customer they might be able to solve his problem. Actually they knew they could do so, quickly and effectively. They were savvy enough not to do so on the spot, as that would have made the approach seem simple and could diminish the preacher's perception of its value. Instead they left the meeting and purposely missed their scheduled flight back to Israel. They chose instead to check into a motel for the long weekend.

On Monday they reappeared at the customer's office, saying they had solved the problem. They solved an even bigger one for struggling BRM. This sale was a million-dollar-plus deal. The sale was actually relatively easy, given their prior success.

Fifth Generation was sold to Symantec, a large acquisitive company. Symantec requested BRM's commitment to continue the development of new products. This relationship proved valuable to the people at BRM, not only for its short-term cash improvement but also for what it taught them. Working with Symantec, BRM learned to augment its cutting-edge technology with a powerful user interface that made Symantec's product much more attractive to customers. This proved invaluable to BRM later.

After some success running their own company, the management team at BRM began segregating a third of the company's earnings for investments in other start-up teams. Beginning as an incubator, Nir quickly realized that incubators were not accorded a lot of respect. They were unable to attract "A Team" players. So they shifted into a form of private equity/venture capitalist status. That also enabled them to screen for companies that could meet the high standards necessary to penetrate the U.S. market.

Nir felt that one of the firm's functions was to mentor and challenge the leaders of their portfolio start-ups, but not to substitute for them. He had mentored soldiers while he was a commander and even his partners when BRM was a young operating company. While being an investor was somewhat different, he needed only to refine and change a few skills, not replace his whole skill set.

INCREMENTAL SKILL MODIFICATION

Nir's use of military skills to become an entrepreneur, entrepreneurial skills to become a venture capitalist, and all of those skills to become a politician may seem extraordinary. But actually, they were merely the result of focused application to new opportunities. They were, in fact, very much like the skills application of Junior Bridgeman at B.F. South, discussed in Chapter 2.

One of the first companies that BRM backed was Check Point, a start-up founded in 1993 by three young men, Gil Shwed, Marius Nacht, and Shlomo Kramer. Obviously Nir and his team understood the business well, so BRM was able to mentor, challenge, and help Check Point in addition to merely investing funds.

Check Point developed a strong firewall technology, but there were other firewalls in the market. The BRM team, as a result of their work with Symantec, understood that adding a groundbreaking user interface to Check Point's products would dramatically increase that company's success. Nir and his partners took a very active role in developing the original Check Point user interface and in working with Shwed and his colleagues so that all agreed to wait until their products with the new user interface were ready for market.

The result exceeded all expectations. Check Point's firewall became an overnight success and remains a market leader to this day. In return for all that, BRM received a substantial minority interest in Check Point. Today, Check Point's revenue exceeds $1.4 billion and its stock market capitalization exceeds $10 billion.

Nir Barkat decided to leave BRM, by that time more of a venture capital firm, in the capable hands of his brother, Eli. Nir's plan was to enter Jerusalem's charitable sector. He wanted to help improve Jerusalem's public elementary education system. He also wanted to make his hometown more inviting to businesses. At the time, Jerusalem was experiencing serious business exoduses.

Nir soon realized that much of what needed to be done was under the control of elected public servants. This motivated him to run for mayor in 2003. As Nir now says, he was fortunate to lose that election. He had gleaned 43 percent of the vote, which told him that he had a good base of support and a realistic shot if he ran again. Most importantly, the loss caused him to rethink how he had waged his campaign. In retrospect, he realized that he hadn't applied what he'd learned from his years at BRM or, for that matter, from his experience in the military. To put it simply, he had tried to change professions without readjusting and changing some skills.

While Israel is an acknowledged fount of high-tech inventors, consider what Israel had been and what had changed in its business community during Nir's lifetime. In the 1970s, when I first did business in Israel, inventors were sent or came to me frequently. Each brought his "black box" idea and asked me to find a business in the United States that could "run with" his dream.

I would go home, check with businesses I thought were suitable. They would tell me they weren't interested in a black box but would be interested if the technology were applied instead to create, say, an "orange ball." When I'd report that to the inventors, many stubbornly said, "I'm sorry. I think the black box is the right answer; I don't want to make orange balls." This was, in effect, developing a solution and then searching for the right problem. It was hardly a productive approach.

A decade or so later, customer-centricity hit Israel, and today the approach is to determine the need and then find a solution. This may be the result of growing technological capabilities that inspired a confidence that they could find solutions. Also, the introduction of U.S.-style marketing education into Israeli universities may have played a role, as did the Internet, which enabled them to better understand the needs of the players in the marketplace.

Nir had applied lessons from his military training and his private equity investor experience—leadership, salesmanship, and charm—to what he had encountered in his political career, but he saw that certain other skills had to be refined and new ones acquired. And others needed work; for example, Nir says, the essential skill of an army commander is to quickly survey the situation, decide how best to accomplish the goal while minimizing risk, and determine who should do what. Implementation was achieved through the expert training of his troops together with his leadership skills that inspired his soldiers to follow his commands. When he was a manager of BRM, he had much the same job with substantially different risks and consequences.

When Nir entered politics, he failed to understand how different his challenges in the public sector were from those in the army, those developing BRM, or as an investor. That may have contributed to his losing his first election for the office of mayor of Jerusalem. He realized, after the fact, that success in politics needed a different approach and somewhat different skills than were needed for success in business.

Most importantly, his constituents were, in effect, his customers. He needed to ask them what they wanted. Then he could use his leadership, management, and venture capitalist mentoring skills to build the confidence of his team. Eventually he could achieve the desired results. The "customers"—his constituents— would come back for more. With his lessons learned, Nir was elected mayor of Jerusalem in 2008.

Although at the time of sitting for my interview, Nir had yet to decide whether or not to run for reelection, I was confident that he would give "his customers" the opportunity to reelect him. That's because he had been asking them what they wanted and saw that it coincided with what he wanted. He knew he could deliver it. And last year, he did indeed run and was elected to a second term as mayor.

Nir's constituents may be somewhat confused. They had grown accustomed to mayors who were managers who negotiated with their constituent factions as a means of getting things done. But that's not who Nir is. He is not a mere manager, but a leader. His brand of leadership—learned when wounded on the battlefield and having to take over when his commander was killed right next to him—guided his partners and the BRM/Check Point team to do what was right.

Actually, Nir's brand of leadership brings to mind the words of Professor Warren Bennis: "Managers do things right. Leaders do the right things." Nir's skill set was modified over time as he moved from soldier to entrepreneur to investor to mayor. Thus Nir was reinvented, but not fundamentally. His skill set was reinvented; his values remained unchanged.

8

When Does the Entrepreneur Need to Let Go?

ONE OF THE MOST CRITICAL ISSUES FOR AN ENTREPRENEURIAL company is when the entrepreneur should relinquish the leadership position to someone who is better equipped to do the job at hand—to move the company to the next curve on the reinvention curve (discussed in Chapter 3). As the company changes and progresses, it may no longer need to include the founder. This decision is ordinarily faced at the time of a reinvention. The occasion is often gut-wrenching for the creator of the business and unpleasant for directors, employees, and stockholders—the company's *other* owners. After all, not only has the entrepreneur birthed the business, he or she has nurtured it through the most difficult years and into maturity. The entrepreneur has every right to feel that no one else could have gotten the business to where it is.

The business will have grown with more employees, stores, offices, suppliers, and customers. It will have larger cash-flow challenges and capital requirements. It will have more sophisticated or more complex investors. And, if the company is publically traded, it will face increased demands by regulators and analysts. The business is no longer able to fly under the radar of competitors. It probably has greater need for strategic planning. There is substantial risk in every decision. There may be more opportunities for growth, perhaps through relationships with larger companies whose top executives may prefer dealing with professional managers than entrepreneurs.

Odds are someone with experience at handling those issues would be better equipped to handle them where this company now sits. Those odds are what drive potential new investors, especially professionals such as venture capitalists and investment bankers, to step in.

Traditionally, the initial investment decisions of a venture capitalist are based on both the horse and the jockey (the horse being the business idea and the jockey being the right entrepreneur to run the first leg in the race). But the venture capitalist's long-term interest is satisfied by a stable of horses. It is not a one-person race; it's a relay race.

Venture capitalists assume they will need someone else, a professional manager, to take the baton at the end of the first leg and manage the business to the point of a liquidity event. A liquidity event, such as an IPO or sale of the business, allows initial investors a chance to remove capital. Venture capitalists pride themselves on being able to find managers who can take over effectively and get to the finish line.

Occasionally but rarely at the end of the first leg they are surprised to find that there is more to the jockey than just entrepreneurial skills. That's the case with Fred Smith, founder of Federal Express, who is still managing FedEx successfully after decades.

Sometimes, those who call the turn blow it. The obvious example is Steve Jobs, the cofounder of Apple, who was fired in 1985 by the board and replaced by John Sculley. Of course, Apple's board ultimately recognized the error of its ways and brought Jobs back. Jobs is best remembered as an extraordinary visionary, but he also became a truly great manager and leader.

There has been no shortage of entrepreneurial "comeback kids," including Michael Dell of Dell Computer, Ron Shaich of Panera Bread, Ted Waitt of Gateway, Charles Schwab of Charles Schwab & Co., and Howard Schultz of Starbucks. Some do well after coming back, others less so, and a few are works-in-progress; Bill Gates's recent return to lead research at Microsoft is different than those who returned as CEO. Of course, no one knows just how different Gates's return will wind up.

I'm sure the words of Nelson Mandela would have resonated with Steve Jobs: "There is nothing like returning to a place that remains unchanged to find the ways in which you yourself have altered."

Howard Schultz Reinvents Starbucks

Starbucks's founder, Howard Schultz, had prepared the company well for the end of the first leg of the race. Remember, here was an entrepreneur who had summed up his experience with a single word: *salesman*. Everyone, Howard included, thought he'd need help. That's why, before the company's initial public offering, several executives were hired whose talent and experience far exceeded Starbucks' immediate needs. The original team—Dave Olsen, Howard Bahar, and Orin Smith—was later enhanced by the addition of others, including Jim Donald.

That team was meant to provide a candidate to be Howard's successor as CEO. So it was no surprise in 2000 that Howard handed the baton to Orin Smith, who had started at Starbucks in 1990 as CFO. Four years later Smith had been promoted to

COO. Now he was CEO. Howard remained chairman of the board and maintained offices down the hall several yards from Orin. During his years as COO, Orin had come to understand the values and culture that Howard had developed, as well as their importance to Starbucks' success.

Howard was pleased with what transpired and spent some of his time starting Maveron, a venture capital firm that invests in start-ups. Howard's knowledge and his experience enable Maveron to distinguish itself from other venture capital firms by bringing more to the table than merely money. Maveron has made several successful investments, including eBay, drugstore.com, Potbelly, Shutterfly, and Groupon. He also bought the Seattle Supersonics, the local NBA team, but in that venture he was less than successful.

Then in 2005 Orin retired, and the baton for the next leg was handed to Jim Donald. During the next few years, Jim opened thousands of stores, and the company's overseas and licensed stores operations grew dramatically. It seemed that Starbucks had the right strategy for the continuing entrepreneurial relay race.

But by 2007 Howard sensed that something was wrong. Late that year, he spelled it out in a memo meant for only a few top executives of the company. Howard stated that the company's soul was endangered. Somehow, the memo was leaked and was widely circulated.

At that same time, the world economy seemed to be unraveling. People everywhere were being laid off. Retirement plans and personal investment portfolios were being decimated, and retirees were being forced to live on a 1 percent return on their savings. The media began to question whether revenue decreases at Starbucks were affected by the economy. If so, it might portend further declines.

Were people no longer willing or able to spend so much for a cup of coffee? It was a perfect storm. McDonald's and Dunkin Donuts, sensing vulnerability at Starbucks, began offering what they said were comparable coffees at much lower prices. Worse, they promoted their new offerings through huge advertising campaigns, while Starbucks continued a feature it had long prided itself on—a near-zero advertising budget.

Howard saw Starbucks ridiculed as "the poster child at that time for excess" during what he called "a cataclysm of the financial crisis, and a combination of self-induced mistakes." He didn't know how bad the financial crisis would get, and he didn't realize the depth of some of the mistakes Starbucks made. Still he recognized the situation as a "tremendous crisis."

Howard Schultz Reinvents with a Retrofit

Howard felt he had to resume control as CEO, because "I knew where the bones were buried. I just didn't know how many were broken."

Howard did his homework. He visited stores, viewing them from the consumers' points of view. Then he took the necessary steps to fix Starbucks. For example, he had determined that automatic brewers killed the atmosphere, deprived customers of fresh brewing's taste and smell, and the brewing devices were so tall that they blocked the view between customers and baristas. And he wanted all personnel retrained to assure a return to his "people company."

He closed 500 stores permanently. He closed all the Starbucks stores for one day. That enabled changes of equipment and retraining. The closing also served as a clear announcement to his customers and former customers that their Starbucks was being reinvented, not to something new but to what it originally had been. It worked.

REINVENTING ISN'T ALWAYS DONE TO CREATE SOMETHING NEW

Howard reinvented Starbucks to regain the spirit (and the soul) he originally had breathed into Starbucks and to make it what it had been before. (The same was true of Jim Sinegal's hot dogs and Chuck Schwab's return to his company. See the next section.)

///

After revenues had slipped dramatically, former customers and new ones began a return to Howard's Starbucks. They liked what they saw. Howard had reinvented with a retrofit. And more recently with the acquisition of Teavana, the tea specialists, Howard has embarked on reinventing Starbucks again, aiming at rolling out tea stores as he did with the progression of Starbucks stores and steeping the tea stores in the coffee company's traditions.

Creating a Glow from a Bare Lightbulb Hanging from a Cord

Charles Schwab & Co. is one of the largest securities brokerage firms in the United States. Its net revenues in 2012 totaled $4.88 billion, with net income of $928 million for a pretax profit margin of 29.7 percent. In all, the company has over 12,500 employees. It may seem just one of many large stockbrokerage firms. The truth is, the company is fundamentally different than most such firms. To understand how it differs, as well as why Schwab and others seem so similar, we must revert to the years preceding the company's formation.

Charles Schwab prefers being referred to as Chuck, possibly to distinguish himself from the eponymous company and possibly to emphasize his feeling that "it's only through a team that you can ever really win something. My success is not due to one individual." The nickname seems more appropriate, given his professional life wherein he championed the cause of the individual investor, the more common Joe. Despite his ultimate listing on the Forbes wealthiest list, the origin of Chuck's company was quite common. When he opened for business, his office space was minimal, and the single room was far from fancy. A bare lightbulb hanging from an electric cord lit the area unevenly.

Just as Howard Schultz didn't create coffee shops and Tom Stemberg didn't create stationery stores, so too Chuck Schwab didn't create stockbrokerage. The stockbrokerage business followed the first broad stock ownership of businesses, likely the East India Company, and expanded in importance after the Industrial Revolution. In all its years of existence there were many changes in its infrastructure, such as communications, accounting, and recordkeeping, but some things remained constant.

The broker's job was to first find buyers to whom he could sell particular stocks and later to convince them that they no longer wanted to own those stocks; then he effected sale of the stocks to others, either directly or through cooperating brokers. The commission rates charged by virtually every broker were the same, and they were high, reflecting a host of services and products that most customers generally didn't want or use. The stockbrokerage commission rate cartel was price-fixing in the extreme. Unchallenged by government, its existence virtually became the law of the land, clearly a fait accompli.

In 1970, when my law firm was founded with several mutual funds and brokerage firms as clients, if you had asked the person on the street or perhaps even on Wall Street, he or she probably would have said that discounting stockbrokerage fees was illegal. I remember facilitating a large stock transaction for a client, in 1971, with Bernie Cantor, founder of the Cantor Fitzgerald firm, who was one of the very few who did "off-market" large volume transactions at deeply discounted commissions without the benefit or assistance of stock exchanges. He simply found a buyer or a seller to fill the order in hand. By avoiding the exchange, he eliminated the impact that a large trade might have had on the stock's price. It also freed him from exchange pressure regarding commission rates.

Of course that type of discount, for volume, seems quite reasonable; volume discounts are granted and allowed in many types of markets. And Bernie did quite well with them, making his firm a great success story and enabling Bernie to become the world's largest individual owner of Rodin sculptures. Still, he was an outlier, and his many transactions had no impact on the brokerage community's ability to keep its thumb on the scale and to prevent discounting by regular stockbrokers.

That was the situation that existed when Chuck Schwab entered the stockbrokerage business. The situation was best described in the saying about stockbrokers—"Where are all the customers' yachts?"—which implies that the brokers did well enough on commissions to afford yachts but the customers were lucky to afford rowboats and needed bailing pails.

Chuck Schwab wasn't your average broker. He attended Stanford University, where he received a BA in Economics and an MBA. Chuck feels that his growing up in Silicon Valley was responsible for his attraction to innovation. Perhaps, however, there is more to it. Chuck says, "I was very interested in stocks and had been since I was 13 or 14."

He began in his early twenties as a securities analyst for an investment advisory firm. In that capacity, he got to work with brokerage firms. Prior to that, he had a summer job selling life insurance. In both positions, he wasn't simply performing the assigned tasks. He was trying to understand how stocks, insurance policies, and mutual funds were sold. He says, "I was a pretty good student about the financial services world. By the time I was 24, I was thinking about it pretty extensively—how each of the financial products was sold, how its brokerage was handled, and how the industries were structured. And by the time I was 25 I had a viewpoint that stockbrokerages, insurance companies, and banks were really set up to make money for themselves and were not at all client or customer focused."

Chuck concluded that they entailed "complete inefficiencies, bad products, and cartel-controlled fee structures." He understood the reasons for the industry getting away with the practices: (1) brokers had always done it that way (cartel inertia is powerful); (2) investors had inadequate sources for information, especially timely information, and in that pre–search engine world would rely on brokerage firms for such knowledge; (3) to protect customers' funds, extensive, complicated, even redundant systems were required, and with antiquated accounting and record-keeping systems, it was difficult to simplify and achieve cost efficiencies; (4) an annual flow of young, new employees, "a whole raft of salesmen" who could be counted on to sell "first to their families and then to hit up their friends," to earn the "huge commissions" being offered (minimum commissions made small transactions extremely costly; commissions on easier investments such as mutual funds had front-end loads nearing 10 percent, and thus the burden was biggest on the average person); and (5) the power of price-fixing—"the fixed-rate structure that was put forth by the traditional brokerage firms, under the so-called Buttonwood Agreement of 1792.

"All these [fixed-rate] arrangements were basically cartels, not official cartels, but they functioned like cartels," says Chuck. As a result, "the little guy, the average investor, was facing these impossible cartels and for the most part [was] almost completely left out. And you had to have a certain amount of wealth almost to go into the front door."

Some things, such as the introduction of data processing, had progressed by the early 1970s, and Chuck, who was by then in his mid-thirties, had experienced, studied, and analyzed the systems for over a dozen years. Certain that "there was a better way that stocks could be sold or distributed at much lower cost," he knew "that doing a discount brokerage was a natural thing for me to do."

Two bases gave Chuck the confidence that there was a demand for such discounted fees. First, he knew what he needed as an investor, and second it was a perfect fit for his friends and customers in Silicon Valley. They knew and in some cases were part of the gang of people who were driving the early stages of the computer revolution. We are talking about 1974. That was three years before Steve Jobs invented the first Apple desktop computer, the Apple II. That was a time when the world was being turned upside down, when companies founded in garages and dorm rooms were going public a few years after being formed, at astronomic valuations. Those in Silicon Valley were in the know and were able to spot potential in friends' or acquaintances' companies. They certainly knew more about those investment opportunities than some broker sitting in New York who had never met the founder of the company and likely never used a computer, let alone understood how it worked or what new invention would help it work better.

There was no way those people in Silicon Valley would accept the advice of such a broker rather than follow their own educated guesses. These people weren't trading on insider information, which would have been illegal; they simply knew the relevant subject matter. Chuck recalls that these people "were interested in many up-and-coming technology companies, like Ampex and Silicon Graphics, and a whole bunch of similarly hot companies. People wanted to buy them on their own, without the [intrusive] help of the stockbroker. The customer[s] didn't want all the other garbage. They just wanted to do a basic buy or sell transaction, because those customers already knew those good growth companies. And it was impossible to trade without unwanted services at that time."

Chuck's customers weren't sitting at home or work waiting for or fielding calls from stockbrokers who wanted to sell them on a particular stock. Chuck also felt that the system was one of stocks being sold by brokers even though his customers knew what they wanted to buy and didn't want to be pushed by "some croupier stockbroker trying to have me do something else like have me buy something else, like a 9.5 percent load mutual fund," where the broker's commission was both high and immediate, or stock of a company with which the brokerage firm had a special relationship.

There's an old joke about the woman who goes into the butcher shop and asks the butcher how much he charges for New York sirloin steaks. The butcher says, "$10 a pound," to which the lady responds, "That's too much," and walks a few blocks to another butcher shop. There she makes the same inquiry. That butcher says, "$6 per pound." But when the lady replies that she'd like six steaks, he says, "I'm sorry, but right now I'm out of New York sirloin steaks." Miffed, she returns to the first butcher and complains, because he was charging $10 while the second butcher was charging only $6. The first butcher asks why she didn't buy them from the second butcher at the lower price, to which she responds that he was out of them. Thereupon the first butcher responds, "When I'm out of New York sirloins, I charge $6 too."

The situation Chuck's customers were experiencing was even worse than the woman in the butcher shop. For them, it was the equivalent of the butcher saying, "Forget the New York sirloin. Instead you should buy butt steak, because it's better for you and you'll like it more. And I can sell you that for $20 per pound." Stockbrokers were convincing their customers to buy what they didn't want and to pay more for it. Chuck's customers didn't want any part of that approach, and Chuck wanted to provide his customers with what they wanted at a reasonable price. So in 1973 he borrowed $100,000 from his uncle and started the Commander Corp. One year later it became Charles Schwab & Co., the country's first discount brokerage firm.

Certainly Chuck wasn't the first person to recognize the latent demand or the patent unfairness of the system. But he was the first to devise a solution and deserves full credit for that. He turned out to be the right person, in the right place, at the right time. First of all, media's love affair with Silicon Valley's high-tech entrepreneurs had just begun. Second, individual investors were becoming far more plentiful, first through their regular savings from improved compensation levels, and also through individual retirement accounts (IRAs), Keogh plans, and other self-directed retirement plans instituted by the new law—ERISA—adopted in 1974.

The media's coverage of those entrepreneurs and their companies, as well as candidate and later President Reagan's public lauding of them, highlighted the investors' lack of need for certain services, such as identifying new, promising companies. What the cartel had done was tie together several services—the buy or sell transactions, advisory services, and analysts' report information—which in total may have justified a higher fee. Generally, tying together different products, where a consumer must buy all the products despite wanting only one of them, can be illegal, a violation of antitrust laws that forbid monopolistic practices.

The famous examples of such practices are when Xerox Corp. required customers who bought their early copy machines to use only Xerox brand paper. And Kodak tried to require customers who bought the company's film to use only Kodak's processors for developing and printing pictures. Unlike those examples, the cartel packaging the brokerage services to include the advisory and analytic services may not have been illegal, as they were all services and not products. (I leave open the issue of price-fixing.) Of course, part of the cartel's reason for high fees was to compensate for the distribution system it chose to employ—namely, hiring brokers to go out and sell particular stocks.

What Chuck did was disassemble the tie-in, enabling those who wanted only the buy-sell brokerage service to buy just that and nothing more. In addition he devised a different distribution and sales model, which eliminated the expensive salesperson. Because Schwab could avoid the costs of the other services and the commissioned salespeople, it could break the price-fixing, thus substantially lowering commissions. No one had ever tried that before.

Reinventing the Established Order

To change institutions fundamentally is never easy, and generally it is brought about by outside forces. By the mid-1970s Wall Street was the ultimate institution of capitalism and had resisted fundamental change for generations. Chuck would become the first to take on the Wall Street establishment; he risked everything. Many in the industry told Chuck not to try it. As he relates: "There were many people who said, 'This is a dumb idea. Don't do it, Chuck. People are sold stocks; they don't buy them.'" Chuck's naysayers actually fell into a couple of camps. First there were friends who really were looking out for Chuck's good, not wanting him to get hurt. (That's not unlike Howard Schultz's and Maxine Clark's experiences.) Second, there were salespeople and brokerage firm partners (at that time no brokerage firms were publicly owned), who liked the system that supported their high commissions and profits and didn't want Chuck to ruin their good thing. Both thought the new model proposed by Chuck—offering unbundled buy/sell services, advertising the availability of discounted commissions services, and hiring account service people, instead of salespeople, to place orders for the customers—would fail.

Given that no one had done this before, you must ask how Chuck decided to do it. He told me, "I didn't do much market research. We were a small company and just had to do it. I knew that people wanted the service. I knew that somewhat, because they weren't so dissimilar from me. I wanted that service available for me, so I assumed that they would want it too."

If that were the only reason, it would have been dangerous. Many entrepreneurs who start a business to supply a product or service that they personally want fail because they didn't check out what their potential customers would actually want. But from conversations with his friends and customers in Silicon Valley Chuck also knew what people were looking for. And then after he started the firm, the curious showed up—the onlookers who mingled with the crowds of customers in and around Schwab offices. They appeared just to see what was going on and why the crowds were so large. (It's natural human behavior to be curious, to want to know what you might be missing.) In this situation the onlookers soon became customers, and customers became repeat customers, both in droves. Chuck could read the numbers and expand.

While Chuck's proof of concept took a while, his proof of scalability was far more rapid. As he relates: "The scale came, the number of clients who were coming in—you just had to walk into my office and you could see the buzz, the calls that were coming in. It was extraordinarily exciting to walk into our office and see the activity. It was all around you. We had people calling us from all over the country, which frankly was very interesting. It wasn't just San Francisco; it was all over. We were getting great PR, in many newspapers, so we were getting broad distribution of the idea, and people thought it was a cool idea. It started small, but it just kept escalating. By then it wasn't too difficult to bring a prospective investor to the office to see what was going on."

It would be difficult to prove a cause/effect relationship, but clearly the volume of stock trades at Schwab has increased dramatically since then. Was that attributable to discounted commissions or to the conditions mentioned earlier that enabled Chuck's new model? Perhaps it was both—a symbiotic relationship for sure. Likewise, it was a first step toward enabling day traders to proliferate. I believe that some part of the stock volume increase was due to customers' higher confidence in their brokers. Brokers had always avoided discussing, let alone explaining, the amounts and basis for their commissions. Now suddenly Chuck had introduced transparency. Indeed, that transparency was part of his marketing message. (In those days, Schwab did nothing more than execute trades.) And increased transparency almost always improves trust. As the late U.S. Supreme Court Justice Louis Brandeis said, "Sunshine is said to be the best of disinfectants." It is not difficult, however, to conclude that a whole new tangential industry exists today as a result of Chuck's success. Companies such as CoolTrade, Prodigio, and RIZM might not exist were it not for him.

In addition, how did Chuck decide what to charge for the simple buy/sell transaction? What example or precedent was there? In fact there were examples in the markets other than with individual investors. For example, large institutions (insurance companies, pension funds, university endowment funds, and so on) that made many trades in large volume blocks of shares negotiated for and received lower commission rates. Brokers willingly gave those discounts (actually rebates that were referred to as "liquidity payments") to get the big business, both for the obvious reason of increasing their commission income without extra work, since institutions did their own research, and for the less obvious reason that the brokerage firms improved their clout with the stock exchanges (NYSE, AMEX, Nasdaq), since the exchanges received fees for the large transactions.

It was clear to Chuck that he would have to reinvent the approach to hiring personnel. He wasn't likely to attract typical stockbrokers who relied on the cartel's commission rates to maintain their yachts. In fact, he didn't want to attract them. Instead he hired salaried (non-commission-based) account representatives. Chuck says that "it was a completely revolutionary way of getting investors [that is, customers]. We never paid, and to this day still don't pay commissions. We pay salaries. We do pay bonuses based upon customer service, not on a commission basis."

But for that to work, he needed to prime the pump, to rev up and redirect demand. He did that by advertising, public relations, and word of mouth. It worked. First he noticed the crowds of people in his office, which was in California. Then as PR articles went national, with the California crowds becoming news items, customers came in from all across the country. New accounts started pouring in from everywhere. The reinvention of the stockbrokerage firm had started. Later the reinvention would gain momentum through online "day trading" and the inevitable copycats.

Like almost all entrepreneurs Chuck had to raise capital. He was extremely passionate about the new venture. One must be passionate to start any new business but especially passionate to do so by tackling the reinvention of an industry, let alone one so steeped in stuffy tradition, rigid regulations, and greed. Often entrepreneurs try to raise capital by demonstrating how passionate they are and by trying to instill prospective investors with the same passion. Chuck decided *not* to do that. He says he tried "to do it with numbers—here is what we've been able to accomplish so far. We've got clients coming in, the number and cost per client are x and y. I tried to do it in a mathematical way, showing how the opportunity for profitability would be there if we just kept going at the same kind of rate. Of course, I never knew for sure whether it was going to be 10 customers or 1 million. (It turns out that it was closer to 10 million and climbing.)" That's not to say Chuck wasn't passionate. He was, and investors do want to see that the entrepreneur is passionate and rationally enthusiastic, optimistic, and yet disciplined. Then they want to see more.

Charles Schwab made the move into discounted commissions based on his understanding of his customers and the securities industry as a whole. Unlike so many in the industry who merely did their job, nothing more, Chuck seriously thought about the industry—what worked and what didn't. Some teachers, coaches, and mentors of entrepreneurs are often asked two questions by students and young potential entrepreneurs: (1) Should I learn a business or industry by working in it before starting a business myself? (2) If so, how do I know when it's been long enough to make the jump across the chasm from employee to entrepreneur? In other words, how much experience should I have, and how will I know when "enough is enough"?

The best answer to the first question is, "It depends." Sometimes, knowing the business means being part of or thinking like what needs to be changed. In such circumstances it may be better to know the general field and not the specifics. (Remember how Tom Stemberg didn't know the office supplies business and how Maxine Clark didn't know kids' toys, but they both knew enough about retail and merchandising to be dangerous to competitors.)

The answers most people give to both questions are correct but inadequate and noninstructive. As to the second question, they say such things as "You'll know" or "It depends." Those are about as helpful as my mother's advice when as a five-year-old I asked how old I'd have to be to drink coffee. She said, "You'll know," which turned out to be accurate, but at the time wasn't helpful.

The best answer would be that time is not the only factor. It doesn't depend so much on how long you spend on a job or even what functions you performed, although both are somewhat relevant. There were brokers with far more stripes than Chuck Schwab had when he started the Commander Corp. when only 37 years old. But Chuck had paid attention, not only to the functions in his pay grade but also to functions and decisions at the highest levels of all the firms where he had worked. He told me that he had been watching what others in the industry had done. That's not terribly dissimilar to Maxine Clark telling how she could negotiate mall space leases "even though I'd never negotiated a lease before" because "I was in every mall in America, as the president of Payless Shoes stores. I'd listened to our legal department talking about it and I had been very curious about it. I was able to acquire by some osmosis process enough knowledge to be successful." Nor is it unlike Howard Schultz, who had never worked as a barista and certainly never ran or owned a coffee shop. But he had paid attention. Being the great salesman that he was, he made note of how his coffee-serving hardware customers had operated, as well as how they served or didn't serve their customers' needs and desires. And Jim Sinegal had observed the brokers in his industry, so when the economy deferred his starting Costco, he was able to do well as a broker in the interim.

When most stockbrokers talked with their customers, they were too busy talking, otherwise known as "selling," to listen. As a lawyer, I was a bit of an anomaly. I could and did meet clients' expectations by being their "mouthpiece." However, I often provided better value by listening and observing. Later as a consultant, I have had family business consulting clients ask me how I was able to help them improve their intrafamily communication, how I was able to tell each of them what to say and do and what to refrain from saying and doing. I told them that my most valuable communications tools were my eyes and ears, not my mouth. So it was with Chuck, Howard, Maxine, and Jim. As you've read, when Howard, Maxine, and Jim encountered things they didn't know, they brought on additional people who had a different background, experience, and knowledge that complemented their own. Chuck did that too.

The stockbrokerage business is generally described as the activity of bringing together buyers and sellers, but it's really more complex than that. There are in the most basic sense two different public stock markets: (1) the primary market, where companies sell their stock to investors, and (2) the secondary market, where investors sell stock they had bought to other investors. In the primary market, the underwriter makes certain commitments to all the selling brokers and the company makes statements about itself that are cleared through the Securities and Exchange Commission (SEC), which provides buyers and their brokers with some assurances. In the secondary markets, the seller is not the company but someone who earlier had bought the stock either from the company or from another investor. News about the company is issued periodically, not at the time of the transaction. And there is no underwriter providing assurances or comfort; no one is doing current due diligence.

The Entrepreneur's Continuing Value Can't Always Be Discounted

Chuck had accomplished the unbelievable, but in so doing he encountered what generally is unexpected even though it is truly almost inevitable. Fortunately, Chuck was sufficiently savvy and experienced to anticipate that with sudden and significant growth, the company would require substantial capital to grow quickly; it would need to do so to stay ahead of copycats who jumped into the pool almost immediately after Chuck had proved that the pool was more than half full of water. Most people assume that second rounds of financing result from entrepreneurs' excess optimism

in projecting timing and extent of success. Entrepreneurs do suf-
fer from such optimism, which is endemic to entrepreneurship.
Underestimating how much capital they'll need is commonplace.
But second-round financings are also needed to fund working
capital and infrastructure, particularly when success exceeds the
most optimistic projections. The good news is that such positive
results facilitate funding (everyone wants to back a winner, especially if he or she can jump on the train while it seems to still be
starting up). The bad news is that such investors' goals may restrict
entrepreneurs from reinventing their businesses at critical times.
Such restrictions may convert reinvention from the agility of turning around a speedboat to trying to navigate an aircraft carrier to
make a U-turn on a dime. That's what happened with Schwab.

In 1983 Schwab secured what must have seemed like an unlimited source of financing when his company became a subsidiary of
Bank of America (BofA), now the second-largest U.S. bank holding company. What happened to Schwab may seem somewhat
like what happened to Edward Bennett Williams, then owner
of the Washington Redskins football team. At the press conference where he introduced his new coach, George Allen, Williams
commented: "I've given him an unlimited budget, and he already
exceeded it."

Schwab sold to BofA for about $55 million. But then both sides
experienced change. Schwab needed (1) to introduce new products, such as mutual fund shares, in a much bigger way and (2) to
adopt new approaches to marketing, including substantially larger
advertising campaigns. Schwab couldn't do certain things because
of bank regulation restrictions, which affected banks and their
subsidiaries. And BofA had problems totally unrelated to Schwab,
including large international loan losses. This, said Schwab, made
BofA "very restrictive on new kinds of endeavors. I wanted to go
much more extensively into mutual funds. I was totally frustrated

by being under the wings of BofA. So I put forth a plan to buy the company back from them, and they needed the capital. In 1987 we bought back the company and got our independence again. We paid them $280 million for the company, which they had bought for $55 million. So they got a good deal."

Today it is clear that Chuck and his backers got a good deal too. But at that time, "it was an enormous risk," says Schwab. "I had a number of associates who thought I was borderline crazy." On the other hand, he says, "There was a whole faction of mine that was very much for it, who were on the team. There were a number who left the company, who thought it was the wrong thing to do, that we were too leveraged, too this, too that. That was a minority. They left, which was fine. But the people who stayed—we had a great team (and as I always say, 'it's only through a team that you can ever really win.')"

Chuck relates that getting financing for the buyback was "problematic for a while, but then we got it. I mean the most difficult time for me to get financing was back in the 1980s when Wall Street was totally against what we were doing. But fast-forward seven or eight years, we had proved the point, and financing was a lot easier."

Schwab says that from 1987 through 2000 the company "had enormous success. We were caught up in the dot-com world. Everyone thought we were one of the fastest growing dot-com companies. We were, and people bought our stock." The exchanges that were so against Chuck and his original ideas less than 20 years earlier were now pleased with the trade volume of Schwab's stock. They were even more pleased with the increased volume that flowed through Schwab offices. At the same time, Chuck relates, "competition came in, as did efficiencies through even newer technologies. Our uniqueness, to some degree, became not so unique."

Schwab had adopted a modified commission plan by this time. "But by 2003," he says, "our average commission dropped dramatically and was still too high. We had to retrench. We had to cut back a lot of expenses that we had built up during the success years. By 2004 we had to restructure [that is, reinvent] the whole company. That included a change of CEO, who rode the crest up. We were spending money like drunken sailors, based upon a commission level that was artificially high and coming down very quickly. [We had] unnecessary services that we were trying to offer, that weren't very well structured. We had huge costs and expansion. All that had to come down."

The board asked Chuck to come back as CEO. They worked at decreasing their cost structure. Chuck tells how the company "had too many executive vice-presidents, with huge infrastructure and people costs below them, too big a structure, and that all had to be revamped. They had to be culled out."

Laying off those people was very difficult for him on a personal basis. After all, it wasn't their fault, and they had been loyal colleagues prior to that. Chuck explained, "We weren't as brutal as you might think. We did a number of things, sending people back to school, giving them scholarships and such. My wife and I put up a bunch of money to send people back to nursing school or teaching school or other things they chose. So we tried to be humane about this, but we had to do it. Reinventing the company was the only way. We had to save the company for the other 70 percent and our clients."

I found it ironic and suggested to Chuck that Charles Schwab & Co. had morphed into the very organization it was founded to displace, namely a higher-service organization whose costs compelled charging excessive fees. Chuck agreed. Even more problematic were the copycats who became his competitors. Where the incumbents whom Chuck had to beat were insulated by the cartel, now Schwab was the incumbent, but sans cartel. He was threatened by competitive pressures from copycats. Chuck was reinventing his firm not to be something new but to be more like what it had originally been. That is much like Schultz's 2008 reinvention of Starbucks and Sinegal's building of a hot dog plant. For Chuck it was reminiscent of the immortal words of Pogo: "We have met the enemy and he is us."

Of course many companies reinvent by moving on to a new CEO or a different kind of CEO, such as Carlson's move to a nonfamily CEO (see Chapter 13). But Charles Schwab & Co. felt it important to bring Chuck back as CEO. "My view of it was that I was the only person who could do it," he says. "Not because I was so brilliant, but it was my baby, and only I could sort of restructure my baby. Nobody else could do that, because you'd have people within the organization say, 'You can't do that because Chuck wouldn't allow that to happen.' I was the only one who had the collective permission to do those kinds of things without completely blowing up the company."

That's important to note—that the founder may be the only person who has what Chuck referred to as "the collective permission." In addition, Chuck, like Schultz, had the unique perspective, the intimate sensitivity to the culture, the values, and the "secret sauce."

Much like Howard Schultz being the only person appropriate to lead Starbucks after its 2008 setback, Chuck was the only person able to fix Charles Schwab & Co. In both cases, the costs and expenses had to be reduced to enable them to compete effectively where no competition existed before. Both required reinvention of the business, but both had to get back to their roots. The reinventions were not to become something new. They were to become what they had been before, at the beginning but in larger measure. Howard referred to removing the tall coffee brewers to reestablish the intimate contact between customer and barista. Chuck talked about "reinvention maintaining the shared values. I think from the very beginning, our values have not really changed. It is really so critical when you get in a stressful situation of going back to the basics that you have the fundamental value system that is baked in and from which you don't deviate. You know, for reinvention to work, it is so crucial to have a group of people that you're convinced have the same ideas and values as you do." To Chuck that fundamental real value system can best be identified in the way they treat customers.

PART 5

Family Business and the Succession Paradox

9

Silver Spoons:
Why Do Some Tarnish
While Others Shine?

FAMILY BUSINESSES ARE NOT JUST "MOM AND POP" CANDY STORES. Some of the world's largest companies are family businesses—Walmart, Ford, SC Johnson, Cargill, Koch, Hallmark, American Greetings, Samsung, ArcelorMittal, Gallo, CitizensBank, First SK Group, BMW, Hyundai, Gerdau—to name a few easily recognized names.

Family businesses account for the biggest part of the U.S. gross domestic product. In some countries, family businesses account for 70 percent—80 percent even—of the nation's gross product. Large family businesses are significantly more profitable than comparable publicly owned businesses. Research by my colleague Professor John Ward and others show that those family businesses have over a 20 percent better return on investment. This is a rosy picture—and it's accurate but actually incomplete. It's incomplete because the picture doesn't account for the fact that a whopping

90 percent of all family businesses fail to make it successfully through the third generation.

The expression "from shirtsleeves to shirtsleeves in three generations" is an ominous one, feared by owners of family businesses everywhere. That is, it is almost inevitable that the successful business that dad or mom passed on to an ambitious son or daughter—a son or daughter who took it to even greater heights—will languish in the next generation. It recalls the saying, "Louis XIV built Versailles, Louis XV lived in Versailles, and Louis XVI died for Versailles."

The grandchild may not have the work ethic, the will, the leadership, the sense of fairness, or the imagination to build on the family success. Indeed, the successes of the first two generations may have created a behemoth business that not even granddad and dad could run, let alone grow. Still, expectations often die hard and actually leverage the need for reinventions.

GENERATIONAL DIFFERENCES AND CHANGES AFFECT COMMUNICATIONS AND CAN BE CRITICAL

We've all heard accusations that society preferring to e-mail rather than talk and young people texting instead of calling will ruin good communication, which is so necessary where family businesses are involved. There are dreary predictions. Let me share a personal story that may lighten the issue: my teenage grandson, Robbie, almost always texts me instead of calling. That's why I was surprised one night at 11 p.m. to see his name come up as my cell phone rang. I answered, "Robbie? Is that you, and is everything OK?" He assured me "I'm OK, Papa" but sounded peculiar. I asked where he was, and he replied, "I'm at a friend's house, Papa. I'm sorry, Papa." His apology seemed peculiar too, so I asked again if he was sure he was OK. "Yes, Papa," he said, "I'm OK. I'm sorry to bother you; I meant to hit the [automatic dial] number for Papa John's Pizza."

Misdirected information, generational or otherwise, is rarely as appealing as this family story. A misdirected e-mail with a confidential message to a family member or a shareholder occurs with the touch of a keystroke and can be explosive.

It may be that there are too many family owners and/or employees with too many interests and too much baggage to be garnered and led. Or the business may crater for the lack of a leader or for the lack of consensus by the family on the *choice* of a leader. Quite often, any grandchild with real potential will prefer to leave the family business for, well, greener or more fertile pastures.

You would think that business families, being well aware of the succession dilemma, would find a way to pass the torch successfully. But far too many family businesses become woeful examples of the shirtsleeves analogy. All too often, the problem arises even before generation three.

VALUES AREN'T VIRAL; THEY ARE IN THE DNA

The great entrepreneurs interviewed for this book had to develop their companies' values from scratch. That's not easy and requires a meaningful individual value system as well as the skills to embed them in a new, rapidly growing, frequently desperate company. While the entrepreneurs remain with their companies, they can continually remind their colleagues of what those values mean to their company's long-term success. Once the entrepreneur leaves, that becomes more difficult, even if there's someone there who cares enough to relate those values.

In family businesses, even though the founders are gone, their values are embedded in the DNA they have passed on to their descendants. Often those values are elusive, especially where the memories aren't kept alive, as they should be, by stories and lore, or by more tangible jogs to memory. Consider carefully the lines in the following stanza of the song "The Mirror" by Joie Scott and Bob Stewart:

It was just a mirror. Didn't mean much to me at the time.
Just a simple piece of glass, but oh, the things it's seen.
Years gone by, good and bad times, family history.
Every time I find myself staring back at myself, I see
there's more in that mirror than just me.

In Chapter 4 you read about individuals' needs to be prepared when opportunities knock, and in Chapter 5 you read about companies such as Intel being prepared to save the day by reinventing. The same is true of family businesses, where the situation is even more complex. The odds of successful succession can go either way. When the pool of potential successors is limited to family, the odds are negatively affected by the pool's limitations but also positively affected by the caring passion of a family member. In addition to the forces that cause individuals and businesses to be prepared, continuity as a family business requires being prepared to overcome challenges external to the business, its founders, and managers. Totally unrelated to the circumstances affecting the business, the death of the owner, who may no longer be running the business, imposes the additional challenge of estate taxes—the inevitable, ultimate rainy day. The sciences of business and genetics must blend; blood becomes the ultimate liquid asset.

The added complication of reinventing a family business might better be understood if seen as two remote-controlled toy magnetic cars, one a business and the other the family that owns it, racing in adjoining parallel lanes. As one car spurts ahead of the other, the opposite magnetic poles attract and the same poles repel. It takes great dexterity and skill to keep the cars in their respective lanes at maximum synchronized speed.

FEELINGS OF ENTITLEMENT: THE SILVER SPOON SYNDROME

Although some family business problems are the result of kids being spoiled, most are not. In the tough business environment of the past several years, kids have learned that the road to succession is cluttered with challenges. They must show that they can overcome those challenges. Outsiders may perceive that children of business owners succeed because they are born with silver spoons in their mouths, but often it is talent and hard work that bring success. Yet those children are tarred with the silver spoon syndrome. Even if the family business is politics and succession plans must be approved by the electorate, there are silver spoon syndromes. And, as in business, some deflect and handle it better than others. In the 1960s, a high percentage of the news about President Kennedy was also about the Kennedy family. They were referred to as being a dynasty.

I was in law school when President Kennedy was assassinated. Months later, his brother Robert Kennedy, the attorney general of the United States, came to our school. He was the man some people expected to become the next president. First he participated in an informal meeting with students, where incidentally he sat on the floor with those of us who couldn't find seats in the overcrowded lounge. Then came a more formal speech in the auditorium to faculty, alumni, and students. He started by saying that when he finished law school he went to work at the Justice Department in Washington, D.C. He explained how he had worked hard, being the first one in and the last out each day. He continued, "And today I am the attorney general of the United States, which just proves: if you work hard, you can achieve any high position, assuming your brother is the president."

Great Leaders Often Intimidate Their Progeny

Many founders so dominate their businesses that their children and even their grandchildren are intimidated. They have witnessed the old man's accomplishments, his intuition, his knowledge, his expertise, and the stature he enjoys in the world. His demeanor may be threatening—even if this is unintentional. His kids—the primary pool of succession candidates—may be too in thrall to take the leadership role, saying, "Dad was a giant. I know I couldn't fill his shoes, so I won't even try." The same can be true when the founder is called "Mom."

Of course, some natural heirs to the leadership role are not deterred. They realize they aren't in direct competition with Dad: that the skills Dad needed to start the business are quite different than the skills needed to build it further. Others have or can develop skill sets for unrelated endeavors. This won't solve the succession problem, but it may be the best course for the daughter or son so inclined.

Often in such cases, that daughter or son must overcome the feeling that leaving the family business to work in another field represents failure or at least a churlish unwillingness to assume familial responsibilities. This is not true, but it may seem that way if expectations are allowed to fester unabated for years or even decades. Then overreactions can exacerbate the problem. Many parents tell their kids to be whatever they want to be but to do it well. You'll see that theme repeated in some of the stories in the following chapters. But implicit messages, emanating from other purportedly unrelated conversations or from body language, may send or be perceived as sending mixed messages that seek loyalty.

To understand the causes and the nature of reinventing new avenues in family business and/or traveling different paths, I am sharing stories of prominent families whose members I have gotten to know through personal conversations. They include Charles Bronfman and Stephen Bronfman (Seagram); Lester Crown, Steve Crown, and Jim Crown (Henry Crown & Co./General Dynamics); Jay Pritzker and Tom Pritzker (Hyatt Hotels); J.B. Pritzker (The Pritzker Group and New World Ventures); Marilyn Carlson Nelson, Diana Nelson, and Wendy Nelson (Carlson Holdings, including Radisson Hotels and TGIF restaurants); and Linda Johnson Rice, Desiree Rogers, and Cheryl Mayberry McKissack (Johnson Publishing, including *Jet* and *Ebony* magazines).

While I have gained much valuable input from them, I also gleaned information from other sources, both private and public. I have separated the chapters relating to the family businesses mentioned above into this section of the book—Part 5. Obviously, all family businesses were started by entrepreneurs who reinvented themselves to found businesses that were later reinvented one or more times. So, why the separation?

Every business carries the DNA of its founder. When management, governance, and/or ownership of a business passes from founder to strangers, the DNA is diluted. In animals, DNA dilution strengthens the strain, often creating exotic beauty and less susceptibility to genetic diseases. This happens with business

DNA as well. It's hard to imagine stronger sets of founder DNA than Thomas Alva Edison's. Yet who can doubt the company he founded, now GE, hasn't gained strength through decades of DNA dilution.

However, when each founder passes on his company to his family, both the nature and the extent of each dilution is different. The effect is dependent not only on the founder and the successors in the business but also on the founder's family who are *not* in the business. That is not to say it is better or worse, but it is certainly more complicated. Therefore, family businesses are best treated separately.

In the opening paragraph of Leo Tolstoy's *Anna Karenina*, he states, "All happy families are alike; each unhappy family is unhappy in its own way." In the family business stories I'm about to share, each family's attempt at successful succession is done in its unique way but offers the basis for lessons to all other families.

10

Col. Henry Crown: The Long Shadow of His Legacy

AT THE END OF WORLD WAR I, HENRY CROWN WAS 23. HE HAD an eighth-grade education, but the prospect of working for others held no interest. Using his wits and his reputation as a go-getter, he managed to borrow $10,000 to bankroll Material Service Corp. His company earned $7,000 in year one, on sales of $218,000, clearly substantial in 1919. The company grew dramatically to become a key Chicago business.

During World War II, Henry Crown, a patriot, enlisted in the U.S. Army at age 45, having memorized the eye chart and spoken during the stethoscope exam to cover weak eyes and a heart murmur. He never lied in business matters but fibbed that time so he could serve his beloved country. When the army learned he was a distinguished businessman he was made head of the Corps of Engineers' Great Lakes Division procurement office. He resigned as president of Material Service and left all boards of directors. He insisted none of those companies be vendors to the army. He then persuaded army suppliers to give discounts, thus saving his country millions of dollars. In the army, Col. Crown developed more skills, which later served him well in commercial business. He retired as a full colonel. Since then, despite fame and fortune as a businessman, he has always been referred to as "Col. Crown," the title he favored most, except for his more revered familial titles of "Dad" and "Grandpa."

Thirty years later, Material Service trucks seemed to be everywhere, laying the foundation for Chicago's postwar building boom. The business was immensely profitable, a virtual cash cow. The company didn't need the excess cash it generated, so Col. Crown allocated it to real estate and other investments. After all, his company supplied the materials for large building foundations, so he—more than most—saw the value of getting in on the ground floor of the postwar Chicago real estate boom. Col. Crown was a thriving Chicago realtor in 1954 when he bagged New York's iconic Empire State Building for his Midwest–based portfolio. But the core of the Crown family's activities and the goose that laid the golden eggs remained his Material Service Corp.

Every Chicagoan around then remembers the red and yellow cement mixing trucks. The colonel's grandson Jim remembers his pride in seeing "The Material Service trucks rumble by you on the street," a pride shared by all family members but none more than Col. Crown. In addition, of course, there is nothing quite like what Costco founder Jim Sinegal referred to as "being king." And Col. Crown was absolutely the king at the highly successful company he had started with a $10,000 loan.

That's what made it so surprising when, in 1959, he parlayed Material Service into the largest ownership position in General

Dynamics, the hugely successful aeronautics and space company. Later General Dynamics was to develop the F-16 fighter jet and F-111 interceptor.

As procurement officer for the U.S. Army during World War II, the colonel understood how that system worked. He recognized that defense had a different business cycle than construction. He didn't need to wait for President Eisenhower's farewell address, some six years later, in which the departing president predicted the "military-industrial complex" would thrive in the "postwar" world of military actions.

With all his accomplishments and his philanthropies Col. Crown was not an intimidating figure. He died with a very small estate because he had given most of what he made to his family and to charity. Yet when he died in 1990, the mantle passed smoothly to his son, Lester, and to Corky Goodman, the son-in-law of Irving Crown, who was Henry Crown's brother. (The Colonel's oldest son, Bob, was the real leader of the second generation. He came into the family office right after his discharge from the navy in 1946 and immediately became his dad's right-hand person. Bob continued in that role until a heart attack robbed the family of his leadership in 1969.)

As every photographer knows, an artificial light casts entirely different shadows depending on whether the light is focused directly on the subject or dispersed and shared with additional subjects beyond the primary subject. So it is with family giants. And the difference in impact is not just on the immediately succeeding generation.

A business giant's shadow has a powerful impact on her or his children that often is not obvious to family members. But when pointed out, it's relatively easy to follow. The impact such a shadow can have on grandchildren, however, is more difficult to follow, even when pointed out.

Lester Crown (with Corky Goodman) has led the family enterprise founded by his father—Henry Crown & Company—with success rivaling and perhaps exceeding that achieved with Material Service Corp. and General Dynamics under his dad, Henry. Under Lester's reign of leadership, followed by the next generation, which was and is led by Henry's grandson Jim, the family wealth grew considerably. But some things didn't change. The family not only continued their extraordinary philanthropic commitment to their community, they also continued their cultural values and practices, stemming from Judaic principles, of using such contributions to honor the memories of their parents and grandparents.

While Lester clearly has run the show since Col. Crown's passing, everyone entering the family's business office learns quickly about the man for whom the company is named. The office is replete with memorabilia and photos, including a large photograph of Col. Crown in uniform. One might think the memorabilia would cast a lingering shadow on Lester and his sons, Steve and Jim, who became executives in the business. But if any shadow existed, it was not that of Henry, but that of Lester.

Honor Thy Father and Thy Mother, but Go Get a Job: Young Steve Crown Bails Out to Reinvent Himself

Mindful of the "shirtsleeves to shirtsleeves in three generations" caveat, Lester was determined to prevent his shadow from blinding his children and their children in turn. Lester was careful to plan for their futures in the family business. He had done his homework, asking questions of other successful families and listening when business leaders spoke of their family issues, problems, and solutions. And he had given considerable thought to how best to resolve the issues. So when his eldest son, Steve, was about to enter the business, Lester was ready. He had Steve work in the family's marine and barge business, located away from the home office. Lester, a caring father and a wise businessman, had Steve report to a capable nonfamily executive.

Lester understood that no matter how talented and hardworking an owner's son was, there could always be a bit of the "silver spoon syndrome." And if the son were asked to join the father in an important meeting, which was how Lester had learned from Henry, nonfamily employees who had worked hard at the business for years might be jealous.

Lester was trying to reinvent the company to adapt to the family's succession plan. Doing so is a wise recognition that both family and business must be considered. Reinvention must bring out the best in both. Surely, thought Lester, the mentor could teach Steve Crown the ropes without the appearance of family favoritism. It didn't work, and Steve left the firm. The stories I'll share from Lester and Steve reveal why it didn't work and ultimately, how they averted the third-generation shirtsleeves curse.

From 30,000 feet up, Lester's approach appears to be textbook smart. It seems that he was thoughtful, sensitive, and deliberate in trying to avoid any missteps that would interfere with Steve's blending into the family firm. It was all that. Yet it failed. Closer examination reveals the reason why.

Lester was totally shocked when Steve came to him, after working at the company for a while, and told him that he was leaving the company. Lester asked why: "Aren't you enjoying what you are doing? Aren't you learning something?" These were questions from the heart; this was, after all, his firstborn. As Lester had been brought into his father's firm, so Lester hoped to bring his son in. There wasn't pressure on Steve to come in, but there still was hope and maybe even expectation. Lester had been so careful to do it the right way.

Steve assured his father that his job was great and worthwhile. He explained that he was leaving because people were, in fact, being too good to him and that if he stayed he would never have the opportunity to fail.

As Lester recalls it, "because it's a family business, someone would pick up and do the things that Steve was supposed to do in order to get it done." As would be expected, Steve's recollection is a bit more specific. He left because he wanted the opportunity to fail, to operate, and to test himself without the benefit of a safety net. He felt that there was always someone covering his back.

Steve wasn't feeling the same as everyone else, which he refers to as "a little equal-plus type of thing." It is reminiscent of George Orwell's Animal Farm where some animals were deemed "more equal than others." He didn't like it. It felt awkward, it deprived him of the opportunity to grow and gain value. It was demeaning. How could he ever be the man he needed to be to fill the big shoes of his father, his uncle, and his grandfather? It was an example of architect Mies van der Rohe's maxim turned upside down. For Steve the unwanted help became "more is less."

Steve's recollection was that, for example, he would prepare a report. Someone else with more experience and knowledge would revise it, modifying both content and form. Then it would be submitted as though Steve had prepared it. This wasn't a team effort or a collaboration where all the players do their part and the team as a whole takes credit. Nor was this a mentor suggesting how the mentee might improve the work.

The drafts weren't red-penned; they were whitewashed. Steve recalls, "I was treated more like a sacred cow or a special case. It was very awkward. That's not the way I wanted to be treated or the way I was told you should be treated."

He also didn't want to be a conduit to the corporate office. He wanted to be held responsible for what he was supposed to do and not to be asked to do what he wasn't supposed to do. It was a difficult situation. Here was a Crown who wanted to be treated like any other employee.

Given Henry Crown & Company's immense success and the resulting increase in family wealth, the concept of "if it ain't broke, don't fix it" seems compelling. Ever respectful of and true to the culture established by the colonel, Lester had told Steve that if anything needed fixing or changing, it would be Steve doing it and not the company.

That's what he said, but Lester was smart enough to know that it was best not to force the issue too much. So he tried to guide the process by not having Steve report to his father or any other family member. But the best-laid plans weren't adequate. The plan's inadequacy wasn't due to a failure to try hard to make things work. It was grounded in the inability to recognize certain natural human behavior: first, no employee wants to be the one who must tell the boss that his son is less than perfect, and second, every employee assigned to mentor the boss's son knows that someday the mentee will be the mentor's boss.

THE FAMILY FACTOR AS A GAME CHANGER

There's an old story about the army captain who called his trusted sergeant. The sergeant had always implemented battle orders as though delivered by the captain himself. So the captain ordered the sergeant to inform Private Schultz that his mother had died. The sergeant asked all his men to line up and commanded, "All you with mothers who are alive, take one step forward . . . ; not so fast, Schultz."

The sergeant who issued the captain's directives as though delivered by the captain himself in battle was off base when an emotional family factor was introduced. Similarly, the loyal executive selected by Lester, who generally ran his department as though Lester was doing so himself, couldn't manage Steve as Lester would have wanted, because the family factor had been introduced.

So Steve did leave the family business. He worked for an independent company situated on the West Coast. There he gained considerable experience and a heightened level of maturity. His employer recognized Steve Crown's considerable contribution. This built Steve's confidence and strengthened his credibility some 2,000 miles to the east.

Eventually, Steve started thinking about coming back to Chicago and reentering the family business. He knew he preferred to settle down in Chicago where his family's roots run deep and are intertwined with every part of the city. His grandfather, the colonel, was getting up in years. Steve relished the opportunity to work with him and his dad to learn from them while he could. That desire was likely bred from his recollection of earlier experiences.

His brother Jim talks about how their father would take them down to the office on Saturdays and tell them, "You should go visit with your grandfather." Henry loved to have his grandsons visit him, even inviting them to sit in on business meetings. The boys loved those visits. Jim says that he considers the colonel "the best storyteller I've sat with in my life. He was involved in some wonderful episodes in American business that had great importance."

Col. Crown had a phenomenal memory, and he'd regale the boys with stories about how "he became an owner of the Empire State Building," says Jim, "or how he came to *not* be an owner of where the United Nations sits now. And sometimes they were human stories of how he observed one behavior in a person and how he knew [from that single trait whether] to trust or not to trust that person. Or how he valued partnerships and friendships, where he could go to the bank, needing help right away, and give the banker a sealed envelope containing collateral documents, which was all he had to offer the bank at that time. And a year later, when he came back to repay the loan, the banker gave him that envelope, and it hadn't been opened."

When the boys were invited to sit in on a business meeting, Col. Crown would tell a story to give the meeting context. Then after the meeting he'd tell more stories to be sure they understood what had transpired and to teach valuable lessons. These stories embodied the values that were critical to their family and its business, and they proved to be great life lessons for Steve and Jim. What Henry was doing and what Lester also did was to prepare the boys for possible future interests in the business, either as direct and active participants or as passive owners.

Does This Compensation Plan Assure Business Immortality?

The colonel and Lester were molding the boys to fit the organization so that a total reinvention of the family business wouldn't be necessary to accommodate heirs and successors. Those values were and are very important to the Crown family, as is often true in family businesses.

An example of how those values are preserved is apparent in Henry Crown & Company's unique compensation system. Every Crown family member receives the same compensation, a relatively modest sum. No matter how long they've worked at the company, no matter what their education or experience when they arrive, no matter what their function or position, and even no matter how much value they bring to the table, all still receive the same compensation.

They admit to being fortunate enough to be able to do this, since all family members derive ample income from investments and dividends. They all live well and would continue living equally well whether they worked at the family firm, worked somewhere else, or didn't work at all.

So Crown family members don't work for the family firm to earn a living. They work there because they love what they do, because they enjoy the challenges and achievements. They work there because it benefits the entire family. Such a family compensation system may not be feasible elsewhere, but it works well there. It's part of the family values and culture. Thus, compensation played no part in Steve's leaving or returning.

DON'T LEAVE YOUR DESCENDANTS UP THE CREEK WITHOUT A PADDLE

For most families the Crown compensation system is not feasible. What's important is not the compensation system itself but the way the Crowns use it to perpetuate a value system—working for self-satisfaction and perpetuating the family business through the principle that family helps family. (Of course, the Crowns also expand that principle through extensive philanthropy to the broader family of community.)

Businesses have value; families have values; and family businesses should have both.

You must determine what values you want to impart to your descendants, and you must recognize that values rarely float from generation to generation without a raft to carry them. Find a system, a technique, or whatever (a mirror?) that will remind your descendants about your family's values and give them the paddles to follow and pass those on.

But the Crown compensation system does demonstrate the nature of the institution and that Lester was at least partially right when he indicated that reinvention—changing to fit in—would be on the family member's side rather than on the company's.

This time Steve knew that his reentry would be handled more smoothly. Despite Lester's admonition regarding who must change, the processes if not the substance of the company's employment of family had been reinvented to assure such smoothness. Indeed the reinvention in that regard is a continuing process in and of itself, as they recognize that each generation has different needs and demands. For if the continuity of Henry Crown & Company is to be assured, continual reinvention is required. And changes have been instituted in anticipation of fourth-generation Crowns entering the business.

In addition Steve knew he too had changed. He had refined some old skills and gained some new skills. He had increased confidence and credibility, and he was sure he could help things go more smoothly. He also felt a responsibility to work in the family business. It wasn't a sense of obligation: no one was twisting his arm. It certainly wasn't for the money. It was a responsibility stemming from the family's values system. His return has proved very successful, and the experience has helped the family develop new and better processes for preparing and welcoming family members into its firm.

11

Changing Times Call for New Skill Sets

Reinvention of entrepreneurs and of their entrepreneurial businesses might best be described with a Gantt chart. This is a horizontal bar chart that illustrates a time sequence with start and finish dates of different phases of the sequence. Each stage overlaps somewhat with those preceding and following it. The stages are a combination of in-series and in-tandem projects but always float in parallel zones. As one leader scales down and a successor is revving up, they are depicted on a Gantt chart by parallel bars that overlap a point of time, say, at the point of succession.

Of course in every company egos, greed, and other emotions become manifest, but they should be overcome with discipline, good governance, and an understanding that what's good for the business is ultimately good for all. These issues are inevitable. Eventually, entrepreneurs must move on. They can sell their businesses, ending their continuum. Some choose to retain ownership and perhaps keep a seat at the board table. Still others hope to pass positions of leadership and governance to their families.

When an entrepreneur chooses to pass the mantle to the children, several additional considerations—both emotional and familial—must be added to the mix. Those new factors may not be consistent with what's good for the business. They tend to conflict, like remote-controlled magnetic toy cars on parallel tracks veering toward each other and perhaps even colliding or being driven off the tracks. For example, as the entrepreneur prepares to step back, there may be two courses of action for the family—selecting a family member or an outsider as successor CEO.

There may even be more than one family candidate. But either way, a host of emotional considerations—for example, DNA, parental instincts, love—may weigh in for continuity in the choice of a family successor. Negatives may play a role: closeness that breeds contempt; a Sophie's Choice selection that inevitably sacrifices a loved one's desires; old baggage; fraternal jealousies, such as son versus nephew choices; or parent-child conflicts. These can slow, even prevent, the planning or the implementation of the reinvention. The result: potential disaster.

Another example, obviously hypothetical, would be a company managed by professional managers but owned by a founder's family. The family has grown accustomed to handsome dividends and well-paying jobs or directorships. Management sees a pending crisis and recommends a bet-the-farm strategy—leaving the existing business and starting a new business—not unlike the Intel situation discussed in Chapter 5. The conflict—to reinvent or to preserve cash for distribution to family owners—is fraught with disaster. The resulting debate and discussion or argumentation and litigation could cause delays that lag beyond the critical point. In that case, paranoids would indeed have real enemies.

Some important lessons of family succession can be recognized in the circumstances of Johnson Publishing.

Linda Johnson Rice

When John Johnson and his wife, Eunice, founded Johnson Publishing Company in 1942 they were creating a new niche industry. Johnson saw that African Americans were not addressed by publications that carried stories of specific interest to them. Yet the African American community was growing in purchasing power. Clearly advertisers would want to reach this community and might feel more comfortable doing so in publications aimed exclusively at them. So the Johnsons created *Ebony* and *Jet*. Along the way the Johnsons founded other companies in unrelated industries. He sensed his readers would become loyal customers of cosmetics and travel designed for them.

The Johnsons' timing, strategy, and implementation were impeccable. The couple succeeded beyond their wildest imagination, becoming business, social, and political powers, which they exploited with great aplomb. As a result, their influence in the African American community was extraordinary but not unexpected. Their acceptance in the general community, while impeded by a general lack of progress regarding race, was revolutionary.

The Johnsons' daughter, now Linda Johnson Rice, was exposed to the business early on. She was always at the company, watching and learning how things were done. By sitting in on high-level meetings with her father, she says she "just sort of . . . [learned] at the foot of the master."

Until she left for college in California, dinners at home were forums where she heard her parents and their guests discuss business, social, and political matters. After receiving her degree in communications and journalism at the University of Southern

California and her MBA from the Kellogg School at Northwestern University, she came back to work at the company. John was confident that Linda had the right stuff, knew the business, and understood how he felt and what he would want.

John Johnson was sensitive to the likely conflict that would arise with family succession in the business. By the time he was ready to pass the mantle, he had employees who had been with the company for four decades. Employees had watched Linda since she was a little girl, and suddenly, she was going to be their boss. John had to reinvent the existing hierarchy—effectively reversing the *i* and the *e* to create an *heir-archy*. He made a typically wise move when he gave staff a heads-up: "I'm putting Linda in this position, and she's going to be vice president and later will be president and eventually CEO. So don't try to backdoor her decisions. You can't [do an end run around her and] come back to me if she's made a decision."

Doing this was important for everyone's expectations to meet his goals when the inevitable reinvention occurred. He took the heat so Linda wouldn't have to be distracted later. That wasn't easy for him.

He definitely had confidence in Linda: he also knew that she generally discussed matters with him before making important decisions. But more to the point, he was preparing the troops, because Linda's "anointment" would be perceived as a dramatic change. And when she replaced her father one day, he knew it would reinvent the company.

Johnson Publishing focused on a unique demographic, but over the past decade or two, all magazine publishing has faced extreme challenges. Even distinguished icons such as *Look*, *Life*, and *Newsweek* have disappeared. Most of the survivors are much smaller, reflecting plunging advertising revenues that threaten their survival. The Internet has brought electronic publishing. Cable TV is also a daunting rival.

Ebony and *Jet* were not immune. Says Linda: "[I] realized that the whole dynamics of our business, the whole landscape of the media business, was changing. Then when 2008 came and everything sort of fell off the cliff, it was a very frightening time for our company—very frightening. I realized that I needed a different skill set to move this company forward."

It was also clear to her that the company "had gotten too large for just one person to run." In addition, much has changed in the African American community: from the conditions preceding Martin Luther King and the Civil Rights Act to having a second-term African American president. The American melting pot has finally begun to blend: African Americans are in the mix. Linda Johnson Rice feels *Ebony* and *Jet* "may appear in different iterations—may not be in the printed form [but will remain relevant], because we know ourselves better than anyone else. We tell our stories. We are the curators of the African American experience, past, present, and in the future." But of course, the future is far less predictable than before, which is another challenge.

Even operational changes have occurred. Johnson Publishing does its own subscription work. Linda explained: "We used to have a whole team of people on one floor who sat at computers and did nothing but type up subscriptions. I would say there were 50 people that did that, because we did all of our fulfillment ourselves. At some point, that becomes completely inefficient, and it's just not economical . . . it just doesn't make sense."

Linda's reference to "one floor" of people leads to another challenge: the Johnson Publishing Building. In 1972, John Johnson had erected a building that could host his entire operation with ample room for the growth contemplated by his entrepreneurial optimism. But he built far more than that. He built a business palace. It was situated near what was then an artificial dividing line between the downtown business community and

Chicago's near South Side, which was becoming a mostly African American neighborhood. The building's grandeur was topped by a big sign—"Johnson Publishing Company." This was meant to send a message to both communities. And that it did. The building was a great source of pride to John Johnson. But in the newly constricted media world the company could no longer afford the Johnson Publishing Building. The Johnsons' future survival dictated a move into rented office space in someone else's office building.

After years of struggling with congestive heart failure, John Johnson passed away in 2005. His wife, Eunice, died in 2010. Although Linda was already the CEO, her father's death was a huge blow to the company. Linda recalls, "When my father passed, to many people across the globe, it was unbelievable . . . it was as if they had lost their own father. But it was also that they felt so much a part of this company, like this was part of them."

And this occurred while Linda was confronted by the publishing industry challenges that were ravaging print media, causing efficiency layoffs and even requiring a need to sell the prized building and relocate. Linda was in the midst of a dramatic do-or-die reinvention and leading it. She sold the building. It was very difficult; she recalls: "It killed me. This is part of history. I knew my father would be turning over in his grave." Then she thought, "Well, here's a way to look at it, Linda. You have the building or you have the business. Which one is more important? Good-bye to the building; hello to the business."

Out of respect to her father and to secure the continuity of both legacies, she sold the building to Columbia College, a local school with a focus on journalism, communications, tech, and fashion, all of which relate to what Johnson does. The college agreed to maintain the Johnson identity, retaining the iconic sign and maintaining John's office for public tours. Linda assured a positive perpetual remembrance, unlike Studebaker's abandoned, decaying building referred to in Chapter 3.

One of the most difficult steps Linda took was modernizing the subscription department. This resulted in dozens of layoffs—pink slips for employees who had been there for decades. This was a painful step she was discussing with her father just before he died. He had said to Linda, "But I can't let those people go; I could never do that. Those people helped me build my business, because these are people who have been here 40 years, doing the same thing." Linda understood that and respected that. But this was her job to do. She did it with a lot of grace and a lot of dignity, because that's the way she wanted people to leave the company. She brought them all together and gave them an indication of their notice.

Then she met with each individually and talked with them personally, even though doing so was very difficult. But she did it because she had known these people all her life. Ultimately, she understood that most of the people had seen the writing on the wall, but that did not make it any easier.

"Dad was a great entrepreneur and businessman," said Linda, "but times had changed and so must the business." It hasn't been easy for Linda, eliminating the products, edifices, and procedures from her Dad's baby. It almost seems like fratricide. But she understands the extreme pressure and challenges facing the publishing industry today. Linda figured out how to preserve the values ("We are the curators of the African American experience: past, present, and future") while embracing the future (technology).

LOYALTY TO THE WRONG PERSON IS DISLOYALTY TO THE RIGHT PEOPLE

Family businesses and entrepreneurs tend to be extremely loyal. After all, how can you not feel loyal to the person who believed in you (or your grandfather) and took a chance when the business was getting started? Linda Rice faced the typical loyalty dilemma with the floor full of subscription people. Her dad couldn't fire them; they had always been there. But notice that he didn't say "these people can't be laid off." He said, "I could never do that," implicitly giving Linda permission to do so. It wasn't that they'd done something wrong. The business had simply outgrown them, so they became the wrong people. If she didn't change to automatic subscriptions systems, the whole company might fold. Then everyone would lose. Charles Schwab faced a similar dilemma in 2004. He stepped up to the plate, just as Linda did.

Linda Johnson Rice's Leadership Team

Today, Ebony.com is an ever-increasing source of *Ebony*'s revenue. Linda struggles to maintain the essence of what *Ebony*, *Jet*, Johnson Publishing, and the company's makeup brand, Fashion Fair Cosmetics, are about. They are about aspirations. But she understands she must listen to the audience and try to follow where they are going. That's where the reinvention comes in.

Linda had the fortitude to confront the challenges, but she knew she lacked some skills needed to run the business. Therefore, she turned to her best friend, Desiree Rogers, who had just returned to Chicago after a year of serving as the Obama administration's White House social secretary. Desiree had many of the skills Linda lacked. Desiree is now the CEO of Johnson Publishing. Linda has moved up to chairperson of the board. Linda describes Desiree as "smart, tenacious, the hardest working person, who is going to get the very best talent she can possibly get. I trust her. I know that she is an incredibly talented person. We understand each other. We understand our friendship. But we both have our eye on the same end goal, and that is to make Johnson Publishing Company a huge success."

Another friend, Cheryl Mayberry McKissack, had worked in electronic media, was smart, and had the rest of the skills that Linda sought. She is now COO of Johnson.

Linda Johnson Rice picked her two long-standing friends because each knew a great deal about reinvention, having already readjusted her skill set in order to reinvent herself.

Desiree Rogers: Johnson Publishing's New CEO

Desiree began her career as a sales trainee at Xerox. But she always knew she "wanted to run a business." As a generalist she had no industry-specific skills and know-how. She would have to develop those skills on her own.

She fleshed out her skills in a practical way. She would not select industries so esoteric that she couldn't understand them. But she *did* select industries she knew nothing about—ones with basics she could master quickly.

She left Xerox and became an executive with the Levy Organization. After getting her MBA from Harvard her first new job was as head of the Illinois Lottery. While that was a lofty job for a 30-year-old, she set to work to improve her skills. She created a team of experts and worked to make them customer-centric. In just six years, she had lottery personnel relating more positively to their customers. Indeed, a focus on customers became the essence of her career.

Desiree's next job was as communications director of male-dominated Peoples Energy, a gas distribution utility formerly known as People's Gas. Everyone with power at the utility was an engineer or a lawyer. "No one could figure out why I was there," she says.

She spent time with the engineers learning what they did. She knew she would never understand their work in depth. But she got to the point at which she understood enough that her questions and suggestions made sense. To gain knowledge of the business, she often went out before dawn to visit work sites where company crews were fixing pipes. She'd don a hard hat and learn firsthand what was going on. Others' acceptance of her grew correspondingly.

Consumer complaints rose as gas prices soared. Meanwhile, the customers were grumbling that the service was becoming less reliable. Her talents recognized, she was promoted to vice president of marketing and customer services. Along the way, she took some risks, forcing attention to serious problems, going above executives in charge of maintenance whose professional determinations had always carried great weight at the company.

But she trusted the crews, the men on the line, and they trusted her with sensitive but important information. They relied on her confidentiality as to source and on her ability to get things done. In one instance that trust combined with Desiree's power of persuasion saved the day, preventing what could have been a major crisis.

After 10 years at the utility, she moved on to a totally different industry, taking an executive position at Allstate Insurance. "I wanted to touch and feel . . . things in different businesses," she says, "because I didn't know what industry I'd end up in. I can't do the same thing over and over. At a certain point, you really hone your craft. What I wanted to do was run a company."

Her stay at Allstate was short-lived. Why? She was asked by her friends, President and Mrs. Obama, to become the White House social secretary. She saw it as a chance to create a branding operation. As she put it, "The White House—there's nothing wrong with that brand."

She left the White House with a new set of added skills. She was asked by her friend Linda Johnson Rice to take over as CEO of the Johnson Publishing business. With *Ebony*, *Jet*, and the cosmetics business, it had iconic brands with amazingly loyal followings. They touch 70 percent of African Americans, over twice the next rival company's share. There may be "nothing wrong with the White House brand," as Desiree says, but it's been a long time since it had that high a loyalty following.

While at the White House, Desiree found she had to disabuse team members of their belief that information is power only if it is held close to the vest and rarely shared. She taught them how power could be found in sharing information. Once at Johnson, she found similar beliefs but now had honed the skill of convincing her team they could benefit by sharing information.

Throughout her career, Desiree has been confronted by naysayers. She has overcome them by trying to understand their perspective. It's a lesson she attributes to her first naysayer, her father. He was in fact a big supporter of Desiree, but he really didn't like her job mobility.

He constantly told her this or that move was a bad idea. Desiree, however, realized that his admonitions were from the perspective of someone who had stayed in one job his whole life. That had worked for him. Wanting only the best for his daughter, he worried about her pension and job security if she jumped from job to job. She took his warnings as messages from a loving father, because she took "the time to understand the orientation of where the commentary was coming from." That approach has guided her professional career and served her well.

Cheryl Mayberry McKissack

Cheryl remembers always having a plan, what she refers to as an "entrepreneurial outside the box plan." Growing up in Seattle, she was one of a small minority population of African Americans, and was thus prepared for and comfortable with being the only female and one of but a few African Americans in her division when she took her first job at IBM.

IBM was known to have a superb sales training program. Cheryl relished what IBM had to offer, and she did well. During her 15 years at the company, she learned sales techniques such as bundling free services with a product to avoid having to discount the product's price. She also watched with some regret as IBM lost mainframe computer market share to the Japanese. The Japanese were able to discount their mainframes to half IBM's price. Despite that, IBM managed to do well for a long time anyway because of Big Blue's outstanding reputation. As noted in Chapter 6, the saying went: "Nobody gets fired for buying IBM." That meant that corporate purchasing agents could buy IBM computers with impunity. If anything went wrong, the purchasing agent wouldn't be judged poorly for having gone with what the world perceived to be the best.

Cheryl was excited to see IBM's creativity surge when the company entered the personal computer business. She viewed that move as a sign of future openness to change and to freedom from always having to do things the old way, the IBM way.

Her 15 years at IBM were satisfying. She had numerous promotions, with what she calls "a fair amount of success." She was reluctant to stay longer because she didn't want to have to implement IBM's new policy of layoffs. Besides, she had settled in to a life in Chicago, having received her MBA from the Kellogg School. After several relocations, she was no longer willing to relocate for IBM, which together with a five-year commitment would have been part of the deal had she stayed.

Cheryl and a fellow IBMer had already started a new business—a women's used clothing store that employed sophisticated technology and was decorated to match the high-end boutiques in its Chicago Gold Coast neighborhood. It failed to scale and progress as originally planned. The two opened a second and then a third location, the last being a franchised store in San Francisco.

But each market was unique. Thus, scaling synergies proved non-existent. Besides, she and her partner each wanted to manage a larger company. So they sold the fledgling business.

Cheryl had loved the feeling of entrepreneurial adrenaline rushes but knew her skills had been developed in and were suited for a huge company. When an opportunity to combine those two characteristics presented itself, she grabbed the brass ring. This was at a company called USRobotics. As director of sales and marketing, Cheryl was able to employ her IBM selling skills while picking up new skills that can only be learned at a start-up.

Ironically, she almost didn't get the job. People at the company feared that Cheryl, coming from IBM, couldn't adapt to their entrepreneurial culture and would get frustrated and leave. Fortunately, she convinced them that she was a "corporate person with an entrepreneurial spirit."

However, in some ways they were right. Cheryl battled within herself the conflict between her corporate habits and her entrepreneurial spirit. She learned how to blend them and continued at USRobotics for five years. Then the company was sold to 3Com for nearly $8 billion. Staying would have meant relocating to Silicon Valley. She had married her longtime boyfriend, Eric McKissack. They had survived a long-distance relationship before and weren't inclined to repeat that. And her stock options at USRobotics had translated into a meaningful nest egg, so she had the luxury of taking time off and focusing on her marriage.

After a while, she was approached by principals from USRobotics who were backing another start-up, Open Port Technology. They felt her skill set was perfect for running this start-up. She had been considering starting a new business, which would have meant learning new skills on her own dime. Open Port would enable her to learn new skills on theirs. Merely using her existing skills was insufficient for Cheryl. Instead she fashioned a position where she could also gain new skills that she lacked. She wanted to manage international operations.

She helped Open Port build meaningful sales to major telecommunications companies. She led and managed the company's global expansion, opening offices in Hong Kong and Paris. However, things at Open Port soon stalled. After three years, she left without a big financial benefit, but she had acquired significant new skills. Now she felt equipped to do what she had always wanted to do—start her own business.

Cheryl speaks of friends who have worked for the same companies throughout their careers. They have been laid off. They developed skills over those years that were useful only to their employers. They hadn't worked at building skills that were transportable. They never even considered moving, let alone considered what they might become and what skill sets they'd have needed to do that. She is so thankful that she did.

She says, "I think you have to have a core set of skills. For me that included technology, marketing, and sales. What I would always try to do was look at the industry." One of her reasons for going to Open Port was that she saw it as "a way to take these core skills and tweak those skills with something that's happening in the industry that would allow me to build a business or build a platform."

She did a self-assessment each year to determine where her skills fit in with the current environment. She knew that change was coming more rapidly, and she never wanted to become overconfident in her skills. Cheryl's idea of doing an annual assessment of her skills is good, provided you can be objective about yourself. For most people, I'd suggest getting someone who can be objective to help make the assessment.

She didn't want to work hard to build the business solely to meet the needs of her employers. She chose to grow their businesses so that it met *her* needs. Still, she gave value to her employers, never giving them short shrift. But she knew that even though they enabled her to learn valuable skills ("I'm very respectful of the lessons I was taught at IBM"), they're not in business to cater to her needs. So Cheryl was happy to move on, taking a job in the one environment where her employer would be in business to cater to her needs. She started her own firm, where she and her colleagues consulted with numerous companies, constantly using and continually adding to her already substantial skill set.

Cheryl's moves from employer to employer, though not as frequent as Desiree's, were quite similar. As part of a generational link from Boomers to Millennials, who change jobs even more frequently, they are good examples of self-reinvention with a goal in mind. That's unlike Dr. Dan, mentioned in Chapter 7, for whom the means drove the end.

One of Cheryl's clients was Johnson Publishing Company. After 12 months, her friends Desiree and Linda invited her to join them full time. Cheryl thought about it for six months. Then they made an offer that Cheryl couldn't refuse—the opportunity to combine the comfort of a corporate executive position and the entrepreneurship she craved. She would be in charge of the Johnson unit that utilized her current skills, president of JPC Digital, which was developing Johnson's entrepreneurial answers to the challenging Internet age, and COO of Johnson Publishing, where she could develop new skills.

PATIENCE IS A TEAM VIRTUE

Patience may have been a skill that Cheryl thought she needed as an executive of Johnson, but obviously she felt comfortable without excessive patience as an entrepreneur, as did all the entrepreneurs mentioned in the book. Patience as an executive

and the drive of an entrepreneur weren't inconsistent traits.
There is an African saying: "If you want to travel fast, go alone. If
you want to travel far, go together."

———

Cheryl saw the iconic brands of Johnson—*Jet* and *Ebony*, for example—as a higher platform. You'll recall that these Johnson publications "revolutionized the way that corporate America saw African Americans," as Linda told me. She saw that platform as the perfect place from which "to leverage the corporate side into the entrepreneurial side." So far she says it's "amazing." Interestingly, she says the first new skill she had to develop was "a little more patience."

12

Differences Between Leading the Family Business and Leading the Family

THE PRITZKER FAMILY OWNS THE HYATT HOTELS; NUMEROUS businesses owned through the family's holding company, Marmon; and untold other real estate and business interests. Their wealth has been substantial for decades. Not so many years ago, one could calculate the wealth of the Pritzkers by examining a single unit, the Pritzker family itself. Now one needs to calculate the net worth of at least 11 members of this remarkably affluent family. Each a billionaire, their aggregate wealth today tallies in excess of approximately $25 billion.

That need to tally resulted from both the transition down from the third to the fourth generation, as well as the impact of recent family disagreements. Over the past decade intrafamily disputes have prompted a media frenzy. To understand what caused the problems and how they were solved, one must consider the family's history.

The Pritzkers—an American Dream

Arriving in the United States in 1881, 10-year-old Nicholas Pritzker spoke no English. He not only became a lawyer, he also became the author of a book through which he passed his values down to his descendants. The book is given to each Nicholas descendant at age 13—at the boy's bar mitzvah or the girl's bat mitzvah. The book is not circulated. No one else is to have a copy.

Nicholas's son, A.N. Pritzker, was a lawyer too, like his father and an extraordinary number of other family members. A.N. Pritzker is where the real story begins.

One of A.N.'s grandsons told me A.N. "was an interesting study, very gregarious and likable." I interviewed A.N.'s oldest son, Jay, 20 years ago. He had a different adjective to describe his father: "intimidating." A.N.'s sons and friends of the family have told stories about how very hard A.N. was on his sons. But A.N. was generally known as being nice to people, so nice "his friends felt fully embraced." A.N.'s grandson, J. B. Pritzker, a successful venture capitalist, private equity investor, and both a business and charity entrepreneur, said that while he had thought of his grandfather as "an outgoing, very nice man . . . the closer you got to him, the more you would see [the intimidation] that my uncle Jay might have been referring to."

A.N. was hard-driving, and he demanded that his three boys be hard-driving too. He was confident that they, like he, were blessed with exceptional intellect and talent. He wanted them to be the best they could be. Through the generations the family mantra seems to have been "I don't care what you do with your life, but whatever it is, be the best at it." The sense is that you were not a failure if you didn't get there, but you had to set your sights high and do your best to make it. Sounds reasonable. So how was it intimidating? And why is the mantra continued by A.N.'s grandchildren in their raising of his great-grandchildren?

The mantra is not what was intimidating; it was A.N. who was intimidating. A.N. was smart and savvy. His grandson Tom told how his grandfather would sit with accountants and tax experts who might suggest changing a deal's discount rate and balloon-payment intervals: "They all pulled out calculators. They were still pushing buttons when, after a few seconds, A.N. would have the answer without benefit of a calculator."

A.N. had left the active practice of law to become a highly successful real estate investor. By the time his sons were ready to join the family business, A.N. had amassed a huge fortune. And by the time his grandchildren came of age he was well known. All that and his "domineering personality" created "a shadow that made him seem very demanding and difficult," according to grandson J.B.

It was inconceivable to A.N. that his sons would not be super-bright and work as hard as he did. They didn't disappoint him. But to pave the way for their success, A.N. was engaged with his sons—even helping with their homework. To A.N. a report card B was a failure.

But he could be fun. He learned to use "new toys" with his sons. That's the phrase Jay used concerning the flying lessons he and A.N. took together. Yet A.N.'s overpowering personality was a serious problem, more for Jay's brothers than for Jay, the oldest son. Jay explained that A.N. was intimidating because "he'd lose his temper." And because he was also extraordinarily energetic, "he'd come across as fierce. . . . Thirty seconds later he'd forgotten that he'd lost his temper. But I didn't forget so quickly," Jay told me.

Jay also attributed A.N.'s intimidating quality to the fact that A.N.'s accomplishments appeared so overwhelming. Jay's brother Don was 10 years younger. That meant that while enduring even more of A.N.'s intimidation than had Jay, perhaps because A.N.

was anxious for Don to prove he was as special as Jay, Don had
to try to equal his older brothers' achievements. Jay finished law
school when he was 20, too young to sit for the bar exam.

Although A.N.'s grandson J.B. was seven when his father, Don
Pritzker, died, J.B. has asked friends and family about his grandfather's influence over his dad. The picture he draws is that Don
felt very intimidated by A.N. Don wanted to please A.N., but at
the same time he wanted to be his own person. Now, Don was
hardly a slacker. A Harvard cum laude graduate and an alumnus
of the law school at the University of Chicago, Don became a
crypto-analyst lieutenant in the navy. He entered the family real
estate business in his mid-twenties, and according to J.B. he "was
absolutely miserable, because he was treated as if he knew nothing and had no education. It didn't take long, I'm told, for him to
realize he had to get out."

Then fate intervened. In 1957, Jay returned from a trip to
California saying that he'd found a great real estate deal, a motel
next to the Los Angeles Airport, but he was reluctant to buy it
because they had no one there to run it. Upon hearing that, Don
called his wife and asked if she'd move to California. According
to J.B., "she knew full well the intimidating influence A.N. had
over her husband, so she was 100 percent in favor. That stiffened
Don's back for approaching his father, who might have deflected
the approach, with his overpowering personality."

Having received his wife's permission, though, Don immediately volunteered. It was his way out. A.N. was absolutely
opposed. Eventually, Jay convinced A.N. that Don should move
to California and oversee the new project. It's unclear whether
Jay, the big brother, knew that his "little" brother needed the distance from their father or Jay, the deal junkie, wanted a trusted
family member on site to run the motel deal which he, Jay, had
found promising. Either way, it's a good thing he stood up for his

brother; the motel was called "Hyatt House." Of course, it became Hyatt Hotels, the biggest jewel in the Pritzker family's portfolio.

That fact was Don's proudest achievement—his way of proving to his father that he could accomplish great things on his own. That was a form of self-appraisal. He felt he hadn't received acknowledgment from his father. According to Jay, A.N. gave a lot of praise about small things but little or no praise on big things. On those, he built huge expectations, which drove his sons and himself.

In 1972, not long after taking Hyatt public, Don passed away. He was 39. By that time, Hyatt was the fastest-growing hotel chain in America.

The intimidating style was not limited to A.N. The majority of Pritzkers had become lawyers. When Don was studying for the bar exam, Jay admitted to slapping Don on the back and saying, sardonically, "Don, don't worry about it. Your grandfather passed. Your three uncles passed. Your brother passed. . . . How bad would it be to have one flunk out of ten?"

Years later, Jay wrote a similar sardonic letter to Don's son, J.B., as the young man was about to take the bar exam. Intimidation, it seems, was a family sport, but its intent was to motivate, not intimidate. More importantly, it was one of many signs that the mantle of leadership had been passed from A.N. to Jay.

Unlike the rest of his family, Bob Pritzker was not a lawyer. He was also smart, driven, and accomplished. He was not immune from A.N.'s dominance. Given his engineering background, he was the perfect candidate to manage Marmon, the family's company used to acquire and own a wide variety of businesses. Controlling ownership of Marmon has since been sold to Warren Buffett's Berkshire Hathaway, with the Pritzker family retaining a 40 percent interest. Marmon was sold to generate liquidity and facilitate the division of assets that would resolve the differences, settle the litigation, and result in each of the fourth-generation Pritzkers becoming his or her own billionaire.

Lack of Information Is a Lack of Power

Keeping business secrets away from family members who were not involved in the business was yet another A.N. and Jay Pritzker quirk. They believed that information about the family's businesses should be shared only with those who were in the business. "Their view was," according to Tom Pritzker, "'If you're in the business, fine, but if you're not, how do you have the experience, how do you have the nuanced feel of 5,149 decisions and the complexity? We're doing all this work. We've committed our lives to this. It's unfair for people who are getting the benefit to sit and sort of throw pebbles in.'"

There is an old saying: "information is power." The corollary would be "the lack of information is a lack of power." That corollary was another form of intimidation.

A.N. authored the idea that family members who weren't involved in the business had neither a need for nor a right to information about the family business. Of course, that also included the family's investments. They were owned by a labyrinth of hundreds of sophisticated trusts, foreign and domestic. The resulting maze was originally known and understood by A.N., Jay, and a talented group of lawyers and advisors. Ultimately the maze proved daunting to the IRS. When A.N. Pritzker died, having accumulated huge wealth, his estate was bereft of serious assets and the estate tax was insignificant.

Pritzker & Pritzker, the family law firm, acted as "house counsel" for the family's interests. The firm limited its practice to handling the family's matters and coordinating the efforts of other law firms that represented the family, its investments, and its businesses.

A.N. and Jay knew where ownership and control of the businesses and investments were actually located. Those trusts were drafted in ways that gave total control to the chosen ones and made it nearly impossible for others to know who owned what. The trust network not only protected the family from the burden of paying income and estate taxes, it facilitated A.N.'s and Jay's ability to maintain a veil of secrecy from the beneficial owners—that is, their relatives. The corpus of those trusts constituted a large and growing fortune.

The trusts, often situated in tax havens such as the Bahamas and the Cayman Islands circumvented beneficiaries' rights to know. Those trusts and compensation paid from them became a public issue when Penny Pritzker, Don's daughter and a savvy businesswoman in her own right, faced U.S. senators during her confirmation hearing for U.S. secretary of commerce. She simply said that the trusts were established before she was born and that she was merely a beneficiary. Apparently that satisfied the Senate. In the Senate the focal issue was whether she paid the appropriate taxes, not governance and transparency in a family business.

Among family members, amounts paid to Penny, Tom, and Nick for their efforts on behalf of but without the knowledge of the family created a firestorm and a chain of unpleasant events. Given the extraordinary successes of A.N. and sons, as well as the sizable income afforded the entire family, no beneficiary wanted to rock the Pritzker boat. Outside of the pressure caused by the family's mantra—to be the best at what you choose to be—family members were free to be whatever they wished to be. The proof of that is the wide diversity of pursuits they chose—rock band musicians, army colonel, Buddhist lama, movie producer, and even the founder of a hotel chain that is *not* part of Hyatt.

So the power of information was limited to those family members in the business. And the dissemination of the information, if and when it was done, was totally controlled by A.N. and later Jay. (Don was gone, and Bob, being an engineer and not a lawyer, had neither the interest nor the concern with the legal intricacies of control. He was free to do what he wanted in the business. Ultimately the secrecy and the plausible deniability resulting from control being elsewhere was a valuable tool in Bob's divorce negotiations.)

A.N. and Jay were not only two of the smartest men around, they were charming and great salespeople. They could be endearing or tough as the occasion demanded. And they retained advisors who were equally smart and convincing salespeople. So again, their talents, skills, salesmanship, and success lulled the family into a willing complacency.

In 1999, with the family's businesses and wealth in great shape, Jay died. Of course the cleverly drawn trusts had provisions to deal with that event. What they did not deal with was the reinvention of the Pritzker family. The changing dynamics were enormous and nearly catastrophic. The American Dream would become a nightmare.

If It Ain't Broke, Why Reinvent It?

With Jay's death, coming 13 years after A.N.'s, someone or some group had to assume the mantle of control that Jay had inherited from A.N. Of course since Don, Bob, and Jay each had more than one child, the geometrics of family growth resulted in more fourth-generation family outside the business and thus outside the sphere of information. Indeed, some fourth-generation family members had founded their own businesses. And a number of fifth-generation family members were coming of age too.

Still, there were capable family members running the Pritzker businesses. There was Tom Pritzker and J.B.'s sister, Penny Pritzker.

(She left the business 14 years later to become U.S. commerce secretary in 2013.) There was also Nick Pritzker, Jay's cousin, who was involved in the company's real estate holdings. These few, by virtue of their involvement in the business, were each thrust into position as stewards and disseminators of information previously held by Jay.

It turned out that neither these few family insiders nor their own families were comfortable with that situation. Tom Pritzker learned much from his father, Jay, and from his grandfather, A.N. That happened not so much at the dinner table, as it did in so many family legends. Instead he learned much, as did the Crowns (see Chapter 10), by being in the office and watching his father and grandfather do their business things. He discovered the importance of selecting and supporting great managers of Pritzker business interests in curious circumstances. Tom watched his father defer to managers concerning important operating decisions despite Jay's contrary view and the fact that Jay owned the controlling shares of that company. Why did he do this? Because at the end of the day, the prime manager—a "hired gun" named Pete in this case—knew best.

Decision making is "important for us," said Tom, "but not everything." He added that the top manager in a given enterprise "should make the call, because he's committed his whole life to this." Referring again to Pete, Tom added that "he lives his whole life doing this, all day, every day. We should give deference; he knows better." Tom summarizes the approach: "Our job is one-third to organize, focus, and give necessary tools to those people. The other two-thirds are to get out of the way and just let them do what they are good at and passionate about." Indeed Jay had taken care to teach his son valuable lessons.

Warren Buffett, without knowing it, echoed the wisdom of that approach. The Pritzker family sold 60 percent of the Marmon

Group to the man known as the Oracle of Omaha. Tom went to visit Buffett and asked, "How do you want to run Marmon?" Buffett replied, "I don't want to run it." Oracle indeed! Buffett's philosophy was the same as that which Jay had taught Tom.

Another example of Jay's business lessons to Tom: the family's wealth gave them long-term staying power. But the entrepreneurs they backed needed cash to live and to buy second homes. They couldn't pass the Pritzker businesses on to their kids. Arrangements had to be made to accommodate those needs even though they had no direct benefit to the Pritzkers and often seemed counterproductive to their current interests.

Tom might have been the "natural" inheritor of A.N.'s and Jay's scepter of information and control, but that would prove the wrong lesson for Tom to learn. The situation was now different. Where there had been two surviving brothers, Jay and Bob, who had dramatically improved and built the family's empire and whose different interests led to compatibility, now there was a mix of siblings and cousins, with varying interests and backgrounds, to contend with. Over a dozen family members seemingly were entitled to share in the success of the enterprise. While the family members were well educated, only a few were in the family business. The majority were not. No fourth generation Pritzker could lay claim to the family's huge success. Quite quickly it became clear that no one could assume all the power that was once Jay's. No one was entitled to control the power-granting information. Jay had done much to provide for the family's future. He had mentored and taught. As J.B. says, his uncles Jay and Bob had acted as substitute parents for J.B. and his siblings: "They felt a kind of tacit guardianship. They felt responsible for us, even though we were still with our mother in California and they were 2,000 miles away. They were actively engaged in making sure we were OK."

Unfortunately, Jay failed to anticipate or plan for the changes that had to occur after he died. Perhaps Jay failed to accept his mortality. Maybe he thought he'd deal with the issues "later." Maybe the lawyer in him and all the lawyers surrounding him focused too much on testamentary conveyances and tax avoidance techniques, resulting in too little attention to the issues of interpersonal family relationships. Whatever the reason, his failure resulted in an all-too-public split among family members, leading to public accusations and litigation. The global Pritzker family had always been represented by one law firm as to its intrafamily relationships. All of a sudden they had numerous law firms protecting their varied interests. The fortress that A.N. had built was suddenly a condominium at war, and the unit owner meetings were anything but pretty.

Jay Pritzker did a remarkable job preparing the family business, its investments, and its ownership vehicles for the future. He should have done better educating the family as to what would be different when he was gone. He ought to have realized that people who are kept out of the information loop become suspicious . . . or worse. The results can be catastrophic.

Suddenly, the family that thrived on privacy, on keeping family business matters secret from the public and even from certain family members, was page one news. Tom and cousins Penny and Nick Pritzker were clearly in the unwelcome spotlight. As Tom puts it, "We had our issues. . . . So who is it that I'm really serving as trustee to my relatives? My view was, 'They all have different skills, ambitions, values. Every one of them is a different package.' So I wasn't sure that forcing them to stay in a family enterprise was the right thing for them and the next generations. And I looked at the companies and particularly the management teams. Quibbling shareholders can damage a company. I didn't want that instability for them. For me, probably holding it together would have been better for me. But I'm not that driven to want to hold it together against all the other people's interests. I decided to sort of let go."

Was This Rocky Reinvention Really Necessary?

The issues were resolved by asset liquidation, selling control of Marmon, and separating out other ownership interests. Family relationships are better now. Put it this way: family members are communicating directly again and not through lawyers.

Reinvention of extremely complex ownership and control has been adapted to the changed circumstances. But in the Pritzker case anticipatory reinvention could have avoided terrible tensions and news media notoriety. I don't know that the resolution would have taken different routes and forms. But certainly there would have been more and better options for the family.

In any family, as family members die, relationships among surviving members change. Not anticipating that situation is foolhardy. Adding complexity to ownership, such as limiting information access through trusts, exacerbates the problem.

13

Reinventing Family Business So Successors' Skills Shine Through

CARLSON COMPANY, OWNERS OF THE RADISSON HOTEL CHAIN, TGI Fridays, and other well-known businesses, is an interesting example of the need to reinvent both the business and the family in order to breed a successful succession to the third generation.

In 1938, Curtis L. Carlson borrowed $55 from his landlord to create Gold Bond Stamps, one of the first customer loyalty programs. This was after he'd noticed another company's stamps in the drawer of a local store in his hometown of Minneapolis. Today, Carlson Company is still family owned. In 2008, the most recent year chronicled, revenues were over $37 billion. Today, the business of Carlson Company is clear for all to see, a far cry from a company started with a $55 loan.

Seeing the opportunity back then was a clear example of Carlson's foresight. He continued to see opportunities and had the guts to bet on his instincts. Not all were winners, but the ones that were built a great company

The Gold Bond of Reinvention

The stamp concept and the business model that Curt developed were brilliant in several respects. Curt sold his Gold Bond Stamps to retail stores, which gave them free to customers—the number of stamps based on the dollars spent in the store. The customers accumulated Gold Bond Stamps until they had enough to "cash in" at a Carlson Redemption Center. The center displayed items that could be bought there only with Gold Bond Stamps, including post–World War II household appliances in great demand following the war and during the subsequent housing boom. Curt even convinced some clergymen to allow congregants to use Gold Bond Stamps to satisfy their church contributions.

Consumers became addicted to the stamps and what they bought. After all, "free" is addictive. By giving the stamps to their customers, retailers assured their loyalty. Thus the retailers, the equivalent of "pushers," became reliant on the stamp program, even fearful of not using them lest their customers shop elsewhere.

Manufacturers of the appliances and other premium items relished the free display space that created mass exposure for their ever-new product lines. Therefore, they discounted the price and gave generous payment terms to Curt.

Carlson was paid up-front by the retailers and didn't have to pay the manufacturers until stamps were cashed in, years later. The resulting float was huge and enabled Curt to pursue other opportunities. And when customers lost or forgot about their stamps or died without telling their kids where they were hidden, the related costs were deferred, possibly forever.

Does the phrase "cash cow" come to mind? It should. Today, the closest comparison is airline affinity programs like United's Mileage Plus program and American Airlines' AAdvantage program. Indeed, these programs have been a top profit center for leading airlines.

One of the investments Curt was able to make, in 1962, as a result of his large cash flow was a minority interest with some friends in the Radisson Hotel located in downtown Minneapolis. As the opportunities presented themselves, Curt bought out his partners one by one until he owned the Radisson outright.

Over the years, Curt saw increasing competition in the stamp business and the inevitable irrelevance and demise of the stamps. He also, however, observed the change in the travel industry. Americans were traveling much more, for both business and pleasure, probably because of the reduced cost of and time needed for air travel, the enhanced availability of cars, the expansion of business markets, the lengthening of paid vacation time, and the expansion of local businesses to national markets. The Radisson Hotel was doing well, so he decided to replicate it. He knew how to run a hotel. Now, he needed to apply his Gold Stamp cash preservation skills to a purely bricks-and-mortar business. Once again he found a way to increase his supply of cash. He franchised the hotel operation to hotel property owners, who gave him lucrative up-front franchise fees. Franchising shifted the burden of raising money and the costs of making renovations to the franchisee.

Later, when overseas travel was growing rapidly, he franchised an overseas hotel group. He also started the business now known as Carlson Wagonlit Travel, which today is a major part of the Carlson empire. His Wagonlit business generates over $27 billion of Carlson's $37 billion in revenue. Along the way he capitalized on the essential link between travel and food. Hotels had restaurants, of course. This resulted in his buying the TGI Fridays chain of restaurants in 1975.

To help you understand the complexity of Curt and his desire to assure continuity of his family's involvement in his businesses, let me share a story. Curt's hotel had a restaurant called the "Flame Room." His kids were disappointed when they went to eat there and saw that there were no flames in the Flame Room. So Curt acceded to the "vote" of his children and had the columns remodeled to have flames. That from a fiercely independent man who described his approach to corporate governance by saying he conducted board meetings "looking in the mirror while shaving."

Curt was keen at observing synergies—or what his daughter, Marilyn, refers to as "adjacencies." Because his hotel had a restaurant, he considered himself to be in the restaurant business too. Being certain that other hotels and restaurants had the same needs he was facing himself, he saw as inevitable his move into the restaurant supply business. When he heard that the TGI Fridays restaurant chain was available, he bought it, in part to build the supply business. How adjacent are those?

That's not dissimilar from his entering the travel business, done at least in part to nurture his hotel business. Curt's overriding goal was to keep Carlson operating as a family enterprise for a hundred years. To achieve that, he knew he would have to reinvent Carlson, perhaps many times. Curt spent a lifetime reinventing the company. Sometimes he acquired something due to a perceived opportunity; other times his acquisition reflected the chance to feed an existing business as well as being an opportunity in and of itself.

Obviously Curt craved reinvention. It's not clear whether he was doing so more as a necessity, opportunity, or addiction. Did he feel that one must reinvent his business to assure survival, or was he an opportunist who saw benefits in related or adjacent areas of business and could not resist the double-barreled benefit?

One thing is definite. His need to reinvent was so much a part of him and so much a series of quick reactions to perceived opportunities that he structured Carlson Company to be sufficiently flexible to accommodate this propensity. A board meeting beyond his shaving mirror would have been an impediment. But as with all of us, age crept up on Curt. He knew he needed help leading and managing his growing operation. He invited his son-in-law, Skip Gage, to be CEO, but eventually Skip didn't meet Curt's expectations. He resigned, and Curt resumed as CEO.

A Feminist Reinvention Yields Unexpected Dividends

Curt's daughter, Marilyn Carlson Nelson, came to work at the company. That was in the early 1960s, after she received an advanced degree in international economics from the Sorbonne. Prior to this she had been the only female analyst at Paine Webber, the large stockbrokerage firm. She signed analytic reports "M. C. Nelson" to hide her gender. When she had her first child, gender hiding was no longer an option. So she left Paine Webber, then one of the largest stockbrokerage houses, for Carlson. She got a quick promotion, but then Curt fired her because she was pregnant for the third time. Curt felt that Marilyn's first responsibility should be to her growing family. She left in tears, although some time later she agreed her dad was right. Curt did truly feel that way. He was also a man of his times—to him, women belonged at home, and the heavy lifting of business should be left to men.

Even when Marilyn was young, she received mixed messages from her father. Curt taught his kids constantly about the business, often in seemingly strange ways. For example, if a restaurant where the family was dining didn't include dessert in the dinner price, he'd convert the dessert decision into a vote on whether to spend the money on dessert or invest it in the family business. Of course everyone knew that Curt's vote counted for more, yet the Carlson Company became the nemesis of their "sweet tooth."

Dinner-table discussions often involved business issues, questions relating to actual decisions regarding Carlson's operations. Sometimes Curt would even act on Marilyn's answers, and he'd thank her for her good advice. Yet, deep down, Marilyn knew how Curt felt about gender in business.

Marilyn spent years away from the company raising four growing children in Minneapolis. As the kids became independent, Marilyn began volunteering for leadership positions in the Junior League, civil rights organizations, and the like. She served as Super Bowl committee chair. Her leadership and her charisma led Minneapolis locals to ask her to run for statewide office. That prospect seems to have been untenable to Curt, who invited her back to the company. Curt told Marilyn that the best way to give back to the community was to create jobs.

Truthfully, it's unclear what caused Curt to invite Marilyn back to the company. Was it his capitalistic convictions, or was he starting to sense his own mortality? Skip hadn't worked out, so Curt needed a new succession plan. It's doubtful that he had changed his attitude about women in business. By hiring Marilyn he wasn't making any succession commitment, but perhaps he was hedging his bet. After all, it might be difficult luring back his daughter if she was the governor or a senator. So she began as a part-time director of community relations, and in 1989 she became a full-time employee.

Marilyn analyzed her skill set, gained from earlier work and her community volunteer work, as well as the skills she lacked. She spent time improving existing skills and learning others. When the time came for Curt, due to his failing health, to step back and select his successor, just months before his death, Marilyn was the obvious choice. She had developed the skill set, was ready for the challenge, and in fact led Carlson through the difficult post-9/11 impact on travel. Then she drove Carlson to new heights.

She was fortunate that when her father had insisted that she focus on raising her family, she was able to learn new skills while performing civic service. Many women start out with civic and charitable organizations filling their résumés. It can prove useful in building skills.

Marilyn continued receiving mixed messages from Curt. He was a nearly constant critic of Marilyn. When she finally questioned his criticism (putting her status on the line), he said, "When I stop yelling at you, that's when you know I'm not interested in you anymore." She had worked hard at reinventing herself and was thus fit for her new assignment and to eventually succeed her father.

Incidentally, when she did succeed Curt, Marilyn took continual steps to revise rules that reflected Curt's attitude about gender. Carlson became one of the friendliest, welcoming places for women to work. The numbers all increased—women employees, women executives, and women directors. In the meantime, the company's infrastructure and its governance were reinvented to allow second- and third-generation family members to assume their responsibilities, including Marilyn's daughters, Diana and Wendy. It just wouldn't do for Marilyn, Diana, and Wendy to use Curt's shaving mirror. Via reinventions, the company was well prepared for the entry of the third generation.

By the time Marilyn was ready to step aside in 2008 the company had grown to a point where a nonfamily professional manager was the appropriate choice to succeed her as CEO. The board selected Hubert Joly, who had been CEO of Carlson Wagonlit Travel, as Marilyn's successor. (Interestingly, in 2012 Joly suddenly and unexpectedly resigned to become CEO of Best Buy. Trudy

Rautio, formerly executive vice president and CFO of Carlson and member of the boards of the travel and hotel subsidiaries, succeeded Joly as CEO.) Marilyn not only reinvented the company's infrastructure to create an environment that welcomed women. By this process she also reinvented the pool from which Carlson could select a successor at a critical time.

Marilyn had the difficult and sensitive burden of retaining the culture and values established by her father while changing the family's approach to succession. She was in the right position to do all that, but she doesn't view such reinventions as being the exclusive province of family members. She has clearly stated that every Carlson CEO must decide what parts of Carlson should be retained and what parts must be changed. She remembers her father's goal—100 years of family control—but has reinvented the company and its governance system so that continuity can be accomplished by the board, instead of solely through the CEO's office. Having said that, she is intent, as are her children, on involving the fourth generation, who now range in age from seven to the mid-twenties. They are given every possibility to learn about Carlson. Who knows what seats, if any, they will fill when the time is right? What matters is that the system is in place.

No Shirtsleeves in This Third Generation

Marilyn was mindful of the skills and talents of her daughters, Diana and Wendy. Diana had been a board member for some years, and in 2013 she became board chairperson. Wendy had been on the professional tennis tour until an injury sidelined her. After that, she got an MBA and moved into private equity with a Chicago firm. Thereafter, she became director of development for Carlson Restaurants. She recently resigned to avoid any conflicts as she became a member of the company's board.

Reinventing the company's governance infrastructure was important, but not sufficient. As in so many family businesses that achieve successful succession, some reinvention of the next generation is also necessary. Wendy shared a story about her reinvention that is instructive. It occurred shortly after she started working for the company. Her first Carlson Restaurants assignment was in Texas. There she was to explore the prospect of opening new facilities. Within a month of joining she observed that the Texas sites had the worst performance in the company. She went to Carlson's restaurant company COO. She told him Texas expansion plans made no sense. She said, "We should focus on expanding in the East where our stores outperform. [Let's] come up with a strategy to turn around Texas before developing more stores."

She failed to convince that COO, so she went to the Carlson Company CEO and COO, her mother and uncle, respectively. But that also failed. Although Carlson was a family business, Wendy's mother and uncle had worked hard to establish and defend a professional environment. They were wise enough to know that such a structure was imperative if they were going to attract and retain the caliber of officers they would need to accomplish their goals.

Many young people who enter the family business, especially those who enter before gaining experience and credibility working elsewhere, throw their weight around and negate other employees' decisions. This can have tragic results. They may ruin their ability to get along with staff, as well as eventually manage or lead the staff. They may also chase good people out the door and create a company reputation that makes it difficult to attract qualified employees. This is not the only reason for the shirtsleeves-to-shirtsleeves dilemma, but it is notable.

The Carlson Company's form of governance had changed from Curt's autocratic style. Someone forgot to alert and train

Marilyn's daughter Wendy. So Wendy's passion for the family's business (every bit as strong as Curt's) caused her to stumble as she tried to use her clout to get her way on business issues. Even though her intentions were good, her behavior was inappropriate and counterproductive.

Fortunately Wendy is a quick study. She went back to work and developed more stores in Texas. She even became vice president of development, with national responsibility. Yet she feels she failed and the company suffered because there wasn't a thoughtful plan to turn around the Texas unit. She was frustrated. Here she was, a family member with supposed "special access" to company leadership. Still she fell short and couldn't make it work.

Her learning curve was still forming. The Hotel Group CEO recruited Wendy to be executive vice president of the Carlson Hotel Real Estate Company. She spent the first three months working the front desk and even making beds. In fact, when friends at a private equity firm heard of a pending Carlson deal, one of them called Wendy and said, "Why didn't you call me?" Wendy responded, "Well, I am at the front desk, not in the boardroom."

That hotel experience showed Wendy many opportunities for improvement. She offered suggestions at weekly executive meetings, but she felt ignored. After all, as a family member she had "been given her job." They felt she hadn't earned her stripes. Think: "silver spoon syndrome." In other words, says Wendy, being "a family member didn't help me; it hurt."

At an executive strategy meeting, someone suggested that they should "aspire to be *one* of the best." Wendy couldn't hold back. "What?" she said, "I have never gone on a tennis court . . . without the desire to win. Why play if we aren't trying to be the best?" She surveyed the room, which, she recalls, "stared aghast and shared all the reasons why we couldn't aspire to be number one."

Her detailed suggestions were based on her concern about the adverse effect on the Carlson brand. But Carlson was predominantly a franchise system. The others were concerned that placing more demands on franchisees would cause them to bolt, adversely affecting company revenues.

Wendy had learned from her prior experience in the restaurant company. She recalls, "I knew a call to the top wouldn't make a difference; it might actually isolate me further from the group." She knew that she had to work from within the group to effect a strategy change. Her considerable reading about how to manage and lead seemed useless; she was stymied.

Then she had an idea, "We had a winning brand—our Radisson brand in Europe." She worked out a scheme to get the group to buy into a simple concept—learn from what we do in Europe. First she went to Europe, returning "with a wonderful story, beautiful pictures, a brand with a soul." She presented a plan for U.S. Radisson and then coordinated a trip for her executives "to visit the best of the best properties in Europe and then visit the worst or average in the U.S." It worked. She had buy-in: the business case for change had been made effectively. When she shared her vision during Christmas dinner with Hubert Joly, who had not yet become CEO of Carlson, he championed the cause. As a result, Wendy is able to say, "Today, I'm proud to report that the company is making great progress toward the goal of being number one in every category in which we operate."

There was Wendy Carlson Nelson, an heir apparent to Curt Carlson. She knew how her grandfather operated (board meetings in his shaving mirror). She had been no less passionate than Curt about the family's business, so she had resorted to a Curt Carlson style governance system in her attempt to fix the restaurant business.

Apparently Wendy didn't get the memo announcing that after Curt left the company, things had changed. Carlson's governance system had been reinvented. Fortunately, she was smart (she is a Kellogg School of Management alumnus) and figured it out quickly on her own. Otherwise, it easily could have gone the other way.

Here is an extraordinarily successful business that seemingly did things right—reinventing the company and its governance system to fit the changed circumstances when Curt Carlson left. He had prepared, against all odds, for a successful succession to the third generation. Yet, Carlson Company failed to prepare the third generation. Fortunately, Carlson did require the third generation to have experience elsewhere, as well as a good education, which prepared Wendy to keep her generation at the top.

14

What's Love Got to Do with It?

WE SAW THAT A.N. PRITZKER INTIMIDATED HIS SONS, A STYLE his son Jay carried to the next generation. Henry Crown was a giant, his venerated presence still evident in office adornments, but his descendants seemed not to feel intimidated by him. Surely in both cases there were parental influences, subliminal and overt, but what happens when Dad is not subtle?

In the huge Broadway musical hit of 1945, *Carousel*, the star character Billy Bigelow sings about his yet-to-be born child, Bill. As he ruminates musically about his son, exploring in his mind what the child will want to be when he grows up, he concludes that Bill can be whatever he wants. That song ends the right way theatrically, but reality isn't always that harmonious. New or about-to-be fathers often plan their children's entire lives. That constitutes the epitome of expectations. And of course expectations are the foundations for disappointments.

Actually, it's only half-bad if one just dreams about what one's child can be. But if one's life, as well as one's child's, are guided, or worse *controlled*, by such expectations, then the longer that illusion continues, the more difficult it becomes to reinvent those lives. And almost always both lives—parent's and child's—will require reinvention if continuity of family control of the business is to have a chance. Indeed, it will generally be necessary if parent and child are to have a good relationship at all.

It's worth exploring family business situations to better understand what does and what does not work well.

The Best Laid Plans ... Oft Gone Awry

Samuel Bronfman was an extraordinarily successful entrepreneur. In a single generation, he had developed a huge liquor distillery in his hometown of Montreal and had created a valuable brand throughout North America and elsewhere, with an efficient and loyal group of distributors. Along the way he had become exceptionally wealthy. The company he founded, Distillers Corp., had acquired Seagram in 1928 and became a pillar of the Canadian economy and one that was respected globally. Although such success always depends on teams of capable people, there is no doubt that Sam was the most important cause of that success.

Sam's son Charles Bronfman told me he loved and revered his dad, but he also said that he was afraid of and intimidated by him. This fear stemmed from witnessing his father lose his temper and yell at other people. Sam never lost his temper at his son, but Charles lived in fear that he might. That would have been enough, but the intimidation had other facets and was quite complex. Charles was so intimidated by his father's capabilities that he was afraid even to consider running the liquor business or, for that matter, any business at all.

Edgar Bronfman, Sam's other son, was also deeply affected by his father's influence, although that may not seem as apparent. It is clear, however, that the two boys took different paths to emerge from their dad's shadow. The two sons understood what Sam wanted them to do, and at first both were sufficiently intimidated to do so. Edgar and Charles entered the liquor business and served alongside their dad. Sam didn't just hire his sons; he sired them. Everyone leaves an imperfect genetic trail. Sam was bucking the odds.

Interestingly, the fear and intimidation the boys felt was similar to that felt by their sister Phyllis. Phyllis was to become a top-notch architect, but she came up with a different design in her struggle to emerge from under her father's shadow. Her ploy was intended to and did establish the fact that her considerable accomplishments were her own. She wanted to separate herself from the family name. Unwilling to offend or embarrass her father, she changed her name when she married.

Edgar went to work for Seagram, eventually running the Canadian operation. Charles, for his part, had been so convinced he could never compete with his father—that he could never lead the distillery business—he headed for the ball field instead. He cofounded and for 22 years was chairman of the Montreal Expos baseball team. In fact, he used his own money to buy the club. Later the team was sold and moved to the U.S. capital as the Washington Nationals.

But Charles did not choose to leave the entrepreneur's playing field. His Operation Birthright is a high-success not-for-profit organization. I'll explore other family stories that Charles shared—with the goal of seeing how he came out from behind Sam's shadow and gained enough confidence to reinvent himself as a successful entrepreneur, and how he viewed the great Vivendi debacle that halved the family wealth.

Charles wanted to help the city of Montreal, but the main reason for his going into baseball was that he knew his father knew nothing about the business or game of baseball. Still, Charles was proud to bring his father to Expo games and to see Sam become a fan before he died. This was a clear manifestation of the feelings he harbored: love (he truly loved his father) and fear (a kind of reverent awe based on Sam's extraordinary accomplishments, primarily in business, and perhaps trepidations due to Sam's outbursts at others).

To honor his father's wishes, after Sam's death, Charles agreed to become cochairman of the liquor business with Edgar. Who says that shadows fade when the sun sets?

When a father's plan for succession in a family business is to make two sons (both one-time officers of the company, by the way) cochairmen, the reasoning is suspect. Sam may have doubted either of them was up to the task by himself. Or was he simply afraid of hurting one son's feelings? We will never know what Sam felt. But clearly he did resort to the default testamentary choice of North American parents: equality. While equality is suitable for political institutions, it is highly overrated for family businesses.

TREATING CHILDREN THE SAME, EQUALLY OR PARTICULARLY

Parents who try to treat their kids the same—for example, buying them the same toys, attending the same entertainment venues, or playing the same games with them—usually fail. Hopefully they learn the lesson: each kid is unique and must be treated uniquely.

When the kids mature and it's time to do estate planning, smarter parents, having learned that all kids aren't the same, then often try treating them equally instead. Parents go through complex contortions to equalize value. For example, if one child works in the business and the other child doesn't, having started his own business, the parents might give the family business to the first child, with the second child getting assets of equal value.

Indeed, if the parents don't have sufficient other assets, they may obligate the first child or the family business to make future cash transfers to the second child. But what if the family business falls on hard times while the second child's business becomes the next Google? That may be the result of the children's unique talents, dedication, or luck. But would you want to exacerbate those factors through decisions made years before? You can decide as you wish, so long as you consider all the possibilities and do more than make knee-jerk reactions to treat the kids equally.

It was not unreasonable for Charles to have thought that Sam doubted his capabilities, which would have been consistent with Charles's intimidation by and awe of his father. Eventually, Charles concluded that having cochairmen was counterproductive and divisive for employees, as well as for stakeholders and other outside relationships. Charles explained his point of view to Edgar, and being a noble warrior for the family and the business, resigned that post. Noble warrior? Yes, but Charles left the cochairman post to avoid a family squabble that he felt would become a war.

Charles knew of family businesses in which such fights often did become wars. After all, Sam had severed business interests with his nephews Peter and Edward, who moved to Toronto and founded a totally separate liquor business. But at the same time Charles's resignation was consistent with his deeply ingrained feelings of business inadequacy. Edgar, also a noble warrior, carried on. He retained the position of CEO and chairman and thus kept doing what his father wanted him to do,

Preventing Repetition of Unintended Consequences

Years later, the different patterns of Charles and Edgar dealing with their respective sons showed both a certain commonality of and differences in their father's impact, not only on them but also on Sam's grandsons.

Both Edgar, whom I did not interview (he passed away in December 2013), and Charles decided that their relationships with their sons would not be at all like theirs with their dad. Charles believes that Edgar, as did Charles, felt intimidated by their father—by his outsized success, as well as by his demeanor and style. Both brothers felt compelled to do what their father wanted them to do and probably also on occasion what they merely *felt* he wanted them to do. Eventually Charles was able to free himself from his father's shadow. That started when he cofounded the Montreal Expos baseball team. But even the fact that he had to escape to an arena not understood by his father was evidence that he felt compelled to follow his father's dictates.

Years later, Charles's son, Stephen, entered a family business, the investment company Claridge. Real estate was the principal activity and expertise of the firm. Originally, Stephen worked under the direction of nonfamily executives.

Claridge was reinvented to make financial investments in businesses, much like a private equity group. While this was happening, the nonfamily real estate team moved on to its own entrepreneurial ventures. This left Stephen to reinvent on two levels, personally and on behalf of the restructured Claridge. He was not totally alone in these efforts. He had an important and highly valued resource behind him, namely his father, Charles.

When Stephen found a prospective investment opportunity, he would do his due diligence and then pass the results of his examination on to his father so they could discuss the prospect. Stephen recalled times he considered reflective of their relationship. In an early instance he was considering two deals. One entailed backing former investment banker Jim McDonald, who was starting a new investment fund. The other was with Michael Cole, a rock-and-roll promoter, who was seeking backing for a Rolling Stones tour. Stephen presented both deals to his father, certain of approval for the investment fund. His confidence there was only exceeded by his certainty that his dad would "hate" the Rolling Stones idea. Despite all this, he presented the two deals to Charles. His dad asked the usual questions, and they started the typical discourse Charles used to be sure his son was learning from the process and indeed had "done his homework."

Stephen was totally surprised when his father said, "The Jim McDonald fund is terrible, so boring. Why would you get involved with a former investment banker who's just starting another fund? You'll really have no fun. . . . You love music. This is the Rolling Stones: it's such a great brand. You'll probably do very well. You'll have fun with it."

Both deals required relatively modest capital. Another private equity deal Stephen did was costly and therefore awkward. Father and son had agreed that the first few deals he would do should be in the $10 million range. Out of nowhere Stephen was approached by an ESPN management team who were seeking financial backing to do a management buyout of the Sports Network of Canada. But the required equity was $50 million, five times the range Charles and Stephen had agreed to.

Afterward Charles did indeed balk, not at the dollar amount but at the business itself. Charles said, "This business is a monopoly. It's strong and well run. I was hoping that you'd buy a broken-down business that you'd have to rebuild, and you'd get into operations and really learn a whole hell of a lot."

Stephen argued that this was an opportunity to learn a new industry from capable managers "in a field I absolutely love [sports]." Ultimately, Charles gave Stephen a thumbs-up.

In both deals—the Rolling Stones tour and the Sports Network—the family wound up doing well financially. But of primary interest for this book is the way that Charles handled it. He continually challenged Stephen, questioning the extent and quality of Stephen's homework as well as the wisdom of his decisions. Then ultimately in each case he let Stephen make the decision. Stephen always knew he had to be prepared for the talks with his father. He knew it was entirely possible that his father would say no. By using this process, Charles was able to avoid being what his own father had been to his sons.

Charles didn't want to dictate what Stephen must do, but he found a communications process that demanded excellence without having to intimidate his son. He had always told his son he could enter any field he chose, so long as he strived to be the best he could be. Of course, A.N. Pritzker said that too but followed it with challenges and jibes meant to intimidate. Charles had found a way to avoid the parental control imposed by Sam without giving Stephen carte blanche.

Charles's brother, Edgar, had served for decades as the CEO of Seagram. Edgar was a successful executive, respected in the industry and in the business community. He succeeded in the role his father chose for him. Of course, that was enabled by Charles's action. Charles says he resigned as cochairman because he lacked confidence that he could run a big company, or as he put it, "I was scared like hell to run a big company." Once he stepped aside, Edgar was left in total charge. There were, however, additional reasons for Charles to resign.

Underlying all of this was what Charles refers to as their "big brother, little brother relationship." As Edgar got older and assumed sizable philanthropic responsibilities (he became the global leader of the World Jewish Congress), he passed the Seagram mantle to his son, Edgar Bronfman Jr. According to Charles, his brother also suffered from the effect of their father's treatment of them. In Edgar's case, that may have resulted in what Charles refers to as "the denouement."

The Denouement

The denouement Charles refers to is the transaction by which Edgar Jr. sold Seagram to the French company Vivendi for the latter company's stock that turned out, almost immediately after the transaction, to be far less valuable than was thought. That resulted in a multibillion-dollar loss to the Bronfman family.

Why did Edgar, a highly successful CEO, fail to prevent his son from doing the Vivendi deal? It wasn't that Edgar was unaware of the nature of Vivendi's industry. Edgar had invested unsuccessfully in MGM years before, and Vivendi, a French concern, was in the media business with TV and films. Why didn't Edgar Sr. do as Charles had done with Stephen, challenging his son to prove the wisdom of his homework?

For that matter, why didn't Charles say something to his brother, if not to his nephew? The lack of oversight by Charles's older brother, Edgar, resulted in enormous losses to the family.

Charles may seem like the best prospect to have used good communication to avoid the disaster. After all, he developed a rapport with his son during presentations about prospective investments. This relationship was the product of his wise communication techniques that made him effective in dealing with highly sensitive matters and tough adversaries.

Years before, Charles grew skilled at communicating with persons who were not members of his own family. He learned a critically important lesson in this regard during his partnership with the famously combative Wall Streeter Michael Steinhardt. Both men were actively engaged philanthropists. The two founded Operation Independence, a not-for-profit charity that funded trips for Jewish kids who wanted to go to Israel. It has proved immensely successful. Early on, the two philanthropists had a serious falling out. But Charles managed to salvage his previously superb working relationship with the crusty investor. Charles thanks his wife for helping him resolve what he believed would be a make-or-break discussion. He told her, "Michael and I have a major difference of opinion and I don't know what to do about it. I don't want to go to war with Michael. I am very fond of him." His wife said, "Well, why don't you tell him that?" Charles realized she had come up with a practical solution. He communicated with Michael as she said and thus preserved a relationship of great value.

To understand Charles's failure to discuss Vivendi with Edgar, keep something in mind: when he stepped out of the management of Seagram, Charles felt it important that he not interfere. That was the clear understanding with his brother when he resigned as cochairman.

But Charles couldn't seem to muster the confidence to have a discussion with his brother and nephew—like the discussions he'd had with Steinhardt and Stephen, at least not until much later, well after the Vivendi deal had imploded. Charles felt that "the risk of war," which he'd feared with Steinhardt, was even more likely in a family situation. He had witnessed a war between his father, Sam, and the cousins, one that resulted in there being two Bronfman families—the Montreal and the Toronto Bronfmans, who communicated through lawyers.

As Charles puts it, "A family relationship is very close, very sensitive, and very compelling. If it goes on long enough, the pecking order is very tough to break. The pecking order with my [older] brother really lasted until after the denouement."

The denouement, as Charles still refers to the Vivendi deal, and its huge impact on the family's fortunes, was serious enough to motivate Charles to call his brother, albeit after the fact, and say, "You and I have to have a real discussion." The discussion took place with a psychologist as facilitator in a hotel meeting room, because Charles thought it best to have it on neutral territory.

TO BE A GREAT COMMUNICATOR, SELECT YOUR COMMUNICATOR ROLE MODEL WISELY

President Ronald Reagan is referred to as "the great communicator" because he could clearly communicate to all Americans simultaneously. In family businesses one can be a great communicator by communicating to a relatively small group of people and may do so using several different messages.

Charles Bronfman wound up being a great communicator, albeit a reluctant one, until his wife urged him to communicate with Michael Steinhardt. It proved that he could communicate without starting "a war." Yet he deferred communicating with Edgar because he feared the risk of a war was more likely in a family. That was because he witnessed the results of his father's war with their cousins, the Toronto Bronfmans.

Given Sam Bronfman's "my way or the highway" approach at dealing with his bright, talented children, I doubt that his

dealing with the cousins was exemplary. Sam was hardly the
best choice for a family communications role model.

Eventually Charles communicated with Edgar. It was too late to
prevent the denouement, but given Edgar's recent passing, it
was timely for a host of reasons.

Charles related the dialogue with Edgar: "I looked him dead
in the eye. I said, 'You never had any regard for me, did you?' He
said, 'No, I didn't.' I said, 'You thought I was dumb.' 'Yes.' I said,
'You now know you're wrong.' 'Yes.'

"Etcetera, etcetera. So this discussion went on. I wanted to
have another one, to really come clean, both of us to come clean.
He wouldn't do it because I think he figured that he would cave.
I said, 'You know, you made just a terrible mistake, just terrible.'
I'd forgotten that he had gone into the movie business one time,
years and years before."

"'Why?' I said, 'You're a bright man. You knew this was the
wrong thing to do. Why?' So now he thought—and he said,
'Well, I'll tell you why.' Now this—this is very telling. He said,
'Father would never, would not let me do what I wanted to do,
and so I vowed I would let my son do anything he wanted to do.'

"I said, 'Well, you're out of your f***ing mind. That's what you
are.' I said, 'You now realize what a terrible mistake it was?' He
said, 'Yes.' But he still loves that son."

And Charles loved his father and his brother. After all, what's
love got to do with it?

Conclusion

Magic Pill? Remember to Refill Your Prescription

WHEN I FINISH READING NONFICTION BOOKS, I SETTLE BACK AND consider: "What did I learn by reading this book?" I recommend that procedure to my students. Now before you finish this book, I'd like to help you prepare for that procedure.

You might wonder why I spell this out now, after you've finished the book and read all the stories, rather than in the introduction. First, I believe that you can better understand how to create your best reinvention designs after you know and fully understand these stories. Second, I didn't want you to skip the stories, to get to the designs more quickly, because I wanted you to enjoy the wonderful stories the interviewees were so kind to share.

We always seek that silver bullet to solve our problems or that single pill to cure all our ills. In fact, there is no silver bullet, no one pill for all ills. But the stories in this book do demonstrate that even the best and brightest have issues, most of which could have been resolved with careful forethought and planning, either alone or with the help of others. The stories in this book may seem so varied as to lack a lesson. There is no single lesson, but there are links among the stories' lessons. Combined, they can help you. This book is clearly one in which the whole is greater than its parts, where 1 plus 1 can equal 3.

Here are three simple lessons taken from all the stories in this book:

1. Reinventions of self, company, and family must be recurring themes if you are to succeed.
2. The examples and stories are intended to help you recognize signs that alert you sufficiently before reinvention is needed, so you have the luxury of consideration and preparation.
3. The approaches taken by these highly successful people should teach you some techniques for designing and implementing your best attempts at reinvention.

The examples in this book demonstrate best practices in their particular circumstances. Best practices may not be the blueprints for your reinvention, but understanding these best practices should help you create next practices which hopefully become the best practices for your situation. Taken separately, the examples may describe too narrow a situation to help you. The intention is that you study them in combinations which can create a pattern from which you can glean your design. I shall explain through examples.

In *Entrepreneurs Are Made Not Born*, I quoted entrepreneurs who advised that to be a successful entrepreneur you should do what you know and love. That doesn't mean you have to start a business just like the one you worked for.

Tom Stemberg didn't start out knowing much about the office supply business, except that it lacked what he as a consumer wanted. He did understand retail; he did great homework to learn what other consumers needed, even though they had no idea themselves; and he loved making lemonade out of lemons.

Maxine Clark knew nothing about teddy bears, but she knew merchandising, she understood that retail had to be entertainment, and she relied on the ultimate teddy bear consumers—kids—to know what entertainment should look like. As to mall lease contracts and much more, she understood that she didn't have to know everything about any particular area of her new business, "just enough not to be dangerous."

Howard Shultz loved coffee and had fond memories of his experiences in European coffeehouses. He had never worked in, let alone run, a coffeehouse. He had observed what was done by good European coffee shops, and by observing how others did it he became confident that he could do it too. He knew it when he saw it, but he struggled because he couldn't explain it.

Dr. Jim Dan learned business and structure by hearing lawyers and accountants and later businesspeople. David Axelrod observed political campaigns sufficiently that with a little help he could run them. And the Crowns, Carlsons, Pritzkers, and Johnsons were important examples of the power of observing, as well as the risk of not.

Those few stories and others in the book give you guidelines within which you can plot your path.

The entrepreneurs I featured are all very smart. Just because you think you're not as smart as they are doesn't mean you shouldn't reinvent yourself as an entrepreneur. First of all, there certainly are satisfactory achievement levels below the achievements of the particular entrepreneurs I featured. Second, if you make incremental changes by changing some skill arrows in your quiver and sharpening others, you can make it work.

By the way, when I say they were smart, that doesn't mean they all went to MIT or the University of Chicago. Anyway, I don't think IQ determines whether you'll be a successful entrepreneur. It may help, as it does with many pursuits, but it also can hurt when intellectualizing prevents trained reactions, such as following your experienced gut. However, those entrepreneurs did do some smart things which are worth emulating:

♦ They observed and learned from what others did.
♦ They learned enough about the industry to know whether competitors were being honest and whether well-wishers knew what they were talking about. They learned who to listen to and who to ignore.
♦ They did great homework. I always tell my students that graduating from graduate school isn't the end of homework; it's the beginning. School is merely training for doing real homework when it counts. Real homework isn't just asking *what* but also *why* and *why not*. (That brings to mind Bobby Kennedy's frequent quote: "There are those who look at things the way they are, and ask, why? I dream of things that never were, and ask, why not?")
♦ Intellectual curiosity means being wary about answers and skeptical about answerers. Nobel laureate Elie Wiesel once told me, "Questions are what bring us together; answers are what drive us apart." Entrepreneurs should always ask themselves: "If I were starting this industry or niche today, should it look like it actually does today?" The answer should almost always be no. Then the challenge begins.
♦ They thought about what the industry's customers wanted but weren't getting.
♦ They created business models to fit their new businesses and not the reverse.

It sounds cool to ignore naysayers, but how do you know whether a naysayer makes sense and whether you should or should not follow his or her advice? Two naysayers with different reasons for saying nay must be considered separately. One may be correct and the other not.

It's simplistic to say you must do great homework and know all you can about the potential issues raised. You actually need to separate real knowledge from superficial knowledge based on rumor, prejudices, hyperbole, common knowledge, folklore, or ill will. That's anything but simple. For instance, Junior Bridgeman couldn't be dissuaded by the silent naysaying that African American jocks couldn't be successful entrepreneurs. But he knew what he could do well and how he could adapt it to restaurant management. And he knew where to get help in the areas he didn't know.

The degrees of obviousness and necessity may vary. You must keep an open mind to seeing what you don't want to see. That's especially difficult for the entrepreneur who seems to be succeeding.

Having successfully ignored naysayings at the time of founding her business, the entrepreneur becomes convinced that her action was correct. And as her business continues to succeed, she becomes certain that ignoring those particular naysayings made good sense. However, changing times bring changed circumstances. The very same warning that was invalid during the pre-start-up stage may be great advice later on. The entrepreneur who remains wed to her earlier decision or who simply can't readjust her warning system may make a tragic mistake by doing exactly what she had done successfully before. As Henry Austin Dobson said in "The Paradox of Time": "Time goes, you say? Oh no! Alas, time stays, we go."

Once you know that reinvention must be considered, you must also determine how extensive a reinvention is appropriate.

Starts and stops in entrepreneurial ventures don't come with built-in critiques or manuals. After a few successful store openings, Costco hit a wall. It happened in the Midwest. That store was closed, and more stores were opened and were successful elsewhere. It would have been easy to blame it on peculiarities of Midwesterners, especially because new stores elsewhere seemed to work. That could lead to a belief that the geographical reinvention was all that was needed. Actually, the Costco team later learned how to succeed in the Midwest, but well before that, they had learned what else needed reinventing in all their stores. Constantly adding new departments proved brilliant. Adding a food department might have sufficed. Adding more and different foods from time to time proved superb. Indeed, Jim discovered that it wasn't just a particular reinvention but also the fact of constant reinvention, so "the operation didn't get stale," that did the trick. And he learned that by observing a shortcoming of his revered mentor and role model, who was slower in realizing that.

Even though Jim didn't know about certain new product lines, he knew which of his executives did know about them from their prior jobs. Alone, the jump to these new products might have been difficult or risky. By involving others, the reinventions became more incremental and feasible.

That's another example of how lessons from various stories can be brought together to guide you. Similarly, the lack of formal market research by most of the entrepreneurs should be compared with the research done by Osher and Stemberg based on their knowledge of particular types of products and retailing in general. The same could be said of Sinegal and Schwab, who knew their industries well but who changed their niches over time.

The change of generations and the resulting successions produce immense challenges and enormous opportunities. The saying "a chip off the old block" is often misunderstood. It is often interpreted to mean that the child has the exact same skills as the parent. First of all, that's highly unlikely in the best of circumstances. Genetics and environmental influences create some similarities but include some mixture of maternal and paternal genes and influences.

A.N. Pritzker used intimidation to cause his sons to be more like him. It may have worked, but it set a pattern that the next generations couldn't implement. Indeed, the secrecy policy that he and later Jay employed resulted in near disaster when the two men failed to inform heirs and assumed the secrets could be part of their family's continuity.

The absence of pure cloning is not at all detrimental. For just as the child won't be exactly like the parent, the family business will have changed over the years as will the family itself. The father may have been the consummate entrepreneur, a loner who ran board meetings in his shaving mirror. The son, or in Carlson's case, the daughter, may be the leader of teams, with the ability to grow but not to start a business from scratch.

The failure of parent and/or child to understand that can result in unfair expectations or false understanding of another's expectations. Even when that is understood by a parent who is sensitive to the needs of himself and others, the failure to anticipate outsiders' reactions may undermine the best of intentions.

Lester Crown made sure that his sons had ample opportunity to learn business lessons from him and his amazing father. His father comfortably entrusted control to the next generation. That was good, but not sufficient. Lester neglected to anticipate how key nonfamily executives would act. This proved a lesson that Lester took to heart in future dealings with family.

Jay Pritzker focused on business relationships to the exclusion of family relationships, which proved complex and troublesome, even more so due to their peculiar secrecy policies. This proved the fault with trying to "control from the grave."

When John Johnson told Linda that he couldn't fire the whole floor full of manual subscription clerks, he said, "I can't," making it clear that he was talking about himself. That's quite different from saying "we can't." By that subtle distinction, he licensed Linda, giving her the freedom to do so when she was convinced that failing to fire the few could result in failing to have jobs available for all their other employees. John just couldn't give up control while alive but arranged for the cord to be cut when he died.

In perhaps the ultimate lack of "controlling from the grave," Marilyn Carlson Nelson decreed that each new CEO, likely nonfamily, would determine what Carlson businesses should stay or go. Thus she delineated critical designs regarding succession— succession of ownership, governance, and management. She dealt with nonfamily executives differently than Crown, and she extended power and authority quite differently than Pritzker.

Sam Bronfman left instructions that upon his death his two sons would be cochairmen of Seagram. That didn't work well. He simply didn't pay attention to what his sons did and didn't want. And his sons didn't understand that succession comes in varying flavors: management succession, governance succession, and ownership succession. Assuming that succession was all or nothing prevented Charles and Edgar from communicating when there were billions of reasons to do so.

Resurgence, a 2014 book by Kellogg Professor Greg Carpenter, Gary F. Gebhardt, and John F. Sherry, enforces the need for reinvention by focusing on extreme reinvention.

Again, pulling together the lessons from different stories can help you decide what approaches you favor for your family business. Joseph Campbell, the American mythologist and writer, asked the rhetorical question: "Are you the hero of your own story?" You have a better chance of being that hero if you have multiple stories of one reinvented self or business after another. Whatever reinvention steps you choose, may you invent, reinvent, and thrive.

Index

About the Author

Lloyd Shefsky coaches family businesses regarding governance, succession, family employment, and entrepreneurial activities within family enterprises. He is also a consultant to entrepreneurs. He has worked with hundreds of entrepreneurial and family businesses, often from start-up to public offerings, sales of the businesses, and succession to founders' descendants. Shefsky has also cofounded businesses and not-for-profit organizations.

Shefsky is Clinical Professor of Entrepreneurship and founder and codirector of the Center for Family Enterprises at the Kellogg School of Management. He has taught and lectured on these subjects internationally and has written professional articles on those and related topics. He is the author of a bestseller, *Entrepreneurs Are Made Not Born*, published by McGraw-Hill. The book has been translated into seven languages.

Lloyd is now Of Counsel to the Chicago-based Taft law firm, which recently acquired Shefsky & Froelich, the Chicago firm he cofounded. He received his JD from the Law School at the University of Chicago and his undergraduate degree from DePaul University. He is also a certified public accountant.